ROAD ATLAS EUROPE

Contents

Road Atlas Europe

Collins
An imprint of HarperCollins Publishers
Westerhill Road, Bishopbriggs,
Glasgow G64 2QT

First published 2009
Revised Edition 2011

Printed in China by South China Printing Co. Ltd.
ISBN 978-0-00-736413-8

All mapping in this title is generated from
Collins Bartholomew™ digital databases.
Collins Bartholomew™, the UK's leading independent
geographical information supplier, can provide a digital,
custom, and premium mapping service to a variety of markets.
For further information:
·˙ ˙44 (0) 141 306 3752
       ˙ˑartholomew@harpercollins.co.uk
          ˑollinsbartholomew.com
                              ips that can be

www.collinsbart...

Country / Capital city / Country identification / National flag	Official language	Currency	Speed limits (Motorway / Dual carriageway / Rural / Town)	Emergency numbers (Police / Fire / Ambulance)	Motoring Organisations
Austria Wien — A	German	Euro = 100 cents	130 km/h / 100 km/h / 50 km/h	112 / 112 / 112	**ÖAMTC** Österreichischer Automobil-, Motorrad- und Touring Club www.oeamtc.at **ARBÖ** Auto-, Motor- und Radfahrerbund Österreichs www.arboe.or.at
Albania Tiranë — AL	Albanian	Lek = 100 qindarka	80 km/h / 40 km/h	19 / 18 / 17	**ACA** Klubi I Automobilit te Shqipërisë www.aca.al
Andorra Andorra la Vella — AND	Catalan	Euro = 100 cents	90 km/h / 50 km/h	110 / 118 / 116	**ACA** Automòbil Club d'Andorra www.aca.ad
Belgium Bruxelles — B	French Dutch Flemish	Euro = 100 cents	120 km/h / 120 km/h / 90 km/h / 50 km/h	112 / 112 / 112	**RACB** Royal Automobile Club of Belgium www.racb.com **TCB** Touring Club Belgium www.touring.be
Bulgaria Sofiya — BG	Bulgarian	Lev	130 km/h / 90 km/h / 50 km/h	166 / 160 / 150	**UAB** Union of Bulgarian Motorists www.uab.org
Bosnia-Herzogovina Sarajevo — BIH	Bosnian Serbian Croatian	Konvertibilna Marka = 100 pfennig	100 km/h / 80 km/h / 50 km/h	122 / 123 / 124	**BIHAMK** Bosanskohercegovački auto-moto klub www.bihamk.ba
Belarus Minsk — BY	Belarussian Russian	Belarus Rouble	120 km/h / 110 km/h / 90 km/h / 60 km/h	02 / 01 / 03	**BKA** Belarussian Auto Moto Touring Club www.bka.by
Switzerland Bern — CH	German French Italian	Swiss Franc = 100 rappen/ centimes	120 km/h / 100 km/h / 80 km/h / 50 km/h	117/112 / 118/112 / 144/112	**TCS** Touring Club Suisse/Schweiz/Svizzero www.tcs.ch **ACS** Automobil Club der Schweiz/Automobil club de Suisse www.acs.ch
Cyprus Lefkosia (Nicosia) — CY	Greek Turkish (North Cyprus)	Euro = 100 cents North Cyprus New Lira = 100 new kurus	100 km/h / 80 km/h / 50 km/h	199/112 / 199/112 / 199/112 / 155/112 / 199/112 / 112 (N Cyprus)	**CAA** Cyprus Automobile Association www.caa.com.cy
Czech Republic Praha — CZ	Czech	Koruna = 100 hellers	130 km/h / 90 km/h / 50 km/h	112 / 112 / 112	**ÚAMK** Ústřední automotoklub České republiky www.uamk-cr.cz **ACCR** Autoklub České republiky www.autoklub.cz
Germany Berlin — D	German	Euro = 100 cents	130 km/h / 100 km/h / 50 km/h	110 / 112 / 110	**ADAC** Allgemeiner Deutscher Automobil Club www.adac.de **AVD** Automobilclub von Deutschland www.avd.de
Denmark København — DK	Danish	Krone = 100 øre	130 km/h / 80 km/h / 50 km/h	112 / 112 / 112	**FDM** Forenede Danske Motorejere www.fdm.dk

Country Capital city Country identification National flag	Official language	Currency	Speed limits 🚗 Motorway 🚗 Dual carriageway 🏘 Rural 🏘 Town	Emergency numbers 👮 Police 🔥 Fire ➕ Ambulance	Motoring Organisations
Spain Madrid E	Spanish Catalan Galician Basque	Euro = 100 cents	120 km/h 100 km/h 90 km/h 50 km/h	👮 112 🔥 112 ➕ 112	**RACE** Real Automóvil Club de España www.race.es
Estonia Tallinn EST	Estonian	Euro = 100 cents	110 km/h 90 km/h 50 km/h	👮 112 🔥 112 ➕ 112	**Eesti Autoklubi** www.autoclub.ee
France Paris F	French	Euro = 100 cents	130 km/h 110 km/h 90 km/h 50 km/h	👮 17/112 🔥 18/112 ➕ 15/112	**L'Automobile Club** Association Française des Automobilistes www.automobile-club.org
Finland Helsinki FIN	Finnish Swedish	Euro = 100 cents	120 km/h 100 km/h 80 km/h 50 km/h	👮 112 🔥 112 ➕ 112	**AL** Autoliitto www.autoliitto.fi
Liechtenstein Vaduz FL	German	Swiss Franc = 100 rappen	80 km/h 50 km/h	👮 112 🔥 112 ➕ 112	**ACFL** Automobil Club Fürstentum Liechtenstein www.acfl.li
United Kingdom London GB	English	Pound = 100 pence	70 mph 70 mph 60 mph 30 mph	👮 999/112 🔥 999/112 ➕ 999/112	**AA** Automobile Association www.theaa.com **RAC** Royal Automobile Club www.rac.co.uk
Greece Athina GR	Greek	Euro = 100 cents	120 km/h 90/100 km/h 50 km/h	👮 112 🔥 112 ➕ 112	**ELPA** Automobile and Touring Club of Greece www.elpa.gr
Hungary Budapest H	Hungarian	Forint = 100 fillér	130 km/h 110 km/h 90 km/h 50 km/h	👮 107 🔥 112 ➕ 104	**Magyar Autóklub** www.autoklub.hu
Croatia (Hvratska) Zagreb HR	Croat	Kuna = 100 Lipa	130 km/h 110 km/h 90 km/h 50 km/h	👮 192 🔥 193 ➕ 194	**HAK** Hrvatski Autoklub www.hak.hr
Italy Roma I	Italian	Euro = 100 cents	130 km/h 110 km/h 90 km/h 50 km/h	👮 112 🔥 115/112 ➕ 118/112	**ACI** Automobile Club d'Italia www.aci.it
Ireland Dublin IRL	Irish English	Euro = 100 cents	120 km/h 60/100 km/h 50 km/h	👮 999/112 🔥 999/112 ➕ 999/112	**AA Ireland** The Automobile Association Ireland Limited www.aaireland.ie
Iceland Rekyavik IS	Icelandic	Krona = 100 aura	90 km/h (tarmac) 80 km/h (untarred) 50 km/h	👮 112 🔥 112 ➕ 112	**FIB** Félag íslenskra bifreiðaeigenda www.fib.is

Country Capital city Country identification National flag	Official language	Currency	Speed limits ▨ Motorway ▨ Dual carriageway ▨ Rural ▨ Town	Emergency numbers ☎ Police ♠ Fire ✚ Ambulance	Motoring Organisations
Luxembourg Luxembourg (L)	Luxembourgish French German	Euro = 100 cents	130 km/h 110 km/h 90 km/h 60 km/h	☎ 113 ♠ 112 ✚ 112	**ACL** Automobile Club du Grand-Duché de Luxembourg www.acl.lu
Lithuania Vilnius (LT)	Lithuanian	Litas = 100 centas	130/110 km/h 110/100 km/h 90 km/h 60 km/h	☎ 112 ♠ 112 ✚ 112	**LAS** Lietuvos automobilininkų sąjunga www.las.lt
Latvia Rīga (LV)	Latvian	Lat = 100 santims	110 km/h 90/100 km/h 50 km/h	☎ 02/112 ♠ 01/112 ✚ 03/112	**LAMB** Latvijas Automoto Biedrība www.lamb.lv
Malta Valletta (M)	Maltese English	Euro = 100 cents	80 km/h 50 km/h	☎ 112 ♠ 112 ✚ 112	**TCM** Touring Club Malta www.touringclubmalta.org
Monaco Monaco (MC)	French	Euro = 100 cents	130 km/h 110 km/h 90 km/h 50 km/h	☎ 112 ♠ 112 ✚ 112	**ACM** Automobile Club de Monaco www.acm.mc
Moldova Chişinău (MD)	Romanian Ukranian	Leu = 100 bani	90 km/h 60 km/h	☎ 902 ♠ 901 ✚ 903	**ACM** Automobil Club din Moldova www.acm.md
Macedonia (F.Y.R.O.M.) Skopje (MK)	Macedonian Albanian	Macedonian Denar	120 km/h 100 km/h 80 km/h 50 km/h	☎ 192 ♠ 193 ✚ 194	**AMSM** Avto Moto Sojuz na Makedonija www.amsm.com.mk
Montenegro Podgorica (MNE)	Serbian (Montenegrin) Albanian	Euro = 100 cents	100 km/h 80 km/h 50 km/h	☎ 92 ♠ 93 ✚ 94	**AMSCG** Auto-moto savez Crne Gore www.amscg.org
Norway Oslo (N)	Norwegian	Norwegian Krone = 100 øre	100 km/h 80 km/h 50 km/h	☎ 112 ♠ 110 ✚ 113	**KNA** Kongelig Norsk Automobilklub www.kna.no
The Netherlands Amsterdam (NL)	Dutch	Euro = 100 cents	120 km/h 100 km/h 80 km/h 50 km/h	☎ 112 ♠ 112 ✚ 112	**ANWB** Koninklijke Nederlandse Toeristenbond ANWB www.anwb.nl **KNAC** Koninklijke Nederlandsche Automobiel Club www.knac.nl
Portugal Lisboa (P)	Portuguese	Euro = 100 cents	120 km/h 100 km/h 90 km/h 50 km/h	☎ 112 ♠ 112 ✚ 112	**ACP** Automóvel Club de Portugal www.acp.pt

Country Capital city Country identification National flag	Official language	Currency	Speed limits 🚗 Motorway 🚗 Dual carriageway 🏘 Rural 🏘 Town	Emergency numbers 👮 Police 🔥 Fire ✚ Ambulance	Motoring Organisations
Poland Warszawa (PL)	Polish	Złoty = 100 groszy	🚗 140 km/h 🚗 120 km/h 🏘 90 km/h 🏘 50/60 km/h	👮 997/112 🔥 998/112 ✚ 999/112	**PZM** Polski Związek Motorowy www.pzm.pl
Kosovo Prishtinë (RKS)	Albanian Serbian	Euro = 100 cents	🚗 100 km/h 🏘 80 km/h 🏘 60 km/h	👮 92/112 🔥 93/112 ✚ 94/112	
Romania Bucureşti (RO)	Romanian	New Romanian Leu = 100 new bani	🚗 120 km/h 🏘 90/100 km/h 🏘 50 km/h	👮 112 🔥 112 ✚ 112	**ACR** Automobil Clubul Roman www.acr.ro
San Marino San Marino (RSM)	Italian	Euro = 100 cents	🚗 130 km/h 🚗 110 km/h 🏘 90 km/h 🏘 50 km/h	👮 112 🔥 887777 ✚ 118	
Russian Federation Moskva (RUS)	Russian	Rouble = 100 kopeck	🚗 110 km/h 🏘 90 km/h 🏘 60 km/h	👮 02 🔥 01 ✚ 03	**VOA** All-Russian Society of Motorists www.voa.ru
Sweden Stockholm (S)	Swedish	Krona = 100 öre	🚗 110 km/h 🚗 90 km/h 🏘 70 km/h 🏘 50 km/h	👮 112 🔥 112 ✚ 112	**M** Motormännens Riksförbund www.motormannen.se
Slovakia Bratislava (SK)	Slovak	Euro = 100 cents	🚗 130 km/h 🏘 90 km/h 🏘 60 km/h	👮 158/112 🔥 150/112 ✚ 155/112	**SATC** Slovenský Autoturist Klub www.autoklub.sk
Slovenia Ljubljana (SLO)	Slovene	Euro = 100 cents	🚗 130 km/h 🚗 100 km/h 🏘 90 km/h 🏘 50 km/h	👮 113 🔥 112 ✚ 112	**AMZS** Avto-Moto Zveza Slovenije www.amzs.si
Serbia Beograd (SRB)	Serbian Albanian Hungarian	Serbian Dinar = 100 paras Euro = 100 cents	🚗 120 km/h 🚗 100 km/h 🏘 80 km/h 🏘 60 km/h	👮 92 🔥 93 ✚ 94	**AMSS** Auto-moto savez Srbije www.amss.org.rs
Turkey Ankara (TR)	Turkish	New Turkish Lira = 100 kuru	🚗 130 km/h 🚗 120 km/h 🏘 90 km/h 🏘 50 km/h	👮 155 🔥 110 ✚ 112	**TTOK** Türkiye Turıng ve Otomobıl Kurumu www.turing.org.tr
Ukraine Kyiv (UA)	Ukrainian	Hryvnya = 100 kopiyok	🚗 130 km/h 🏘 90 km/h 🏘 60 km/h	👮 02 🔥 01 ✚ 03	**FAU** Federation Automobile d'Ukraine

Country	Official website	Tourism website
Albania	www.km.gov.al	www.albaniantourism.com
Andorra	www.andorra.ad	www.andorra.ad
Austria	www.oesterreich.at	www.austria.info
Belarus	www.government.by	www.engbelarustourism.by
Belgium	www.belgium.be	Flanders: www.visitflanders.com
		Wallonia: www.opt.be
Bosnia-Herzegovina	www.fbihvlada.gov.ba	www.bhtourism.ba
Bulgaria	www.government.bg	www.bulgariatravel.org
Croatia	www.vlada.hr	www.croatia.hr
Cyprus	www.cyprus.gov.cy	www.visitcyprus.com
Czech Republic	www.czech.cz	www.czechtourism.com
Denmark	www.denmark.dk	www.visitdenmark.com
Estonia	www.valitsus.ee	www.visitestonia.com
Finland	www.valtioneuvosto.fi	www.visitfinland.com
France	www.premier-ministre.gouv.fr	www.franceguide.com
Germany	www.bundesregierung.de	www.germany-tourism.de
Greece	www.greece.gov.gr	www.visitgreece.gr
Hungary	www.magyarorszag.hu	www.hungarytourism.hu
Iceland	www.iceland.is	www.visiticeland.com
Ireland	www.irlgov.ie	www.discoverireland.ie
Italy	www.governo.it	www.enit.it
Kosovo	www.ks-gov.net	www.visitkosova.org
Latvia	www.saeima.lv	www.latviatourism.lv
Liechtenstein	www.liechtenstein.li	www.tourismus.li
Lithuania	www.lrv.lt	www.travel.lt
Luxembourg	www.gouvernement.lu	www.visitluxembourg.lu
Macedonia (F.Y.R.O.M.)	www.vlada.mk	www.exploringmacedonia.com
Malta	www.gov.mt	www.visitmalta.com
Moldova	www.moldova.md	www.turism.gov.md
Monaco	www.monaco.gouv.mc	www.visitmonaco.com
Montenegro	www.montenegro.yu	www.visit-montenegro.com
Netherlands	www.overheid.nl	www.holland.com
Norway	www.norway.no	www.visitnorway.com
Poland	www.poland.gov.pl	www.poland.travel
Portugal	www.portugal.gov.pt	www.visitportugal.com
Romania	www.guv.ro	www.romaniatourism.com
Russian Federation	www.gov.ru	www.russiatourism.ru
San Marino	www.consigliograndeegenerale.sm	www.visitsanmarino.com
Serbia	www.srbija.sr.gov.yu	www.serbia-tourism.org
Slovakia	www.government.gov.sk	www.slovakia.travel
Slovenia	www.gov.si	www.slovenia.info
Spain	www.la-moncloa.es	www.spain.info
Sweden	www.sweden.se	www.visit-sweden.com
Switzerland	www.admin.ch	www.myswitzerland.com
Turkey	www.mfa.gov.tr	www.goturkey.com
Ukraine	www.kmu.gov.ua	www.tourism.gov.ua
United Kingdom	www.direct.gov.uk	www.visitbritain.com
Vatican City	www.vaticanstate.va	www.vaticanstate.va

International country identification

A	Austria	Autriche	Österreich
AL	Albania	Albanie	Albanien
AND	Andorra	Andorre	Andorra
B	Belgium	Belgique	Belgien
BG	Bulgaria	Bulgarie	Bulgarien
BIH	Bosnia - Herzegovina	Bosnie Herzégovine	Bosnien-Herzegowina
BY	Belarus	Bélarus	Belarus
CH	Switzerland	Suisse	Schweiz
CY	Cyprus	la Chypre	Zypern
CZ	Czech Republic	République tchèque	Tschechische Republik
D	Germany	Allemagne	Deutschland
DK	Denmark	Danemark	Dänemark
DZ	Algeria	Algérie	Algerien
E	Spain	Espagne	Spanien
EST	Estonia	Estonie	Estland
F	France	France	Frankreich
FIN	Finland	Finlande	Finnland
FL	Liechtenstein	Liechtenstein	Liechtenstein
FO	Faroe Islands	Iles Féroé	Färöer-Inseln
GB	United Kingdom GB & NI	Grande-Bretagne	Grossbritannien
GBA	Alderney	Alderney	Alderney
GBG	Guernsey	Guernsey	Guernsey
GBJ	Jersey	Jersey	Jersey
GBM	Isle of Man	île de Man	Insel Man
GBZ	Gibraltar	Gibraltar	Gibraltar
GR	Greece	Grèce	Griechenland
H	Hungary	Hongrie	Ungarn
HR	Croatia	Croatie	Kroatien
I	Italy	Italie	Italien
IRL	Ireland	Irlande	Irland
IS	Iceland	Islande	Island
L	Luxembourg	Luxembourg	Luxemburg
LT	Lithuania	Lituanie	Litauen
LV	Latvia	Lettonie	Lettland
M	Malta	Malte	Malta
MA	Morocco	Maroc	Marokko
MC	Monaco	Monaco	Monaco
MD	Moldova	Moldavie	Moldawien
MK	Macedonia (F.Y.R.O.M.)	Ancienne République yougoslave de Macédoine	Ehemalige jugoslawische Republik Mazedonien
MNE	Montenegro	Monténégro	Montenegro
N	Norway	Norvège	Norwegen
NL	Netherlands	Pays-Bas	Niederlande
P	Portugal	Portugal	Portugal
PL	Poland	Pologne	Polen
RKS	Kosovo	Kosovo	Kosovo
RO	Romania	Roumanie	Rumänien
RSM	San Marino	Saint-Marin	San Marino
RUS	Russian Federation	Russie	Russische Föderation
S	Sweden	Suède	Schweden
SK	Slovakia	République slovaque	Slowakei
SLO	Slovenia	Slovénie	Slowenien
SRB	Serbia	Sérbie	Serbien
TN	Tunisia	Tunisie	Tunisien
TR	Turkey	Turquie	Türkei
UA	Ukraine	Ukraine	Ukraine

km

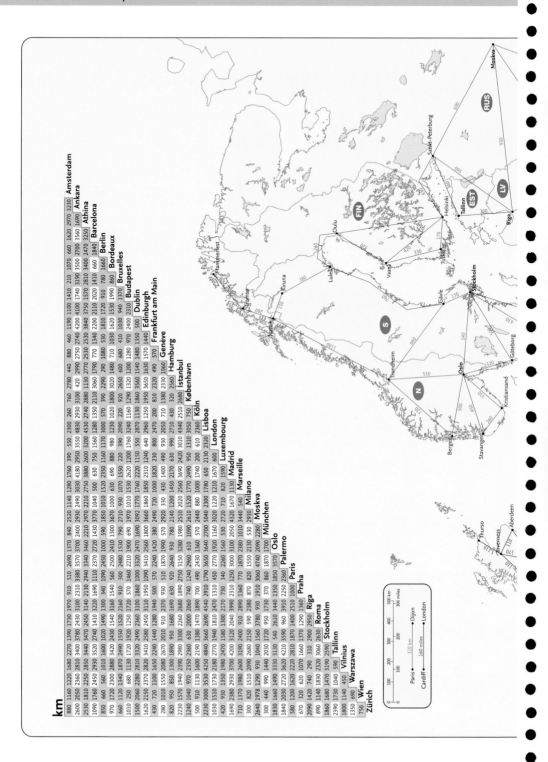

	Zürich	Wien	Warszawa	Vilnius	Tallinn	Stockholm	Roma	Rīga	Praha	Paris	Palermo	Oslo	München	Moskva	Milano	Marseille	Madrid	Luxembourg	London	Lisboa	Köln	København	İstanbul	Hamburg	Genève	Frankfurt am Main	Edinburgh	Dublin	Budapest	Bruxelles	Bordeaux	Berlin	Barcelona	Athina	Ankara
Amsterdam	880	1160	1220	1680	2270	1390	1730	1970	910	510	2690	1370	840	2520	1140	1280	1760	390	550	2300	260	760	2780	440	880	460	1190	1100	1410	210	1070	660	1620	2970	3230
Ankara	2600	2050	2360	2810	3400	3780	2430	3100	2310	3380	3570	3700	2400	2930	2490	3030	4180	2950	3550	4830	2930	3100	420	2990	2750	2740	4200	4100	1740	3190	3500	2700	3560	1690	
Athina	2530	1810	2250	2850	3440	3470	2450	3140	2130	2940	3340	3460	2210	2970	2210	2750	3880	2600	3200	4530	2740	2880	1130	2770	2530	2530	3840	3750	1570	2810	3400	2470	3250		
Barcelona	1090	1760	2450	2930	3520	2740	1410	3220	1690	1110	2370	2720	1430	3770	1040	500	630	750	1560	1280	1350	2110	3060	1790	770	1340	2200	2110	2020	1410	660	1840			
Berlin	850	660	560	1010	1600	1020	1490	1300	340	1090	2450	1000	590	1850	1010	1520	2350	1160	1170	3000	570	390	2290	290	1080	530	1810	1720	910	780	1660				
Bordeaux	970	1720	2300	2880	3420	2430	1540	3160	1540	560	2500	2410	1300	3670	1000	630	690	880	980	1230	1020	1800	3020	1480	710	1030	1620	1530	1990	860					
Bruxelles	660	1120	1340	1870	2490	1550	1520	2160	910	300	2480	1530	790	2710	930	1070	1550	220	390	2090	220	920	2650	600	680	410	1030	940	1370						
Budapest	1010	250	680	1130	1720	1920	1250	1720	570	1460	2210	1900	690	1970	1010	1530	2620	1200	1760	3240	1160	1290	1320	1200	1280	970	2400	2310							
Dublin	1500	2060	2280	2810	3320	2490	2360	3100	1860	1000	3320	2470	1690	3092	1770	1760	2220	1150	550	2870	1130	1860	3560	1540	1480	1350	500								
Edinburgh	1620	2150	2370	2820	3410	2580	2450	3110	1950	1090	3410	2560	1800	3660	1860	1850	2310	1240	640	2960	1250	1950	3650	1630	1570	1440									
Frankfurt am Main	430	720	1100	1650	2240	1440	1280	1940	500	570	2240	1420	380	2490	720	1000	1820	230	800	2470	200	810	2320	490	570										
Genève	280	1010	1550	2080	2670	2010	910	2370	930	510	1870	1990	570	2920	330	430	1400	490	930	2050	710	1380	2330	1060											
Hamburg	820	950	850	1300	1890	950	1680	1690	630	920	2640	930	780	2140	1200	1450	2170	630	990	2710	430	320	2560												
İstanbul	2230	1570	1940	2390	2980	3300	2260	2680	1890	2750	3150	3280	1980	2510	2020	2560	3690	2420	3010	4340	2510	2680													
København	1240	1040	970	2350	2360	630	2000	2060	740	1240	2960	610	1090	2610	1520	1770	2490	950	1310	3050	750														
Köln	500	910	1130	1600	2190	1380	1470	1890	700	490	2430	1360	570	2440	880	1000	1740	200	610	2360															
Lisboa	2230	3000	3530	4250	4840	3660	2690	4540	2910	1790	3650	3640	2700	5040	2300	1780	650	2130	2320																
London	1030	1510	1730	2180	2770	1940	1810	2470	1310	450	2770	1920	1160	3020	1220	1210	1670	600																	
Luxembourg	420	930	1350	1980	2470	1580	1300	2170	730	340	2260	1560	530	2720	710	820	1590																		
Madrid	1690	2380	2930	3700	4200	3120	2040	3990	2310	1250	3000	3100	2050	4320	1670	1130																			
Marseille	710	1370	1980	2600	3190	2400	910	2890	1360	770	1870	2380	1010	3440	540																				
Milano	300	820	1510	2090	2680	2150	590	2380	870	820	1550	2130	530	2930																					
Moskva	2640	1978	1290	930	1040	1560	3780	930	1910	3060	4740	2090	2280																						
München	300	440	990	1440	2030	1720	950	1730	370	860	1870	1700																							
Oslo	1830	1660	1490	3330	3130	540	2610	3440	1350	1850	3570																								
Palermo	1840	2030	2720	3620	4210	3590	960	3910	2250	2360																									
Paris	580	1200	1620	2220	2810	1870	1400	2510	1000																										
Praha	670	320	620	1070	1660	1370	1290	1360																											
Rīga	2090	1420	740	290	310	2900	2950																												
Roma	890	1140	1830	2320	3060	2630																													
Stockholm	1860	1680	1470	3190	2590																														
Tallinn	2390	1730	1040	590																															
Vilnius	1800	1140	450																																
Warszawa	1350	690																																	
Wien	750																																		

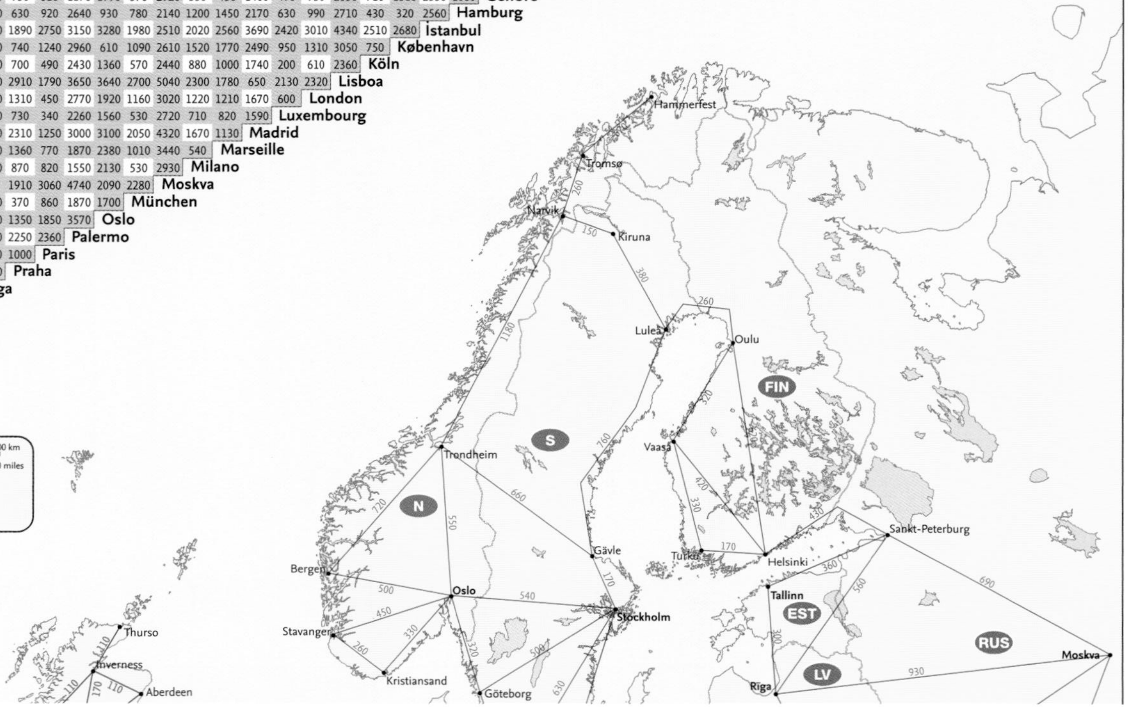
0 100 200 300 400 500 km
0 100 200 300 miles
Paris 310 km Dijon
Cardiff 160 miles London
Hammerfest
Tromsø
Narvik
Kiruna
Luleå
Oulu
Vaasa
Turku
Helsinki
Sankt-Peterburg
Tallinn
Rīga
Moskva
Trondheim
Gävle
Stockholm
Bergen
Oslo
Stavanger
Kristiansand
Göteborg
Thurso
Inverness
Aberdeen
FIN
S
N
EST
LV
RUS

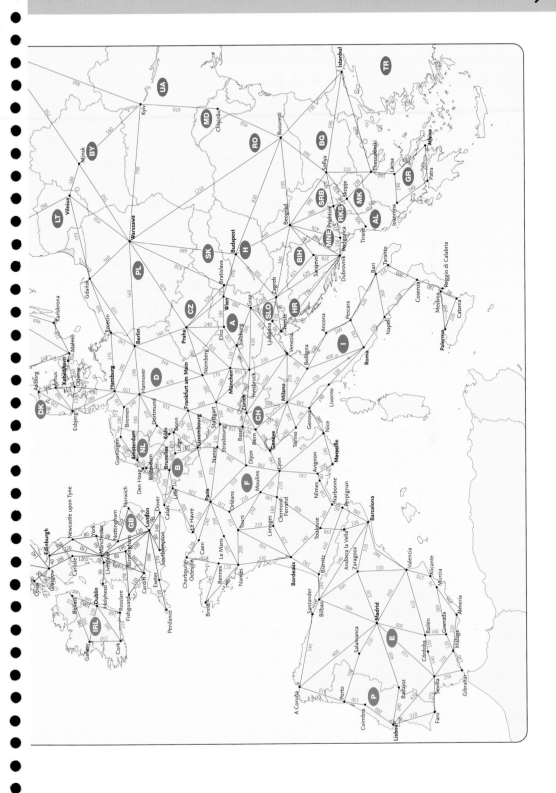

Motorway
Autoroute
Autobahn

 Motorway
Autoroute
Autobahn

 End of motorway
Fin d'autoroute
Ende der Autobahn

 End of motorway
Fin d'autoroute
Ende der Autobahn

 Lane for slow vehicles
Voie pour véhicules lents
Fahrsspur für langsam
fahrende Fahrzeuge

 'Semi motorway'
Route pour automobiles
Kraftfahrstraße

 End of 'Semi motorway'
Fin de route pour automobiles
Ende der Kraftfahrstraße

 European route number
Numéro européen de route
Nummernschild für
Europastraßen

 Priority road
Route prioritaire
Vorfahrtstraße

 End of priority road
Fin de route prioritaire
Ende der Vorfahrtstraße

 Priority over oncoming vehicles
Priorité par rapport aux véhicules
venant en sens inverse
Gegenverkehr muss warten

 One way street
Rue à sens unique
Einbahnstraße

 One way street
Rue à sens unique
Einbahnstraße

 No through road
Route sans issue
Sackgasse

 Hospital
Hôpital
Krankenhaus

 Parking
Parking
Parkplatz

 Pedestrian crossing
Passage pour piétons
Fußgängerüberweg

 First aid post
Premiers secours
Erste Hilfe

 Information
Informations
Fremdenverkehrsbüro
oder Auskunftsstelle

 Hotel/Motel
Hôtel
Autobahnhotel

 Restaurant
Restaurant
Autobahngasthaus

 Mechanical help
Assistance mécanique
Pannenhilfe

 Filling station
Station essence
Tankstelle

 Telephone
Téléphone
Fernsprecher

 Camping site
Zone de camping pour tentes
Zeltplatz

 Caravan site
Zone de camping pour caravanes
Wohnwagenplatz

 Youth hostel
Auberge de jeunesse
Jugendherberge

 Right bend
Virage à droite
Kurve (rechts)

 Left bend
Virage à gauche
Kurve (links)

 Double bend
Succession de virages
Doppelkurve

 Roundabout
Circulation en sens giratoire
Kreisverkehr

 Intersection with
non-priority road
Intersection avec
une route non-prioritaire
Vorfahrt

 Traffic merges from left
Rétrécissement sur la gauche
Verkehr ordnet sich von links ein

 Traffic merges from right
Rétrécissement sur la droite
Verkehr ordnet sich von
rechts ein

 Road narrows
Chaussée rétrécie
Verengte Fahrbahn

Road narrows at left
Chaussée rétrécie à gauche
Einseitig (links) verengte
Fahrbahn

Steep hill – descent
Descente ou montée à
forte inclinaison
Gefälle

Road narrows at right
Chaussée rétrécie à droite
Einseitig (rechts) verengte
Fahrbahn

Give way
Cédez le passage
Vorfahrt gewähren

Slippery road
Chaussée glissante
Schleudergefahr

Uneven road
Cassis
Unebene Fahrbahn

Tunnel
Tunnel
Tunnel

Opening bridge
Pont mobile
Bewegliche Brücke

Road works
Travaux
Baustelle

Loose chippings
Projection de gravillons
Splitt, Schotter

 Level crossing with barrier
Passage à niveau avec barrière
Bahnübergang mit Schranken
oder Halbschranken

 Level crossing without barrier
Passage à niveau sans barrière
Unbeschrankter Bahnübergang

 Tram
Tramway
Straßenbahn

 'Count down' posts
Balises pour passage à niveau
Bake vor Autobahnausfahrt

 'Danger' level crossing
Attention au train !
Achtung Bahnübergang

 Low flying aircraft
Avions volant à basse altitude
Flugbetrieb

 Falling rocks
Chutes de pierre
Steinschlag

 Cross wind
Vents contraires
Seitenwind

 Quayside or river bank
Débouché sur un quai
ou une berge
Ufer

 Two-way traffic
Circulation dans les deux sens
Gegenverkehr

 Traffic signals ahead
Annonce de feux tricolores
Lichtzeichenanlage

 Pedestrians
Piétons
Fußgänger

 Children
Endroit fréquenté par
les enfants
Kinder

 Animals
Passages d'animaux
Viehtrieb, Tiere

 Wild animals
Passage d'animaux sauvages
Wildwechsel

 Other dangers
Autres dangers
Gefahrstelle

 Beginning of regulation
Début de prescription
Anfang

 Repetition sign
Panneau de rappel
Wiederholung

 End of regulation
Fin de prescription
Ende

 End of all restrictions
Fin de toutes les limitations
Ende sämtlicher Streckenverbote

 Halt sign
Stop
Halt! Vorfahrt gewähren!

 Customs
Douanes
Zollstelle

 No stopping ("clearway")
Arrêt interdit
Halteverbot

 No parking/waiting
Arrêt et stationnement interdits
Eingeschränktes Halteverbot

 Priority to oncoming vehicles
Priorité aux véhicules venant
en sens inverse
Dem Gegenverkehr Vorrang
gewähren!

 Use of horns prohibited
Avertisseur sonore interdit
Hupverbot

 Roundabout
Circulation en sens giratoire
Kreisverkehr

 Direction to be followed
Obligation de suivre la direction
indiquée par la flèche
Vorgeschriebene Fahrtrichtung

 Pass this side
Obligation de suivre la direction
indiquée par la flèche
Rechts/Links vorbei

 Minimum speed limit
Vitesse minimum autorisée
Vorgeschriebene
Mindestgeschwindigkeit

 End of minimum speed limit
Fin de vitesse minimum
Ende der vorgeschriebenen
Mindestgeschwindigkeit

 All vehicles prohibited
Interdit à tous les véhicules
Verbot für Fahrzeuge aller Art

 No entry for all vehicles
Interdiction d'entrer pour
tous les véhicules
Verbot der Einfahrt

 No right turn
Interdiction de tourner à droite
Rechtsabbiegen verboten

 No u-turns
Interdiction de faire demi-tour
Wendeverbot

 No entry for motor cars
Accès interdit aux
automobiles motorisées
Verbot für Kraftwagen

 No entry for all motor vehicles
Accès interdit à tous
les véhicules motorisés
Verbot für Kraftfahrzeuge
und Kraftwagen

 Motorcycles prohibited
Interdit aux motocycles
Verbot für Krafträder

 Mopeds prohibited
Interdit aux motocylettes
Verbot für Mofas

 No overtaking
Interdiction de dépasser
Überholverbot für
Kraftfahrzeuge aller Art

 End of no overtaking
Fin d'interdiction de dépasser
Ende des Überholverbots für
Kraftfahrzeuge aller Art

 Maximum speed limit
Vitesse maximum
Zulässige
Höchstgeschwindigkeit

 End of speed limit
Fin de limitation de vitesse
Ende der zulässigen
Höchstgeschwindigkeit

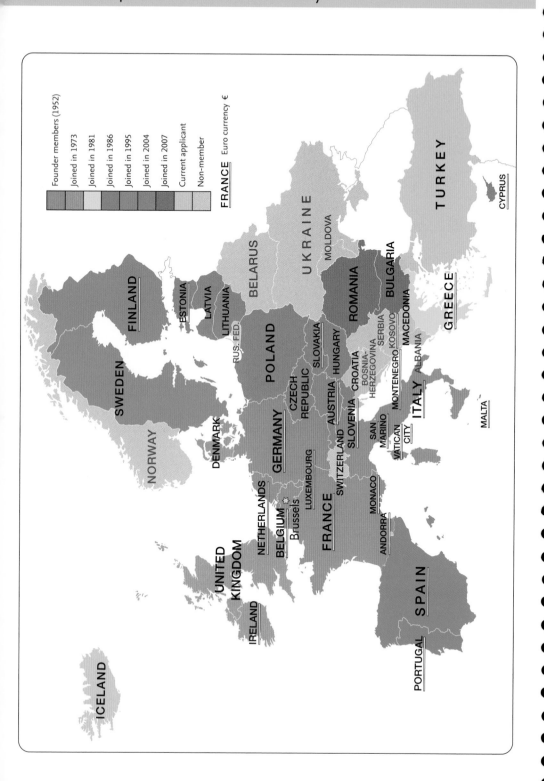

Founder members (1952)

Joined in 1973

Joined in 1981

Joined in 1986

Joined in 1995

Joined in 2004

Joined in 2007

Current applicant

Non-member

FRANCE Euro currency €

ICELAND

NORWAY

SWEDEN

FINLAND

DENMARK

ESTONIA

LATVIA

LITHUANIA

RUS. FED.

BELARUS

UKRAINE

MOLDOVA

UNITED KINGDOM

IRELAND

NETHERLANDS

BELGIUM

Brussels

LUXEMBOURG

GERMANY

POLAND

CZECH REPUBLIC

SLOVAKIA

HUNGARY

AUSTRIA

SWITZERLAND

FRANCE

SLOVENIA

CROATIA

BOSNIA-HERZEGOVINA

SERBIA

KOSOVO

MONTENEGRO

MACEDONIA

ALBANIA

ROMANIA

BULGARIA

GREECE

TURKEY

CYPRUS

SAN MARINO

VATICAN CITY

ITALY

MONACO

ANDORRA

SPAIN

PORTUGAL

MALTA

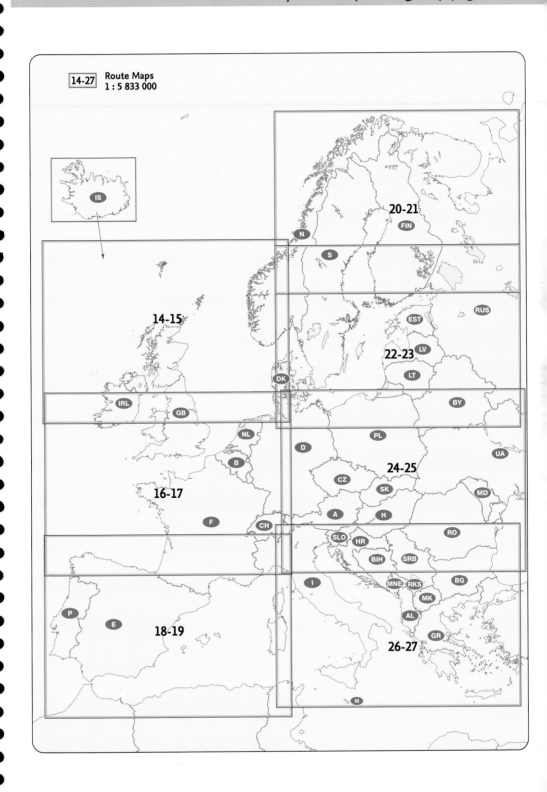

14-27   Route Maps
1 : 5 833 000

IS

14-15

20-21

N

FIN

S

EST

RUS

LV

22-23

LT

DK

IRL

GB

BY

NL

PL

B

D

UA

CZ

24-25

16-17

SK

MD

A

H

F

CH

SLO

HR

RO

BIH

SRB

I

MNE RKS

BG

MK

P

AL

E

18-19

GR

26-27

M

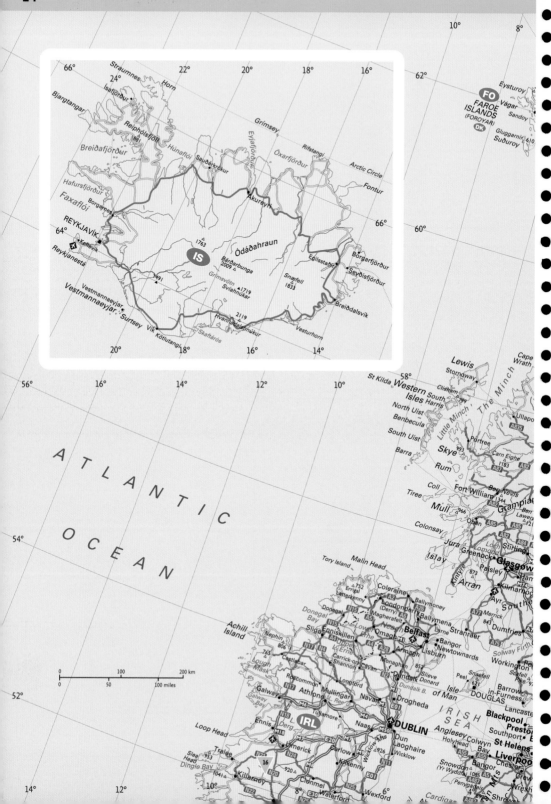

10°
8°

22°
20°
18°
16°

66°
62°

Straumnes
Horn

24°
Ísafjörður

Bjargtangar
Grímsey

Reiphólsfjöll 861
Rifstangi

Breiðafjörður
Húnaflói
Eyjafjörður
Öxarfjörður

Saudárkrokur
Arctic Circle

Hafursfjörður
Borgarnes
Akureyri
Fontur

Faxaflói
66°
60°

REYKJAVÍK
64°
Keflavík
△1763
Bárdarbunga
Ódáðahraun

Reykjanestá
IS
Borgarfjörður

2009 △
Egilsstaðir
Seyðisfjörður

Vestmannaeyjar
△1491
Grímsvötn
△1719
Snæfell
1833

Vestmannaeyjar Surtsey Vík
Sváhnúkar

△2119
Breiðdalsvík

Kötlutangi
Hvannadalshnúkur
Vesturhorn

Skaftárós

20°
18°
16°
14°

FO
FAROE
ISLANDS
(FØROYAR)
DK
Eysturoy
Vágar
Sandoy
Gluggarnir 610
Suðuroy

Lewis
Cape
Wrath

St Kilda
58°
Stornoway
Western South
Isles Harris
Clisham

56°
16°
14°
12°
10°
North Uist
Benbecula
Ullapo
A835

South Uist
Skye
993
Portree
Carn Eighe
1183
A87
A82

Barra
Rum

Coll
Beg Nevis
Fort William
144

A T L A N T I C
Tiree
Mull △966
A85
Grampia

Colonsay
Oban
A85
Lawe
Ber

O C E A N
Jura
Greenock
Loch
Stirling
A84

54°
Islay
Paisley
Glasgow
873

Tory Island
Malin Head
Kintyre
Arran
Kilmarno

Errigal △752
Coleraine
Ayr
South

Letterkenny
Ballymoney
Merrick
843
Dumfries

Donegal
(Derry)
Magherafelt
A6
A75

Achill
Nephin
Bay
Sligo
Enniskillen
Omagh
Ballymena
Larne
Stranraer
Solway Firth

Island
806
Castlebar
765
Carrick-on-
Shannon
Monaghan 852
Armagh
Lisburn
Bangor
Newtownards
Peel
Snaefell
621
Workington

Lough
Mask
Roscommon
Cavan
Slieve
Donard
Isle
DOUGLAS
in-Furness
Scafell
978

Galway
Athlone
Longford
Navan
Drogheda
Dundalk B.
of Man
Barrow-
Pike 773
Lancaste

Galway
Mullingar
M3
IRISH
Blackpool
Preston

Bay
Tullamore
M1
DUBLIN
SEA
Southport
St Helens

Loop Head
Ennis
M7
Naas
Dun
Laoghaire
Anglesey
Colwyn
Bay
Holyhead
Liverpool

Tralee
953
Limerick
Carlow
Wicklow Mts
926
Kilkenny
Snowdon
1085
Bangor
Chester

Slea
Head
1041
Killarney
Clonmel
N24
Waterford
E01
Penygadair
Wexford
Shrew

14°
12°
10°
8°
6°
Cardiga

0   100   200 km
0   50   100 miles

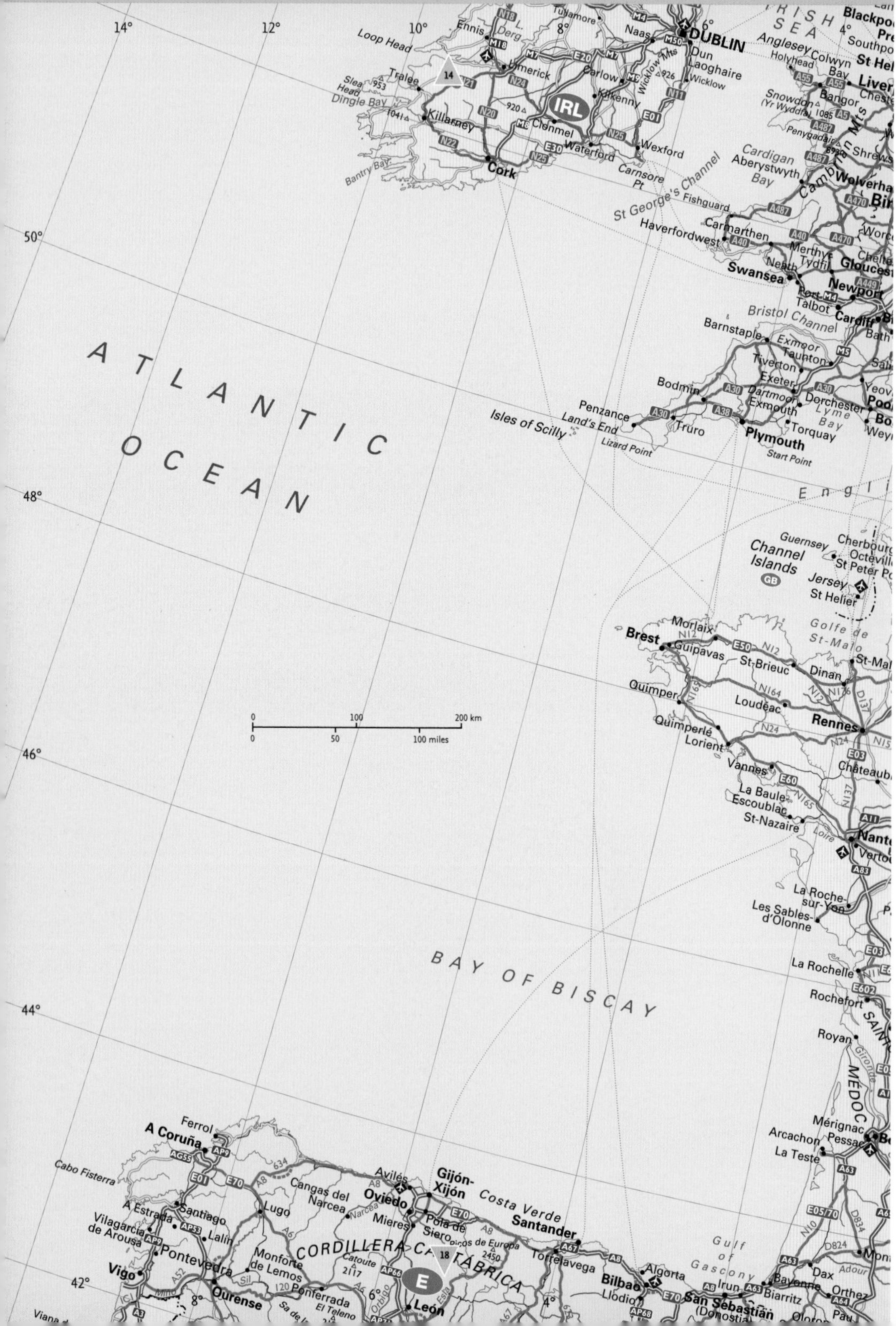

ATLANTIC

OCEAN

BAY OF BISCAY

IRISH SEA

Blackpoo
Pre
Southpo
Anglesey Colwyn St Hel
Holyhead Bay Liver
Snowdon Bangor Chest
(Yr Wyddfa) A5 Shrews
Penygadair 1085
Wolverha
Bi

Loop Head 10°
Ennis Tullamore 8° Naas DUBLIN
L. M50 Dun
Derg M1 Laoghaire
Tralee Limerick Carlow Wicklow 926
953 M8 Clonmel E20 Kilkenny
Slea 1041 N20 Cahir N25 Wexford
Head N8 E30 Waterford Carnsore
Dingle Bay Killarney M8 Pt
N22 Cork
Bantry Bay

Cardigan
Aberystwyth Cam
Bay

St George's Channel
Fishguard A487
Haverfordwest A40 A40 Word
Carmarthen A470
Merthyr Glouces
Swansea Tydfil
Neath M4 Newport
Port M4 A40
Talbot Cardiff A40 Bath
Bristol Channel
Barnstaple Exmoor Bath
Tiverton Taunton M5
Bodmin Dartmoor Exeter Dorchester Po
Penzance A30 Exmouth Bo
Land's End Truro A30 A30 Torquay Weyr
Isles of Scilly Plymouth Lyme
Lizard Point Start Point Bay

Eng l

48°

Channel Cherbour
Islands Octeville
GB St Peter Po
Guernsey
Jersey
St Helier

Golfe de
St-Malo
Morlaix
Brest N12
Guipavas E50 St-Brieuc St-Mal
N12
Quimper Dinan
N165 N12 D13
Loudéac
Quimperlé Rennes N15
Lorient N24
Vannes E60 Châteaubr
La Baule- E603 A11
Escoublac Nant
St-Nazaire Loire Vert
A83

La Roche-
sur-Yon
Les Sables-
d'Olonne E03
P

La Rochelle
Rochefort E602 SAIN
Royan
MÉDOC

Mérignac B
Arcachon Pessac
La Teste A63

Ferrol
A Coruña AP9
AG55 Avilés Gijón-
Cabo Fisterra E01 A8 A8 Xijón Costa Verde Santander
A9 Cangas del Oviedo Pola de
A Estrada Narcea Narcea Mieres Siero 18 Torrelavega
Santiago Lugo A66 A8 Bilbao Algorta
Vilagarcía AP53 Lalín Monforte Pola de A8 Llodio San Sebastián
de Arousa Pontevedra de Lemos Sil A67 Bayonne
Vigo CORDILLERA-CANTÁBRICA Irún Biarritz
Ourense Ponferrada 2117 León Dax
Viana El Teleno AP66 AP68 Pau
8° 6° 4° 2°

100 km
0 100 200 km
0 50 100 miles

14° 12° 10°
50°
48°
46°
44°
42°

MÉDOC
LONGE
Angoulême
Limoges
LIMOUSIN
Ussel
Riom
Roanne
sur-Saône
Ambérieu-
en-Bugey
Monthey
Bellinzona
Domodossola
Lugano
Périgueux
Clermont-
Ferrand
Thiers
Villeurbanne
Lyon
Annecy
Cluses
Martigny
Sion
Omegna
Varese
Com
Mérignac
Pessac
Bergerac
Dordogne
Isle
Ibourne
Brive-
la-Gaillarde
St-É
Issoire
Le-Puy-
en-Velay
Annonay
Vienne
Aix-les-Bains
Mt Blanc
Aosta
Arona
Monz
Bordeaux
GUYENNE
Tulle
AUVERGNE
Tournon-
sur-Rhône
Grenoble
Voiron
Massif de la Vanoise
Ivrea
Busto Arsizio
Novara
Mi
Marmande
Agen
Moissac
Cahors
Figeac
CENTRAL
Romans-
sur-Isère
Valence
Alpes
Briançon
Torino
Alessandria
Pavia
Voghera
Mont-de-Marsan
Montauban
Carmaux
Rodez
Millau
Dauphiné
Gap
Cuneo
Fossano
Ovada
Genov
Dax
Auch
Albi
Cévennes
Alès
Montélimar
Digne-
les-Bains
Savona
La Spe
Toulouse
Nîmes
Avignon
Cavaillon
Nice
MONTE CARLO
San Remo
Golfo di
Genova
Tarbes
Lourdes
PYRÉNÉES
Montpellier
Arles
Manosque
Salon-de-Provence
Grasse
Cannes
Antibes
Imperia
Albenga
Foix
Béziers
Sète
Agde
Aix-en-Provence
Marignane
St-Raphaël
Côte d'Azur
LIGURIAN SE
Narbonne
Carcassonne
Marseille
Aubagne
La Ciotat
Toulon
Îles d'Hyères
Cap Corse
Monte Stello 1307
Ba
ANDORRA
LA VELLA
Perpignan
Port-Vendres
Étang de Leucate
Golfe du Lion
CORSE
(CORSICA)
Monte Padro 2393
Monte Rotondo 2622
Huesca
Figueres
Golfe de Sagone
Monzón
Vic
Olot
Costa Brava
Ajaccio
Pte Porto-
d'Ovace Vecchio
agoza
Lleida
Manresa
Girona
Capo Pertusato
la Ma
Igualada
Sabadell
Blanes
SARDEGNA
(SARDINIA)
El Prat de Llobregat
Mataró
Barcelona
Vilanova i la Geltrú
Golfo dell'Asinara
Porto
Torres
Olb
Tarragona
Golf de
Sant Jordi
Sassari
Alghero
Tempio
Pausania
Ozieri
Tortosa
Castellón de la Plana
Burriana
MALLORCA
(MAJORCA)
Cap de
Formentor
Menorca
(Minorca)
Ciutadella
Mahón
Nuoro
Oristano
gunto
Palma
de Mallorca
Inca
Manacor
Macomer
ncia
Eivissa (Ibiza)
Terralba
Guspini
Eivissa (Ibiza)
Illa de
Cabrera
Villacidro
Iglesias
era
día
Formentera
ISLAS BALEARES
(BALEARIC ISLANDS)
Carbonia
Sant' Antioco
Cagliari
Quartu Sar
Golfo di
Cagliari
Dorm
rosa-La Vila Joiosa

0   100   200 km
0   50   100 miles

M   I   T   E   R   R   A   N   E   A   N   S   E   A   38°

ALGER
Aïn
Taya
Dellys
Collo
Ténès
Gouraya
Tipasa
Koléa
Boumerdes
Skikda
Annaba
Mateu
led Farès
Kerba
Cherchell
Larba
Tizi Ouzou
Bejaïa
Jijel
El Mila
El Hadjar
El Tarf
El Kala
Tébourba
L'Ari
Aïn Defla
Miliana
Médéa
Akbou
Bougaa
Mila
Azzaba
Dréan
Béja
Bin
Ech Chélif
Theniet El
Had
Ksar
el Boukhari
Sour el
Ghozlane
Sétif
Chelghoum
el Aïd
Constantine
Jendouba
Souk
Ahras
Le Kef
TN
Tissemsilt
DZ
Sidi Aïssa
Bordj Bou
Arréridj
El Eulma
Oued Zénati
Sédrata
M'Daourouch
Siliana
Chahbounia
Aïn el
Hadjel
Aïn Oulmene
Aïn-M'Lila
El Aouinet
Tiaret
Mahdia
Aïn Oussera
M'Sila
Aïn Azel
Oum el
Bouaghi
Aïn Beïda
Morsott
Atlas Tellien
Zenzach
Batna
hemeret
Souguet
Ksar Chellala
Bou Saâda
Barika
Kalaa

halvøya
Vardø
E75
gerhalvøya
Mys Nemetskiy
Vadsø
E6
Varangerfjorden
Kirkenes
Nikel'
Zapolyarnyy
E105
Polyarnyy
Severomorsk
Tumannyy
M. Kanin Nos
Vozv. Kanin Kamen'
M. Laydennyy
Gorn
69°
Murmansk
Kola
M u r m a n s k i y   B e r e g
Gremikha
M. Svyatov Nos
Indigskaya
M. Mikulkin
Guba
nanijärvi
Lovozero
M. Konushin
Poluostrov Kanin
Kaninskiy Bereg
Cheshskaya
Guba
Olenegorsk
Vozvyshennost' Keyvy
O. Morzhovets
Mezenskaya
Guba
66°
Monchegorsk
Oz. Ekostrovskaya
Kirovsk
M. Voronov Guba
Mezen
Lokan
tekojärvi
Apatity
E105
Mezen
Kovdor
Polyarnye Zori
Oz. Imandra
Arctic Circle
T e r s k i y   B e r e g
Oz. Kolvitskoye
Kandalaksha
Ūmba
Kuzomen
G o r l o   B e l o g o   M o r y a
Z i m n i y   B e r e g
65°
Alakurtti
Kandalakshshkiy Zaliv
Dvinskaya
Kemijärvi
Salla
Loukhi
Guba
Severodvinsk
Arkhangel'sk
Kemijärvi
E63
Kitka
Kesten'ga
Oz. Pyaozero
K a r e l ' s k i y   B e r e g
E105
Solovetskiye
Ostrova
Isakogorka
Novodvinsk
64°
järvet
Myojärvi
E63
Kuusamo
Oz. Topozero
M18
Rabocheostrovsk
Taivalkoski
Kalevala
Kem
Onezhskaya Guba
Onega
Voynitsa
Oz. Verkhneye
Kuyto
Yushkozero
Kiantajärvi
Belomorsk
P o m o r s k i y   B e r e g
Ämmänsaari
E63
Kostomuksha
E105
Bereznik
M8
Hyrynsalmi
912
Mirnyy
62°
jjärvi
22
Kajaani
Kuhmo
Reboly
Oz. Leksozero
Segezha
Oz. Vygozero
E63
76
75
Segozerskoye
Vdkhr.
M18
Ozero
Vodlozero
Nyandoma
Kiuruvesi
Nurmes
Lieksa
Sukkozero
Oz. Gimol'skoye
Medvezh'yegorsk
isalmi
87
Pielinen
E105
Podyuga
Konosha
E63
Kuopio
Kallavesi
Outokumpu
Joensuu
Pyhäselkä
Kondopoga
Oz.
Syamozero
Onezhskoye
Ozero
Pudozh
Kargopol'
Ozero
Lacha
Suonenjoki
Oriyesi
Suoyarvi
Petrozavodsk
Sheltozero
Vytegra
Ozero
Vozhe
järvä
Pieksämäki
A131
M18
järkylä
E63
Varkaus
Savonlinna
Sortavala
Pitkyaranta
A130
Podporozh'ye
Ozero
Beloye
Belozersk
Sheksninskaya
Vdkhr.
Heinola
Mikkeli
Saimaa
Lakhdenpokh'ya
E105
Olonets
Loadeynoye
Pole
Ozero
Kubenskoye
60°
Lahti
Kuusankoski
Svetogorsk
Priozersk
Ladozhskoye
koski
Lappeenranta
Imatra
Pielavesi
Mäntsälä
Orimattila
Hamina
A124
Ozero
23
Volkhov
Tikhvin 34°
a Gryada
Babayevo
36°
38°
Kaduy
Cherepovets
E75
E18
Kotka
Sertolovo
Vsevolozhsk
E105
oretsk

FIN

RUS

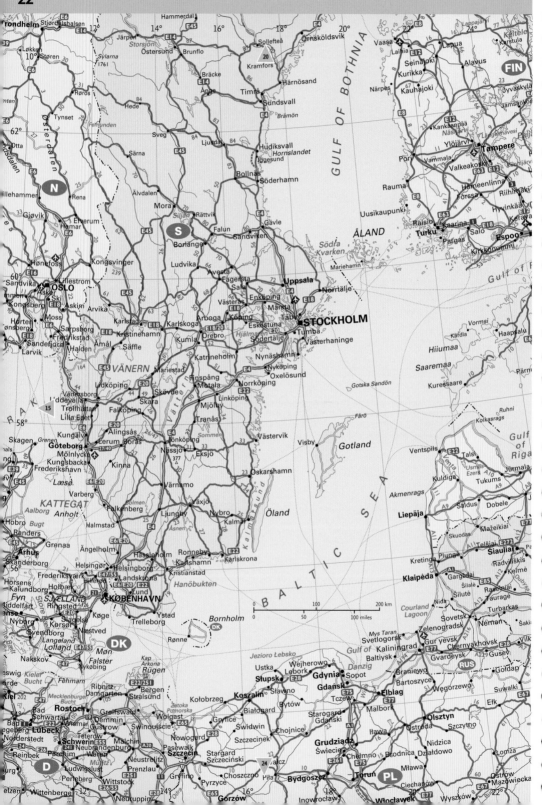

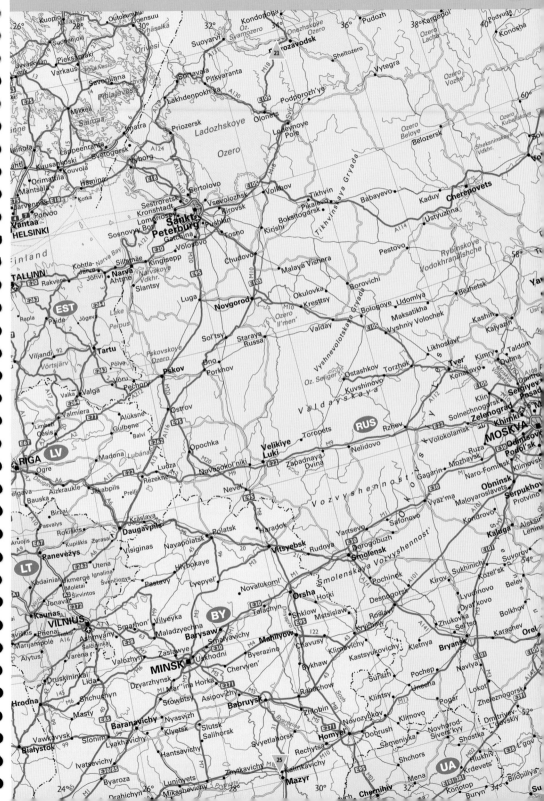

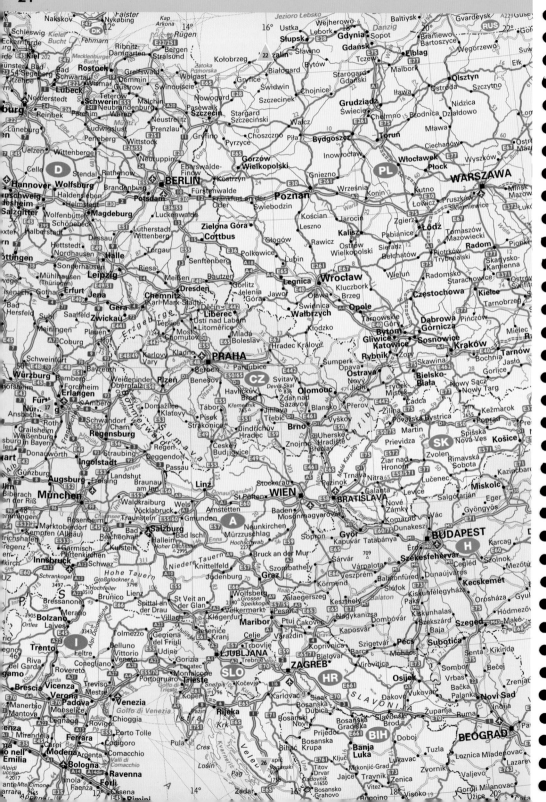

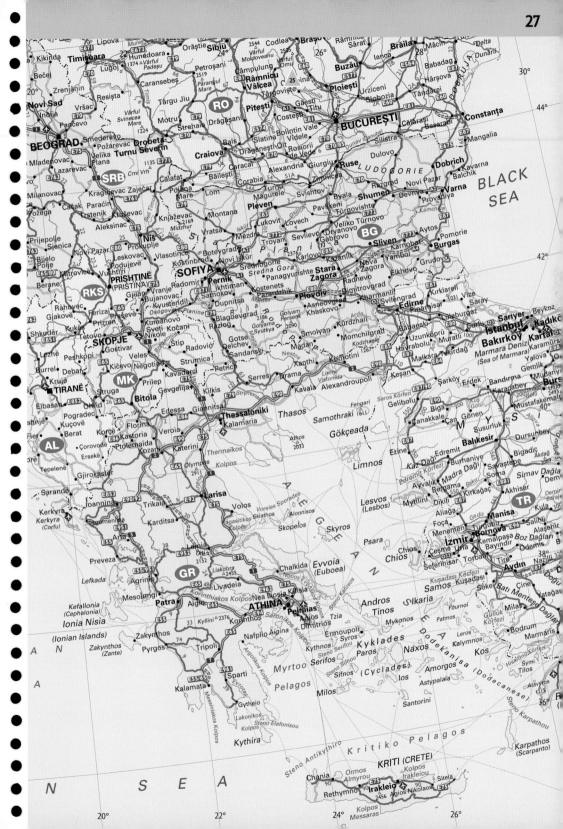

	Road maps	Carte routière	Straßenkarten
E55	Euro route number	Route européenne	Europastraßennummer
A13	Motorway	Autoroute	Autobahn
	Motorway – toll	Autoroute à péage	Gebührenpflichtige Autobahn
47	Motorway junction – full access	Echangeur d'autoroute avec accès libre	Autobahnauffahrt mit vollem Zugang
12	Motorway junction – restricted access	Echangeur d'autoroute avec accès limité	Autobahnauffahrt mit beschränktem Zugang
	Motorway services	Aire de service sur autoroute	Autobahnraststätte
309	Main road – dual carriageway	Route principale à chaussées séparées	Hauptstraße - Zweispurig
	Main road – single carriageway	Route principale à une seule chaussée	Hauptstraße - Einspurig
516	Secondary road – dual carriageway	Route secondaire à chaussées séparées	Zweispurige Nebenstraße
	Secondary road – single carriageway	Route secondaire à une seule chaussée	Einspurige Nebenstraße
	Motorway tunnel	Tunnel (autoroute)	Tunnel (Autobahn)
	Main road tunnel	Tunnel (route principale)	Tunnel (Hauptstraße)
	Motorway/road under construction	Autoroute/route en construction	Autobahn/Straße im Bau
	Road toll	Route à péage	Gebührenpflichtige Straße
2587	Mountain pass (height in metres)	Col (altitude en mètres)	Pass (Höhe in Metern)
	International airport	Aéroport international	Internationaler Flughafen
	Railway	Chemin de fer	Eisenbahn
	Tunnel	Tunnel	Tunnel
Rotterdam	Car ferry	Bac pour autos	Autofähre
▲2587	Summit (height in metres)	Sommet (altitude en mètres)	Berg (Höhe in Metern)
▲	Volcano	Volcan	Vulkan
	Canal	Canal	Kanal
	International boundary	Frontière d'état	Landesgrenze
	Disputed International boundary	Frontière litigieuse	Umstrittene Staatsgrenze
D	Country abbreviation	Abréviation du pays	Nationalitätszeichen
	Urban area	Zone urbaine	Stadtgebiet
28	Adjoining page indicator	Indication de la page contiguë	Randhinweis auf Folgekarte
	National Park	Parc national	Nationalpark
	Scenic route	Parcours pittoresque	Landschaftlich schöne strecke

Road numbers in France are currently being modified and are subject to change.	En France, le numérotage routier est en cours de modification; des changements sont donc possibles.	Die Straßennummerierungen in Frankreich werden zur Zeit geändert.

1 : 2 000 000

| 0 | 20 | 40 | 60 | 80 | 100 kilometres |
| 0 | | 20 | | 40 | | 60 miles |

1 cm = 20 kilometres
1 cm = 12.5 miles

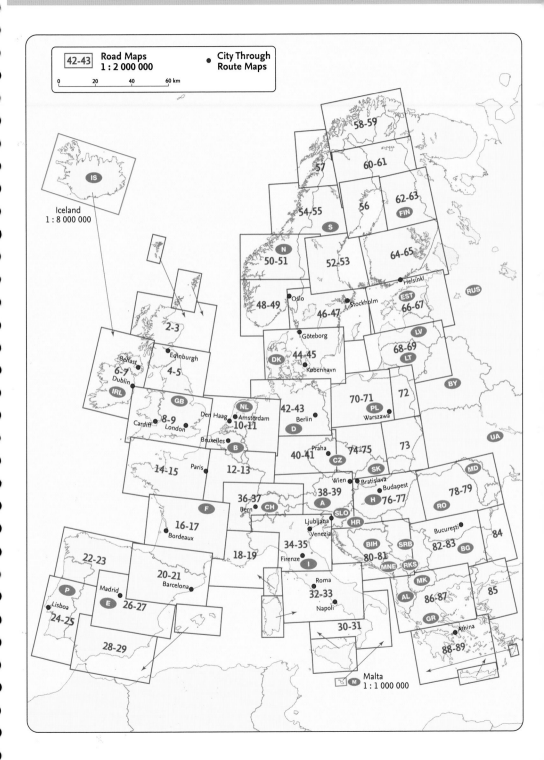

Road Maps
1 : 2 000 000

42-43

0   20   40   60 km

City Through
Route Maps

Iceland
1 : 8 000 000

IS

58-59

57

60-61

54-55   56   62-63   FIN

S

N   50-51   52-53   64-65

48-49   Oslo   46-47   Stockholm   EST   RUS

Göteborg   66-67

2-3   DK   44-45   Helsinki   LV

Edinburgh   68-69

Belfast   4-5   København   LT

6-7   BY

Dublin

IRL   GB   NL   70-71   72

8-9   Den Haag   Amsterdam   42-43   PL

Cardiff   London   10-11   Berlin   Warszawa   UA

Bruxelles   D

B   Praha   74-75   73

14-15   Paris   12-13   40-41   CZ

SK   MD

36-37   38-39   Wien   Bratislava   Budapest   78-79

F   Bern   CH   A   H   76-77   RO

16-17   SLO   Ljubljana

Bordeaux   HR   Venezia   Bucureşti   84

34-35   BIH   SRB   82-83   BG

22-23   20-21   18-19   Firenze   80-81   MNE   RKS   MK

P   Madrid   Barcelona   I   Roma   AL   86-87   85

Lisboa   E   26-27   32-33   GR

24-25   Napoli   Athina

28-29   30-31   88-89

Malta
1 : 1 000 000   M

1 2 3 4 5 6

B

Westray
Westray
Rousay
Brough Head
Birsay
Mainland
ORKNEY
ISLANDS   Stromness
Ward Hill 479
Hoy   Flotta

Cape Wrath

Pentland Firth
Island of Stroma
Dunnet Head
Strathy
Point   Scrabster
Thurso

Butt of Lewis

Cranstackie
Foinaven 915
Arkle 787
Beinn Hope
Ben Hope 764
Beinn Stumanadh
927   Ben
Loyal 527   CAITHNESS   Wick

C

Flannan
Isles

Muirneag
248
Tolsta Head
Tiumpan Head
Eye
Peninsula

Handa
Island   Ben Hee
Ben Stack 721
Quinag 808

SUTHERLAND

Morven
706   Scarben
626

Great
Bernera
Mealisval 574
LEWIS
Beinn
Mholach 292
Stornoway

Ben Klibreck 961
Ben More
Assynt 998
Canisp 846   Loch
Cul Mor   Shin

Ben
Klibreck
521
Ben Horn

Scarp
Tirga Mor 679
Beinn
Mhòr 798   672
Tarbert
Kebock Head

Rubha
Coigeach
Suilven 731
Stac
Pollaidh 613   Carn
Chuinneag 898
Carn
t-Sabhail 379
Dornoch Firth

THE MINCH

D

Pabbay
Berneray
South
Harris   Rodel
Scalpay
Shiant
Islands
Rubha Reidh

Greenstone
Point

Summer
Isles

Meall
Liath Choire 635   548

Ullapool

Beinn
Dearg
1084   Carn
Gorm   Easter Ross
Beinn
Tharsuinn 692
Alness

Lossiemouth
Elgin
Forres
Mill Buie
371

North Uist   Lochmaddy

Sound of Harris

Vaternish
Point
Ben Geary 284
Loch
Snizort   Trotternish

An Teallach 1062
Mullach Coire
Mhic Fhearchair 1019
Liathach 1110
Slioch 980
Sgurr
Mor   Ben
Wyvis
1046

Dingwall
Black
Isle   Nairn   Spey

Carne
na Loine   Ben Rinnes

Monach
Islands
Baleshare
Benbecula

Sound of Monach

Loch
Maree
Beinn Alligin 985
Liathach 1054
Sgorr
Ruadh 960   Sgurr
a'Mhuilinn 879
Sgurr
a'Chòire Ghlais 1083

Inverness

Grantown-
on-Spey 549   Cook's

South
Uist   Beinn Mhòr 620
Lochboisdale

Healabhal
Bheag 488
Portree
SKYE   The
Storr 719
Raasay
Scalpay

Beinn Bhan 896
Beinn
Sgritheall   Aonach
Buidhe 899   Glen Affric
Loch
Ness   GB
Carn
Odhar
802   Badenoch
Aviemore

Cairn Gorm 840
Carn Mor 804

E

Barra
Vatersay   Castlebay

Sea of the
Hebrides
Canna

Cuillin Hills 993
Sgurr
Alasdair
Bla
Bheinn 928
Soay
Ardvasar
Ladhar Bheinn 1020

Kyle of
Lochalsh
A'Chraolaig 1120
Sgurr
na'Ciche 1040
935   Carn
Chuilinn 788
Carn Dearg 816
Creag
Meagaidh 926
Cairn Gorm
Ben Macdui 1309 1245
Cairn Toul 1291

CAIRNGORMS
Ben Avon 1171
Meall
Chuaich 951
An Sgarsoch 1006   Lochnagar
1155

Eriskay
Sandray
Pabbay
Mingulay
Berneray

Rum 812
Askival
Eigg 393
Sound of Arisaig
Muck

Mallaig
Loch Morar
Gulvain 987
Loch Arkaig
Loch
Lochy   Braemar
Glas Maol
1068   Mayar 928

F

Coll

Tiree

Ardnamurchan
Ben Hiant 528
Ben Resipol 845

Fort William
Ben Nevis 1344
Binnein
Mor 1128
Glen Coe
Bidean
nam Bian 1150   Ben
Alder
1148
Beinn Dearg 1008
Carn nan
Gabhar 1121   928

Schiehallion 1083
Loch
Lyon   Pitlochry
Blairgowrie

Treshnish Isles
Staffa
Ulva 966
Craignure

Lochaline
Duart
Gleann 717

Fuar
Bheinn 765
Beinn
Sgulaird 932
Stob
Ghabhar 1087
Meall
Heasgarnich 1076
Ben
Lawers 1214

Breadalbane
Ben
Chonzie   Perth

Mull

Iona
Ross
of Mull
Fionnphort

Oban
Ben Bute
Ben More

Ben Cruachan 1126
Loch
Etive
Ben Buie 717
Loch Awe   Beinn
Bhuidhe 948
Ben More 1130   Ben
Vorlich 985   Crieff

G

Colonsay

Oronsay

Scarba
Cruach
Scarba
Luing 449
Lochgilphead

Kerrera
Seil
Easdale
Beinn
Resipol 515
Beinn
Chapull 526

Beinn
Bhreac 943
Vorlich
811   Ben More
Ben
Ledi 879
Callander
Dunblane 720

Stirling
Cowdenbeath
Glenrothes

Jura
Tarbert
Beinn
an Oir
Paps of Jura 785

Beinn Mhor 742
Doune
Hill 734
Loch
Lomond   Gargunnock
Hills 570
Denny   Alloa
Grangemouth
Falkirk
Bo'ness   Edinburgh

Islay
Port Askaig
Feolin
Ferry   Bridgend 491
Ardpatrick
Point   Gigha
Beinn an Tuirc 454   Hill of Stake 522   Greenock
Dunoon
Helensburgh
Alexandria
Dumbarton
Clydebank
Paisley
Barrhead
Beith   Glasgow
Cumbernauld
Bathgate
Coatbridge
Motherwell
Wishaw   Livingston

H

Machir Bay
Portnahaven
The Oa
Mull Of Oa   Port
Ellen

Knapdale
Sound
of Bute
Rothesay
Largs
Ardrossan
Saltcoats
Brodick
Irvine   Kilwinning
Troon   Kilmarnock
Galston
Crosshands

East Kilbride
Hamilton
Lanark
Blackhope
Scar
Peebles
Tweeddale

1

Kintyre
Goat Fell 874
Arran
Ard Bheinn
512
Goat Fell

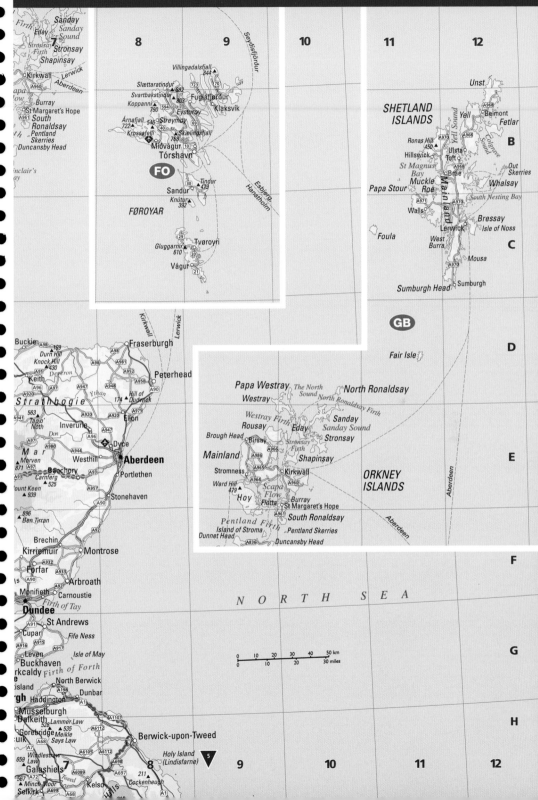

7 **8** **9** **10** **11** **12**

Sanday
Eday
Sanday
Sound
Stronsay
Shapinsay
Firth
Stronsay
Firth
Kirkwall
Lerwick
Aberdeen
A960
Burray
St Margaret's Hope
South
Ronaldsay
Pentland
Skerries
Duncansby Head
Sinclair's

Villingadalsfjall
844
Slættaratindur 882
Svartbakstindur 803
Koppanni
790
594
Fuglafjørður
Eysturoy
Klaksvík
Árnafjall
722
546
Streymoy
Krossafelli
40
768
Skælingsfjall
Midvágur 10
Tórshavn

FO

Tindur
479
Sandur
Knútur
392

FØROYAR

Gluggarnir
610
Tvøroyri
29
20
Vágur 21

**SHETLAND
ISLANDS**

Unst
A968
Yell
Belmont
Fetlar
Ronas Hill
450
A970
Ulsta
Toft
A968
Out
Skerries
Hillswick
St Magnus
Bay
Brae
A971
Muckle
Roe
Whalsay
Papa Stour
A970
South Nesting Bay
Walls
A971
A970
Bressay
Isle of Noss
Foula
West
Burra
Lerwick
A970
Mousa
Sumburgh Head
Sumburgh

GB

B

C

Serdisfjördur
Esbjerg
Hanstholm

Kirkwall
Lerwick

Fair Isle

D

Buckie
A98
199
Durn Hill
Knock Hill
430
A95
A96
A97
A952
A981
A950
A947
A948
174
Hill of
Dudwick
A975
A90
Keith
Deveron
Fraserburgh
Peterhead
Strathbogie
563
Tap o'
Noth
Ythan
A920
A920
A941
Don
A920
A96
A947
A980
A944
Ellon
A93
Inverurie
Dyce
Aberdeen
Westhill
Portlethen
Mar
871
Morven
A97
Banchory
Carnferg
525
A93
Stonehaven
ount Keen
939
A957
A90
896
Ben Tirran
A92
Brechin
Kirriemuir
Montrose
Forfar
A933
A90
Arbroath
A92
Monifieth
Carnoustie
Firth of Tay
Dundee
St Andrews
A91
Cupar
A916
A915
A917
Fife Ness
Leven
Isle of May
Buckhaven
rkcaldy Firth of Forth
sland
North Berwick
gh Haddington
A198
Dunbar
Musselburgh
Dalkeith
A1
Gorebridge
520
Lammer Law
535
Meikle Says Law
A1107
ulk
A68
A7
Berwick-upon-Tweed
Windlestraw
659 Law
A6105
A6112
A698
Holy Island
(Lindisfarne)
Galashiels
A72
211
567
Minch Moor
A6089
A697
Cockenheugh
Selkirk
A68
A1

Papa Westray
Westray
The North
Sound
North Ronaldsay
North Ronaldsay Firth
Westray Firth
Rousay
Sanday
Sanday Sound
Brough Head
Eday
Stronsay
Birsay
Stronsay
Firth
Shapinsay
Mainland
A986
A966
Stromness
A965
Kirkwall
A964
A960
Ward Hill
479
Scapa
Flow
Hoy
Flotta
Burray
St Margaret's Hope
A961
South Ronaldsay
Pentland Firth
Island of Stroma
Pentland Skerries
Dunnet Head
A836
Duncansby Head

**ORKNEY
ISLANDS**

Aberdeen

Aberdeen

E

F

N O R T H   S E A

G

0 10 20 30 40 50 km
0   10   20   30 miles

H

7 **8** **9** **10** **11** **12**

5

7
8
9
10
11
12
B
C
D
E
F
G
H
St Andrews
Fife Ness
Isle of May
Leven
Buckhaven
Firth of Forth
North Berwick
Dunbar
Haddington
Musselburgh
Lammer Law
Meikle Says Law
Gorebridge
Berwick-upon-Tweed
Holy Island (Lindisfarne)
Windlestraw Law
Galashiels
Kelso
Cockenheugh
Selkirk
The Cheviot
Hawick
Teviotdale
Cheviot Hills
Windy Gyle
Carter Bar
Alnwick
Amble
Roan Fell
GB
NORTHUMBERLAND
Ashington
Morpeth
Blyth
Kielder Water
Bedlington
Cramlington
Ponteland
Whitley Bay
NORTH SEA
Newcastle upon Tyne
South Shields
Hexham
Prudhoe
Gateshead
Sunderland
Stanley
Washington
Consett
Durham
Seaham
Peterlee
Cross Fell
Chapelfell Top
Spennymoor
Ferryhill
Hartlepool
IJmuiden
Penrith
Bishop Auckland
Billingham
Redcar
Newton Aycliffe
Teesdale
Stockton-on-Tees
Middlesbrough
Helvellyn
Barnard Castle
Guisborough
Darlington
Yarm
Whitby
Harter Fell
Cleveland Hills
North York Moors
Round Hill
High Seat
Richmond
Windermere
The Calf
Kendal
Northallerton
Scalby
Scarborough
Eastfield
Pickering
Filey
Vale of Pickering
Thirsk
Yorkshire Dales
Whernside
Ingleborough
Great Whernside
Pen-y-Ghent
Pennines
Vale of York
Flamborough Head
Ulverston
Carnforth
Ripon
Norton
Yorkshire Wolds
Bridlington
Bridlington Bay
Lancaster
Ward's Stone
Knaresborough
Haxby
Driffield
Skipton
Harrogate
York
Pocklington
Barnoldswick
Ilkley
Otley
Wetherby
Hornsea
Thornton
Pendle Hill
Keighley
Tadcaster
Clitheroe
Colne
Beverley
Boulsworth Hill
Bradford
Leeds
Garforth
Selby
Anlaby
Kingston upon Hull
Preston
Blackburn
Burnley
Halifax
Rothwell
Withernsea
Accrington
Knottingley
Goole
Leyland
Dewsbury
Barton-upon-Humber
Chorley
Todmorden
Elland
Wakefield
Immingham
Spurn Head
Rochdale
Huddersfield
Thorne
Scunthorpe
Mouth of The Humber
Ormskirk
Bolton
Bury
Honley
Hatfield
Grimsby
Cleethorpes
Wigan
Oldham
Brigg
Kirkby
Middleton
Holmfirth
Barnsley
Doncaster
St Helens
Salford
Manchester
Chapeltown
Margery Hill
Rotherham
Rotterdam, Zeebrugge
Liverpool
Sale
Glossop
Kinder Scout
Louth
Widnes
Warrington
Stockport
Sheffield
Gainsborough
Lincolnshire Wolds
Runcorn
Wilmslow
Peak District
Dronfield
Worksop
Ellesmere Port
Knutsford
Shining Tor
Buxton
Staveley
Northwich
Macclesfield
Bolsover
Ollerton
Lincoln
Skegness
Chester
Middlewich
Chesterfield
Mansfield
Sandbach
Congleton
Matlock
Sutton in Ashfield
Coningsby
Crewe
Leek
Alfreton
East Fen
West Fen
Nantwich
Kidsgrove
Belper
Ripley
Newark-on-Trent
Wrexham (Wrecsam)
Audley
Stoke-on-Trent
Hucknall
Heanor
Sheringham
Newcastle-under-Lyme
Cheadle
Carlton
Sleaford
Boston
The Wash
Cromer
Whitchurch
Ilkeston
Nottingham
Fakenham
Stone
Derby
Long Eaton
Grantham
North Walsham
Market Drayton
Uttoxeter
Burton upon Trent
Ashby de la Zouch
Loughborough
Melton Mowbray
Bourne
Spalding
King's Lynn
Stafford
Taverham
Newport
Rugeley
Coalville
Stamford
Market Deeping
Dereham
Wellington
Cannock
Lichfield
Syston
Oakham
Wisbech
Norwich
Telford
Oakengates
Tamworth
Leicester
Uppingham
The Fens
Wymondham
Walsall
Atherstone
Oadby
Peterborough
0 10 20 30 40 50 km
0 10 20 30 miles

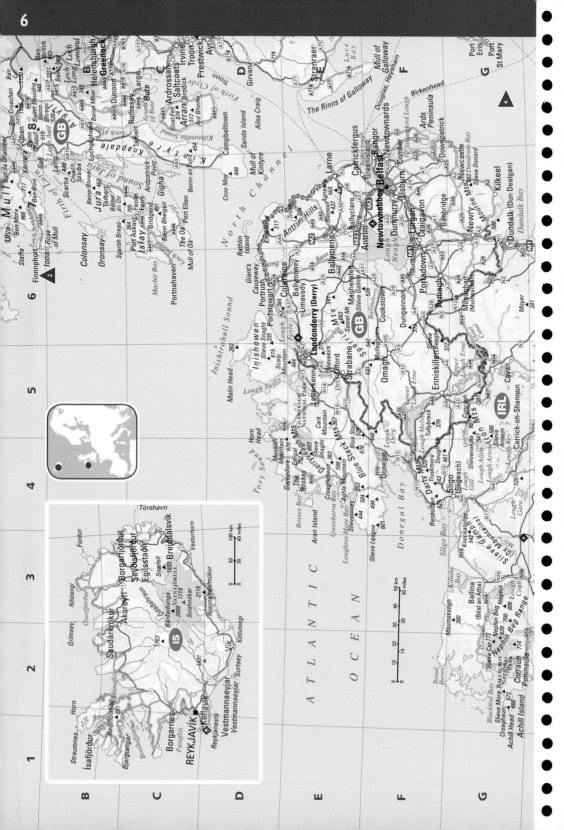

IRISH SEA

ST GEORGE'S CHANNEL

Douglas
Holyhead
Liverpool
Newport Bay
Fishguard
Strumble Head
St David's Head
Ramsey Island
Skomer Island
St Ann's Head
Milford Haven
Haverfordwest (Hwlffordd)
Pembroke
Pembroke Dock
Swansea
Cherbourg, Roscoff
Roscoff
Carnsore Point
Saltee Islands

Drogheda (Droichead Átha)
Balbriggan
Skerries
Malahide
Portmarnock
Swords
DUBLIN (BAILE ÁTHA CLIATH)
Dún Laoghaire
Lucan
Leixlip
Celbridge
Bray (Bré)
Greystones
Wicklow (Cill Mhantáin)
Wicklow Head
Bray Head
Djouce Mountain
Mullaghcleevaun
WICKLOW MOUNTAINS NATIONAL PARK
Lugnaquilla
Arklow (An tInbhear Mór)
Wexford (Loch Garman)
Wexford Bay
Enniscorthy
New Ross
Waterford (Port Láirge)
Tramore (Trá Mhór)

Navan
Hill of Tara
Naas (An Nás)
Newbridge (Droichead Nua)
The Curragh
Carlow (Ceatharlach)
Athy
Kilkenny (Cill Chainnigh)
Blackstairs Mts
Mount Leinster
Brandon Hill
Booley Hills
Carrick-on-Suir
Clonmel
Dungarvan (Dún Garbhán)
Youghal (Eochaill)
Youghal Bay

Mullingar (An Muileann gCearr)
Lough Ennell
Tullamore (Tulach Mhór)
Portlaoise
Slieve Bloom Mts
Thurles (Durlas)
Tipperary
Golden Vale
Slievenamon
Knockmealdown Mts
Midleton
Cobh (An Cóbh)
Great Island
Old Head of Kinsale

Longford
Athlone (Baile Átha Luain)
Ballinasloe (Béal Átha na Slua)
Nenagh (An tAonach)
Silvermine Mts
Arra Mts
Silvermine
Limerick (Luimneach)
Slievefelim
Galtee Mts
Galtymore
Ballyhoura Mts
Mallow
Nagles Mts
Cork (Corcaigh)

Roscommon
Lough Ree
Lough Derg
Slieve Aughty Mts
Slieve Bernagh
Ennis (Inis)
Burren
Mullaghareirk Mts
Boggeragh Mts
Musheramore
Killarney (Cill Airne)
Macgillycuddy's Reeks
Carrantuohill
Mangerton
Shehy Mts
Knockaboy

Castlebar (Caisleán an Bharraigh)
Westport
Murrisk
Croagh Patrick
Mweelrea
Benmore
Maumturk Mts
Connemara
Clifden
Iar Connaught
Galway (Gaillimh)
Galway Bay
Aran Islands
Inishmore
Inishmaan
Inisheer
Hag's Head
Liscannor Bay
Loop Head
Kerry Hd
Tralee (Trá Lí)
Tralee Bay
Dingle (Daingean)
Mish Mts
Brandon Mountain
Slieve Mish
Iveragh
Knocknadober
Valencia Island
Bray Head
Great Blasket I.
Dursey Island
Beara
Bear Island
Bantry Bay
Sherkin Island
Cape Clear
Clear Island

North Sound
Mouth of the Shannon

Clew Bay
Clare Island
Inishturk
Inishbofin
Inishshark

IRISH SEA

DUBLIN (BAILE ÁTHE CLIATH)
Dún Laoghaire
Malahide
Portmarnock
Douglas
Dublin Bay
Bray (Bré)
Greystones
Djouce Mountain
Wicklow (Cill Mhantáin)
Arklow (An tInbhear Mór)
IRL
Rosslare

Holyhead (Caergybi)
Holy Island
Anglesey (Môn)
Llandudno
Prestatyn
Rhyl
Colwyn Bay
Bangor
Caernarfon
Menai Strait
Snowdon
Snowdonia
Caernarfon Bay
Ffestiniog
Lleyn Peninsula
Bardsey Sound
Bardsey Island
Tremadog Bay
Cadair Idris
Penygadair
Cardigan Bay
Plynlimon
Aberystwyth
St George's Channel
Strumble Head
Fishguard (Abergwaun)
Newport Bay
Fishguard Bay
St David's Head
Ramsey Island
Mynydd Preseli
St Bride's Bay
Skomer Island
Pembrokeshire Coast
St Ann's Head
Milford Haven
Pembroke Dock
Pembroke
Haverfordwest (Hwlffordd)
Carmarthen (Caerfyrddin)
Carmarthen Bay
Tenby
Llanelli
Gorseinon
Swansea (Abertawe)
Port Talbot
Porthcawl
Llantwit Major
Barry
Ammanford (Rhydaman)
Pontardawe
Neath (Castell-y-Nedd)
Aberdare
Pontypridd
Bridgend
Penarth
Cardiff (Caerdydd)
Llanfairfechan
Denbigh
Connah's Quay
Flint
Buckley
Wrexham (Wrecsam)
Rhosllanerchrugog
Oswestry
Newtown (Y Drenewydd)
Builth Wells
Brecon
Brecon Beacons
Black Mountains
Ebbw Vale
Merthyr Tydfil
Blaenavon
Abertillery
Abergavenny (Y Fenni)
Pontypool
Cwmbran
Risca
Caerphilly
Caldicot
Newport (Casnewydd)
Portishead
Weston-super-Mare
Bristol Channel
Ilfracombe
Braunton
Barnstaple
Bideford
Hartland Point
Lundy Island
Bideford Bay
Exmoor Forest
Minehead
Highbridge
Dunkery Beacon
Bridgwater
Taunton
Wellington
Tiverton
Crediton
Exeter
Dartmoor
High Willhays
Launceston
Tavistock
Bodmin Moor
Liskeard
Saltash
Plymouth
St Austell
Newquay
Redruth
Truro
Camborne
St Ives
Penzance
Land's End
Mount's Bay
Helston
Falmouth
Isles of Scilly
Hugh Town

Birkenhead
Liverpool
Wallasey
Hoylake
Bootle
Crosby
Widnes
Runcorn
Ellesmere Port
Neston
Chester
Northwich
Sandbach
Crewe
Nantwich
Whitchurch
Market Drayton
Newcastle-under-Lyme
Stoke-on-Trent
Cheadle
Shrewsbury
Wellington
Telford
Wolverhampton
West Bromwich
Dudley
Stourbridge
Halesowen
Kidderminster
Bewdley
Stourport-on-Severn
Redditch
Worcester
Droitwich Spa
Leominster
Ludlow
Bridgnorth
Hereford
Ross-on-Wye
Gloucester
Monmouth (Trefynwy)
Chepstow
Lydney
Dursley
Chipping Sodbury
Bristol
Kingswood
Keynsham
Bath
Melksham
Trowbridge
Frome
Badstock
Wells
Glastonbury
Street
Bridgwater
Chard
Crewkerne
Yeovil
Sherborne
Blandford Forum
Dorchester
Bridport
Seaton
Sidmouth
Exmouth
Dawlish
Teignmouth
Newton Abbot
Torquay
Paignton
Brixham
Dartmouth
Start Bay
Lyme Bay
Weymouth
Isle of Portland
Bill of Portland
St Alban's Head
Swanage
Poole
Wimborne Minster
Ringwood

Manchester
Salford
Stockport
Warrington
Sale
Glossop
Wilmslow
Macclesfield
Congleton
Leek
Stafford
Rugeley
Cannock
Walsall
Evesham
Tewkesbury
Cheltenham
Stroud
Salisbury
Warminster
Gillingham

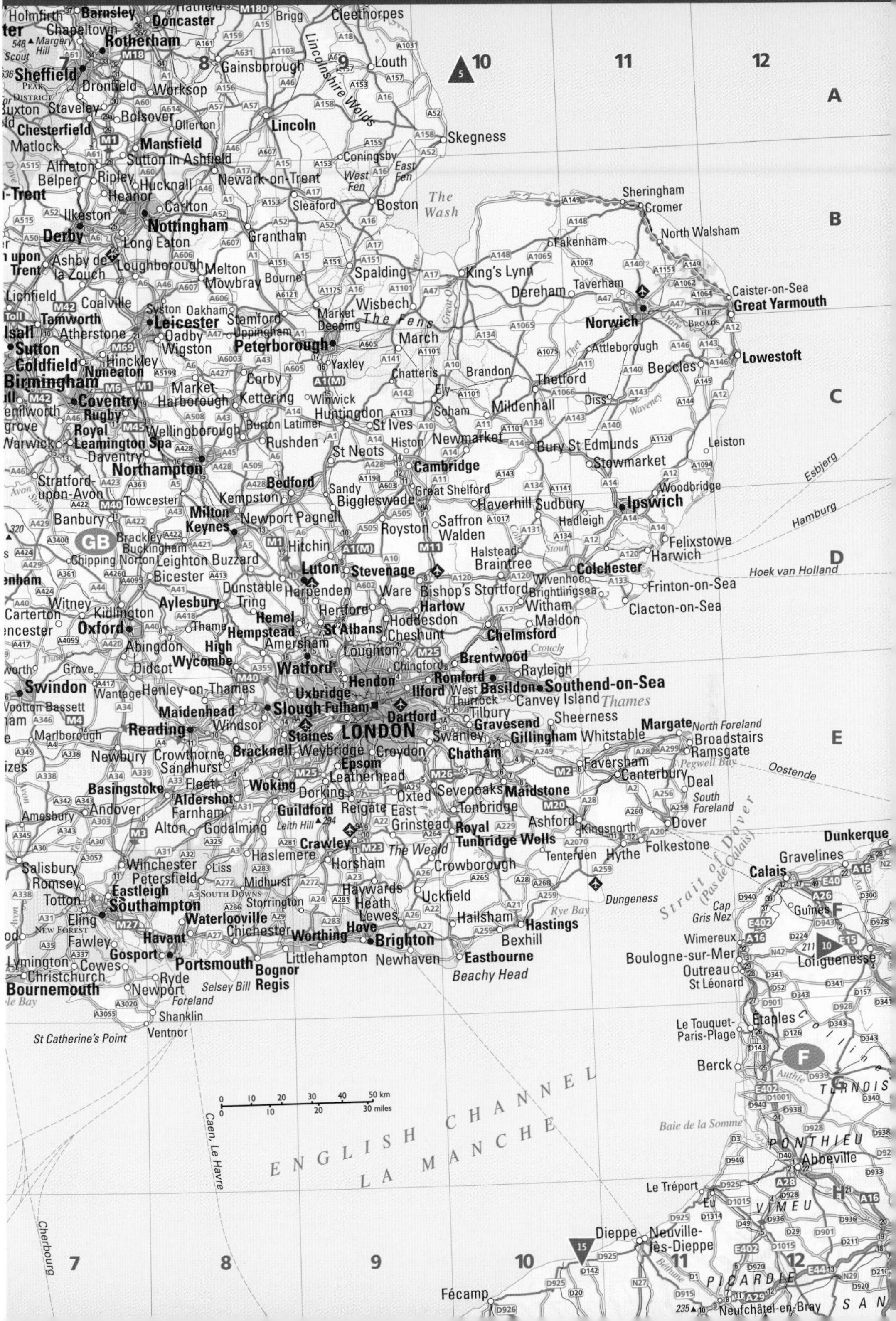

10
11
12
A
B
C
D
E
F
G
H
7
8
9
10
11
12
Barnsley
Doncaster
Holmfirth
Chapeltown
Rotherham
Margery Hill
Sheffield
Peak District
Dronfield
Worksop
Gainsborough
Brigg
Cleethorpes
Louth
Lincolnshire Wolds
Buxton
Staveley
Bolsover
Chesterfield
Ollerton
Lincoln
Skegness
Matlock
Mansfield
Sutton in Ashfield
Coningsby
Alfreton
Ripley
Belper
Hucknall
Heanor
Newark-on-Trent
West Fen
East Fen
Carlton
Nottingham
Ilkeston
Sleaford
Boston
The Wash
Sheringham
Cromer
North Walsham
Fakenham
Derby
Long Eaton
Grantham
Ashby de la Zouch
Loughborough
Melton Mowbray
Bourne
Spalding
King's Lynn
Dereham
Taverham
Caister-on-Sea
Great Yarmouth
Lichfield
Coalville
Syston
Oakham
Leicester
Stamford
Market Deeping
Wisbech
The Fens
Norwich
The Broads
Tamworth
Atherstone
Oadby
Wigston
Uppingham
Peterborough
March
Attleborough
Lowestoft
Sutton Coldfield
Hinckley
Nuneaton
Yaxley
Chatteris
Brandon
Thetford
Beccles
Birmingham
Coventry
Market Harborough
Corby
Kettering
Winwick
Ely
Mildenhall
Diss
Waveney
Kenilworth
Rugby
Huntingdon
Soham
Royal Leamington Spa
Warwick
Wellingborough
Burton Latimer
St Ives
Histon
Newmarket
Bury St Edmunds
Leiston
Daventry
Rushden
St Neots
Stowmarket
Northampton
Cambridge
Esbjerg
Stratford-upon-Avon
Bedford
Sandy
Great Shelford
Woodbridge
Biggleswade
Haverhill
Sudbury
Ipswich
Towcester
Kempston
Milton Keynes
Newport Pagnell
Royston
Saffron Walden
Hadleigh
Hamburg
Banbury
GB
Brackley
Buckingham
Hitchin
Halstead
Felixstowe
Harwich
Chipping Norton
Leighton Buzzard
Luton
Stevenage
Braintree
Colchester
Hoek van Holland
Bicester
Dunstable
Harpenden
Ware
Bishop's Stortford
Wivenhoe
Brightlingsea
Frinton-on-Sea
Witney
Aylesbury
Tring
Harlow
Witham
Clacton-on-Sea
Carterton
Kidlington
Hemel Hempstead
Hertford
Hoddesdon
Maldon
Oxford
Thame
St Albans
Cheshunt
Chelmsford
Abingdon
High Wycombe
Amersham
Loughton
Crouch
Grove
Didcot
Watford
Chingford
Brentwood
Rayleigh
Swindon
Wantage
Henley-on-Thames
Hendon
Romford
Basildon
Southend-on-Sea
Uxbridge
Ilford
West Thurrock
Canvey Island
Thames
Wootton Bassett
Maidenhead
Slough
Fulham
Dartford
Tilbury
Sheerness
Windsor
Gravesend
Margate
North Foreland
Marlborough
Reading
Staines
LONDON
Swanley
Gillingham
Whitstable
Broadstairs
Newbury
Crowthorne
Bracknell
Weybridge
Croydon
Chatham
Ramsgate
Sandhurst
Epsom
Faversham
Pegwell Bay
Oostende
Fleet
Woking
Leatherhead
Canterbury
Deal
Basingstoke
Dorking
Oxted
Sevenoaks
Maidstone
Aldershot
South Foreland
Andover
Farnham
Guildford
Reigate
East Grinstead
Tonbridge
Amesbury
Ashford
Kingsnorth
Dover
Alton
Godalming
Leith Hill
Royal Tunbridge Wells
Dunkerque
Crawley
The Weald
Tenterden
Hythe
Folkestone
Haslemere
Gravelines
Salisbury
Winchester
Liss
Horsham
Crowborough
Calais
Romsey
Petersfield
Midhurst
Strait of Dover (Pas de Calais)
Eastleigh
South Downs
Haywards Heath
Cap Gris Nez
Totton
Southampton
Storrington
Uckfield
Dungeness
Guînes
Eling
New Forest
Waterlooville
Lewes
Hailsham
Rye Bay
Fawley
Havant
Chichester
Worthing
Hove
Hastings
Wimereux
Gosport
Brighton
Bexhill
Lymington
Cowes
Portsmouth
Littlehampton
Newhaven
Eastbourne
Boulogne-sur-Mer
Longuenesse
Christchurch
Ryde
Bognor Regis
Beachy Head
Outreau
Bournemouth
Newport
Selsey Bill
St Léonard
Foreland
Shanklin
Étaples
Ventnor
Le Touquet-Paris-Plage
St Catherine's Point
F
Berck
Authie
TERNOIS
0 10 20 30 40 50 km
0 10 20 30 miles
Caen, Le Havre
ENGLISH CHANNEL
LA MANCHE
Baie de la Somme
PONTHIEU
Abbeville
Le Tréport
Eu
VIMEU
Dieppe
Neuville-lès-Dieppe
Cherbourg
Béthune
PICARDIE
Fécamp
Neufchâtel-en-Bray
SAN

1 2 3 4 5 6

Newcastle upon Tyne
Kingston upon Hull
Esbjerg
Hamburg
Wadd
Terschelling

NORTH SEA

0 10 20 30 40 50 km
0 10 20 30 miles

Vlieland
Texel
Den Burg
Engelschmangad

B

Sheringham
Cromer
North Walsham
Den Helder
Anna Paulowna
Schagen
Langedijk
Bergen
Heiloo
Alkmaar
Hoorn
Medemblik

Norwich
Caister-on-Sea
Great Yarmouth
Attleborough
Beccles
Lowestoft
Castricum
Heemskerk
Beverwijk
Wormerveer
Marker

C
Diss
GB
Zuid-Kennemerland
Zaandam
Haarlem
AMSTERD

Stowmarket
Leiston
NORDSEE
Heemstede
Hoofddorp
Hillversum

Ipswich
Woodbridge
Noordwijk-Binnen
Katwijk aan Zee
Wassenaar
Leiden
Zoetermeer
Utrecht

D
Felixstowe
Harwich
'S-GRAVENHAGE
(DEN HAAG)
Monster
Delft
Gouda
Veen

Frinton-on-Sea
's-Gravenzande
Europoort
Rotterdam

Clacton-on-Sea
9
Vlaardingen
Spijkenisse
Dordrecht

Middelharnis
De Biesbosch
Made
Breda
Oosterhout

E
Zierikzee
Zevenbergen
Tilburg

Margate
North Foreland
Broadstairs
Ramsgate
Middelburg
Goes
Roosendaal
Essen
Eindho

Canterbury
Pegwell Bay
Vlissingen
Westerschelde
Zandvliet
Brecht
Turnhout

Deal
South Foreland
Knokke-Heist
Blankenberge
De Haan
Terneuzen
Antwerpen
(Anvers)
Kasterlee

Dover
Folkestone
Oostende (Ostend)
Westende
Damme
Zelzate
Zwijndrecht
Borsbeek
Geel

Brugge
(Bruges)
Gistel
Beernem
Lier

Strait of Dover
(Pas de Calais)
Koksijde
Gent
(Gand)
Wichelen
Beringen

Dunkerque
Staden
Roeselare
(Roulers)
Tielt
Deinze
Zulte
Dendermonde
Zemst
Mechelen
(Malines)
Hasselt

Gravelines
Ieper
St-Martens-Latem
BRUXELLES
(BRUSSEL)
Schaerbeek
St-Truiden

Calais
Guines
Wormhout
Gullegem
Anzegem
101
Dilbeek
Halle
Grez-Doiceau

Cap Gris Nez
Wimereux
Mons des Cats
Comines
Wevelgem
Kortrijk
Brakel
Hernel
Braine-l'Alleud
Hannut

Boulogne-sur-Mer
Outreau
St Léonard
Bailleul
Mouscron
Herne
Tubize
Soignies
Echezee

Longuenesse
Tourcoing
Roubaix
Leuze-en-Hainaut
Namur

G
Le Touquet-Paris-Plage
Berck
Etaples
Lille
Seclin
Tournai
Mons
Anzin
Charleroi
Ciney

Béthune
Divion
Avion

Baie de la Somme
F
Arras
Maubeuge
Rochefort

H
Abbeville
Doullens
Cambrai
Aulnoye-Aymeries
Avesnes-sur-Helpe
Couvin

Le Tréport
Eu
12
Caudry
Fourmies

VIMEU
Albert
Peronne
VERMANDOIS
Oise

Amiens

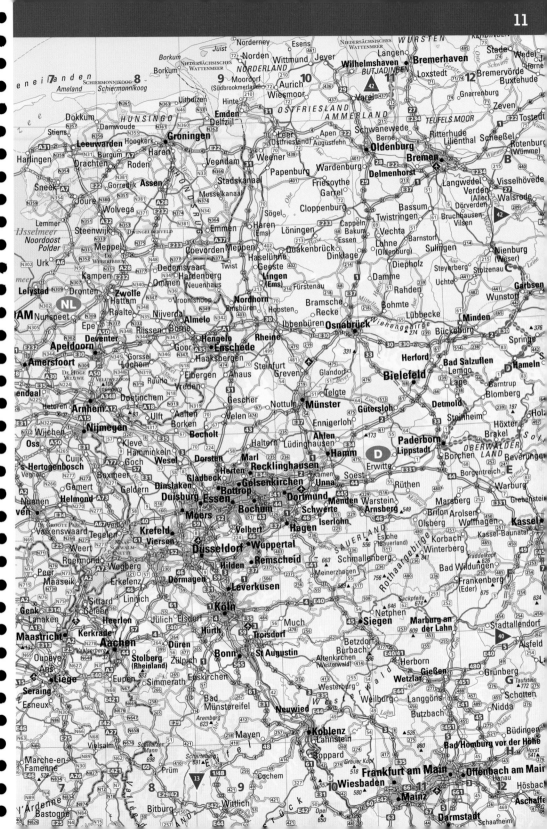

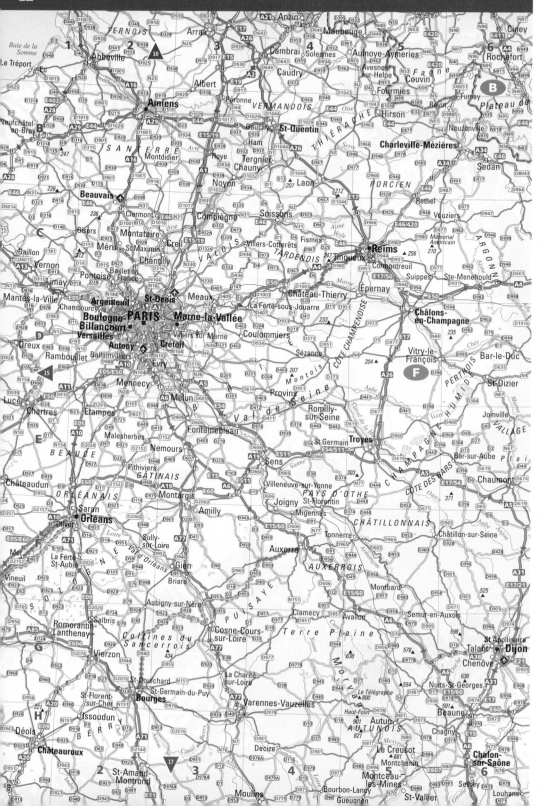

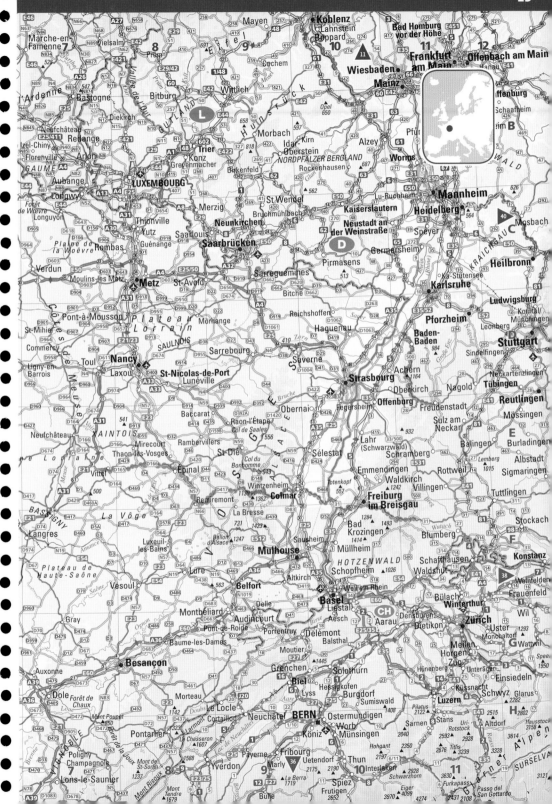

ENGLISH CHANNEL

LA MANCHE

CHANNEL ISLANDS

Golfe de St-Malo

Mer d'Iroise

BRETAGNE

PAYS DE LEON

CORNOUAILLE

PENTHIÈVRE

TRÉGORROIS

GRANDE BRIÈRE

PAYS DE RETZ

Plymouth, Saltash, Ivybridge, Paignton, Brixham, Dartmouth, St Austell, Truro, Redruth, Camborne, Falmouth, Helston, Lizard, Mount's Bay, Start Bay

Rosslare, Cork

Cherbourg-Octeville, Tourl, Valognes, Carteret, Coutances, Granville, Alderney, Guernsey, Vale, St Sampson, St Peter Port, Sark, Jersey, St Saviour, St Brelade, St Helier

Perros-Guirec, Roscoff, Lannion, Paimpol, St-Pol-de-Léon, Plouguerneau, Ploudalmézeau, Île d'Ouessant, Landivisiau, Morlaix, Guingamp, Plérin, St-Brieuc, Ploufragan, Lamballe, Dinard, St-Malo, Dol-de-Bretagne, Dinan, St-Renan, Gouesnou, Landerneau, Plouzané, Guipavas, Le Conquet, Pte de St-Mathieu, **Brest**, Mont d'Arrée, Carhaix-Plouguer, Loudéac, Rennes, Betton, Vezin le Coquet, St-Jacques-de-la-Lande, Cesson-Sévigné, Bruz, Crozon, Châteaulin, Montagnes Noires, Pontivy, Ploërmel, Guichen, Guer, Bain-de-Bretagne, Douarnenez, Le Cap, Pte du Raz, Ergué-Gaberic, Scaër, **Quimper**, Rosporden, Pont-l'Abbé, Penmarch, Pte de Penmarch, Concarneau, Quimperlé, Hennebont, Landes de Lanvaux, Redon, Blain, Nort-sur-Erdre, Savenay, **Lorient**, Ploemeur, Lanester, Larmor-Plage, Île de Groix, Auray, Ploeren, Vannes, St-Avé, Sarzeau, Pontchâteau, Presqu'île de Quiberon, Baie de Quiberon, Quiberon, Belle-Île, Guérande, Trignac, La Baule-Escoublac, St-Nazaire, St-Herblain, Bouguenais, **Nantes**, Rezé, Vertou, St-Philbert-de-Grand-Lieu, Orvault, Carquefou, Pornic, Machecoul, Noirmoutier-en-l'Île, Île de Noirmoutier, Marais briton, Challans, St-Jean-de-Monts, Île d'Yeu, St-Hilaire-de-Riez, St-Gilles-Croix-de-Vie, Aizenay, La Roche, Gijón-Xixón

0 10 20 30 40 50 km
0 10 20 30 miles

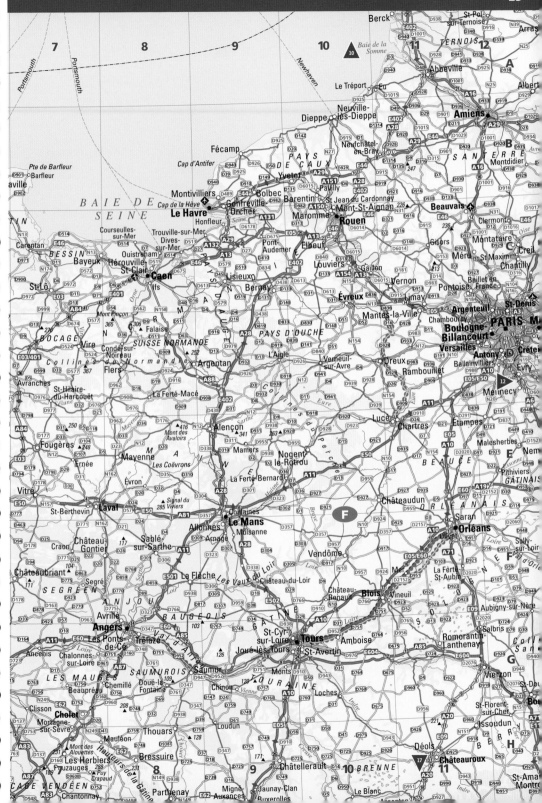

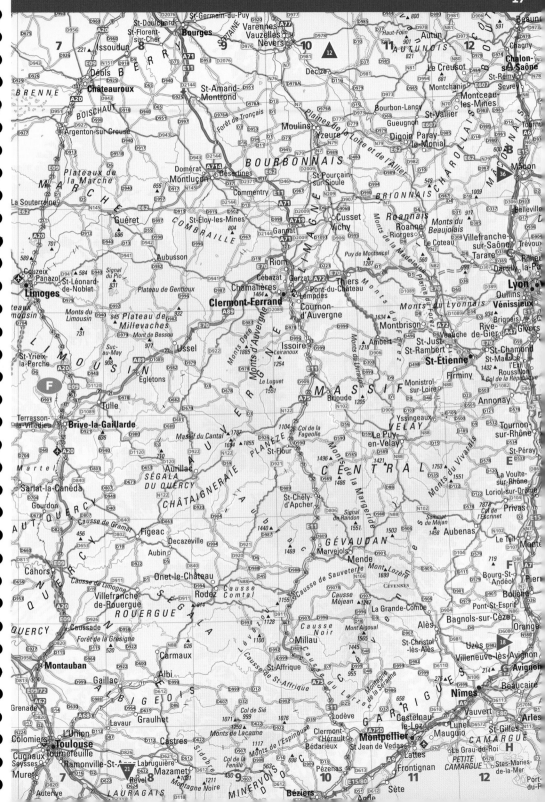

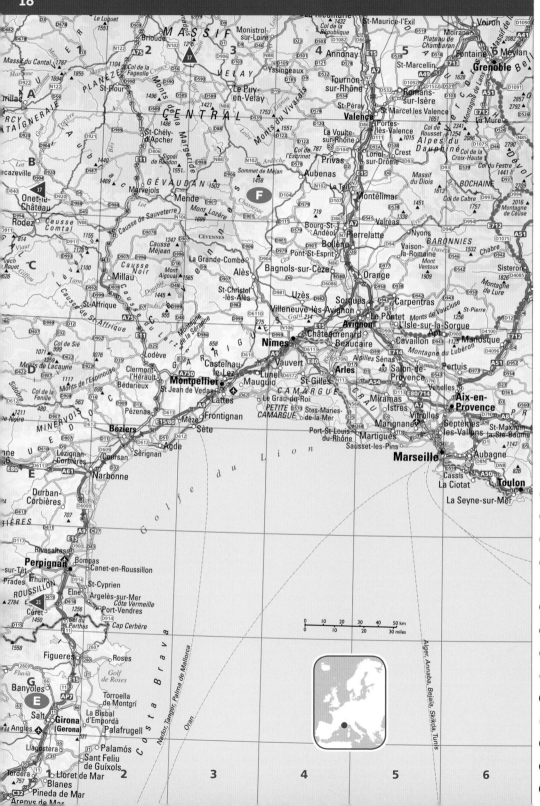

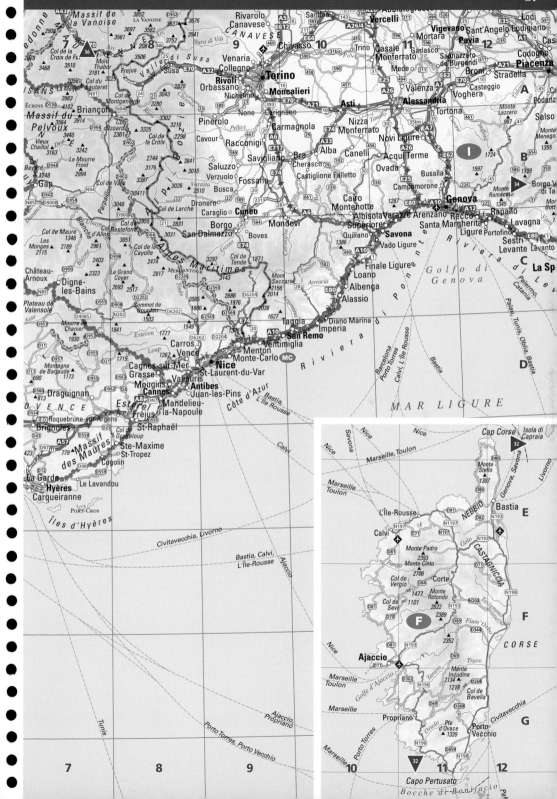

1   2   3   4   5   6

Golfe de Gascogne
Golfo de Gascuña

Mont-de-Marsan
Soustons
St-Paul-lès-Dax
Dax
Capbreton
Tarnes
Bayonne Boucau
Biarritz Anglet
Côte d'Argent
St-Jean-de-Luz
Hendaye
Hasparren
Mourenx
Lescar
Billère
Pau
Jurançon
Tarbes
Orthez
Salies-de-Béarn
Vic-en-Bigorre
Aire-sur-l'Adour

Santoña
Laredo Castro-Urdiales
Bermeo
Algorta
Santurtzi
Portugalete Arizgoiti
Barakaldo
Bilbao (Bilbo)
Basauri
Gernika-Lumo
Donostia-San Sebastián
Irun
Errenteria
Ondarroa
Zarautz
Andoain
Anoeta
Bizondo
Oloron-Ste-Marie
Lourdes

Balmaseda
Llodio
Amorebieta
Durango
Ermua
Eibar
Billabona
Tolosa
Villasana de Mena
Amurrio
Arrasate
Zumarraga
Legazpi
Beasain
Altsasu
Urduña
Puerto de Urquila
Puerto de Velate

Medina de Pomar
Vitoria-Gasteiz
Puerto de Azáceta
Berriozar
Barañáin
Burlada
Pamplona (Iruña)
Ansó
Col d'Aubisque
Torla
ORDESA-MONTE PERDIDO

Miranda de Ebro
CONDADO DE TREVIÑO
Estella
Jaca
Sabiñánigo

BUREBA
Briviesca
Haro
Tafalla
Santo Domingo de la Calzada
Nájera
Logroño
RIBERA NAVARRA
Sierra de la Demanda
Calahorra
Arnedo
BÁRDENAS REALES
CINCO VILLAS
Huesca
Sierra de Guara
SOMONTANO

Puerto de Piqueras
Corella
Cintruénigo
Alfaro
Tudela
Ejea de los Caballeros

Puerto de Oncala
Tarazona
Tauste
Esteban
Zuera
EL CASTELLAR
LOS MONEGROS

Ardal
Soria
Sierra de Cabrejas
Alto del Moncayo
LLANO DE PLASENCIA
Alagón
Zaragoza

de Duero
Hinojedo
El Burgo de Osma
CAMPO DE
Almazán
Alto Cruz
Cabezo de Morés
La Almunia de Doña Godina
La Muela

MARQUESADO DE BERLANGA
GÓMARA
Calatayud
CAMPO DE CARIÑENA
LLANOS DE
E

Caballera
Ocejón
La Bodera
Ministra
Judes
Santa Cruz
Herrera
Cucutas
DESIERTO DE CALANDA
Caspe
Alcañiz

Sigüenza
Puerto de Marannchón
Aragoncillo
Sierra de Caldereros
Aguila
Valdellosa
Retuerta
Andorra

Pinoso
Guadalajara
Berninches
LA ALCARRIA
Serranía de Cuenca
Juez
Nevera
San Ginés
Puerto de Minguez
San Just
Carrascal
Puerto de Cabrillas
Ares

Alcalá de Henares
Torrejón de Ardoz
Mejorada del Campo
Arganda del Rey
Embalse de Buendía
Caimodorro
Puerto de Pozondón
Zaragozana
Peñarroya
EL MAESTRAZGO

Teruel
Puebla de Escalón
Javalón
Peñagolosa

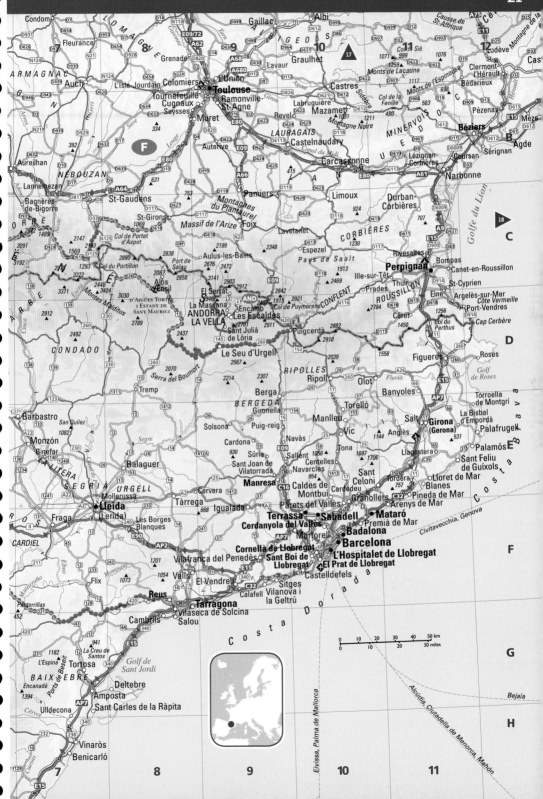

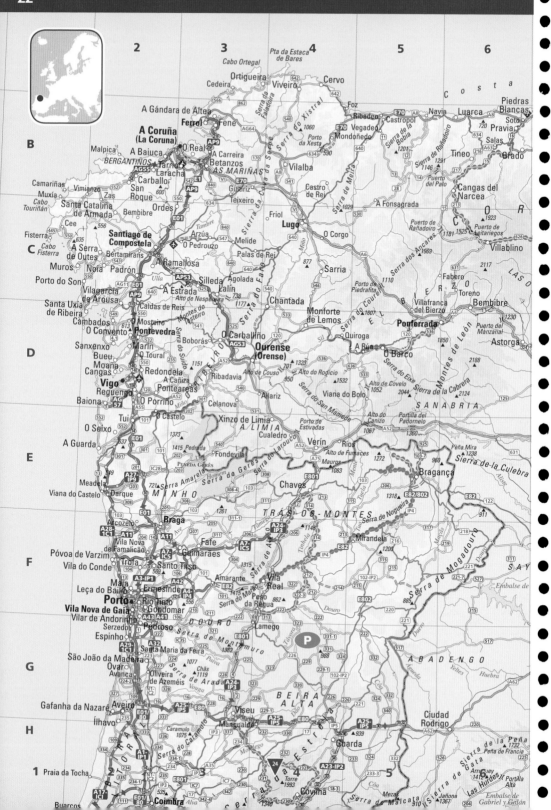

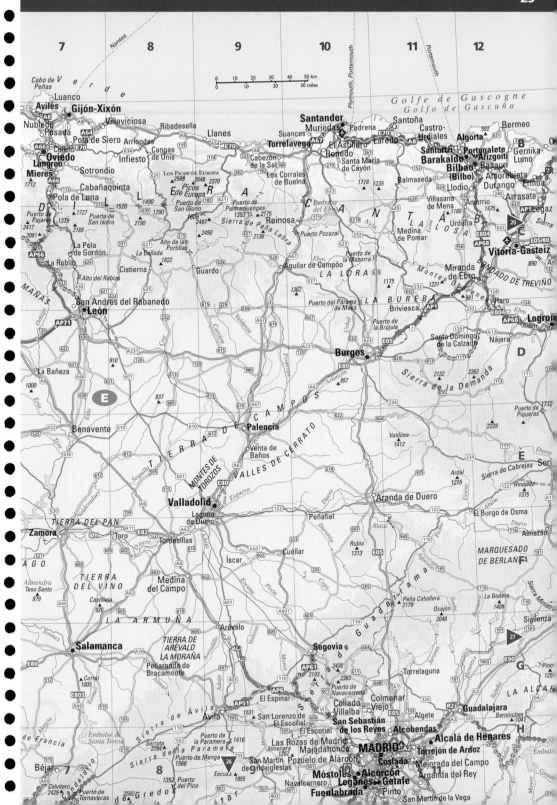

B 1 2 3 C D E F G R

Scale

50 km
30 miles
0 10 20 30 40 50

Portugal / Spain region map

Aveiro, Gafanha da Nazaré, Ílhavo, Praia da Tocha, Buarcos, Figueira da Foz, São Pedro de Muel, Vieira de Leiria, Nazaré, Marinha Grande, Peniche, Ericeira, Mafra, Sintra, Odivelas, Cacém, Amadora, Estoril, Costa do Estoril, Costa da Caparica, Almada, Barreiro, LISBOA, Moscavide, Alverca, Vila Franca de Xira, Benavente, Cartaxo, Santarém, Almeirim, Torres Novas, Torres Vedras, Caldas da Rainha, Alcobaça, Rio Maior, Leiria, Pombal, Pedrógão, Coimbra, Viseu, Mangualde, Guarda, Covilhã, Fundão, Castelo Branco, Penamacor, Abrantes, Tomar, Vila Nova de Ourém, Fátima, Entroncamento, Vendas Novas, Montemor-o-Novo, Setúbal, Costa da Galé, Bafa de Setúbal, Costa Bela, Cabo Espichel, Costa do Sol, Évora, Estremoz, Portalegre, Alter do Chão, Elvas, Vila Viçosa, Olivença, Badajoz, Campo Maior, Arronches, Valencia de Alcántara, San Vicente de Alcántara, Alburquerque, La Atalaya de Santiago, Arroyo de la Luz, Cáceres, Malpartida, Coria, Moraleja, Montehermoso, Plasencia, Béjar, Candeleda, Jaraíz de la Vera, Talavera la Real, Mérida, Don Benito, Villanueva de la Serena, Campanario, Quintana de la Serena, Castuera, Zalamea de la Serena, Hinojosa del Duque, Peñarroya-Pueblonuevo, Fuente Obejuna, Azuaga, Llerena, Fuente de Cantos, Zafra, Villafranca de los Barros, Almendralejo, Montijo, Olivenza, Los Santos de Maimona, Fuente del Maestre, Jerez de los Caballeros, Fregenal de la Sierra, Oliva de la Frontera, Navalmoral de la Mata, Trujillo, Miajadas, Guareña, Mirandilla, Santa Olalla, Cabeço de Vide, Estena, Monsanto, Guarda, Ciudad Rodrigo, Sierra de Gata, Sierra de Guadalupe, Sierra de San Pedro, Sierra de Montánchez, TIERRA DE BARROS, LLANOS DE OLIVENZA, LA SERENA, CAMPO ARAÑUELO, SIERRA DE GREDOS, BEIRA ALTA, BEIRA BAIXA, RIBATEJO, SERRA DA ESTRELA, VERA-VALLE

Embalse de Valdecañas, Embalse de Orellana, Embalse de la Serena, Embalse de Santa Teresa, Embalse de Gabriel y Galán, Embalse de Alange

Rivers: Tejo, Tâmega, Guadiana, Tormes, Mondego, Zêzere, Sorraia, Sado, Ardila, Guadámez, Búrdalo, Salor, Jerte, Tiétar, Alagón

Serra de Lousã, Serra do Caramulo

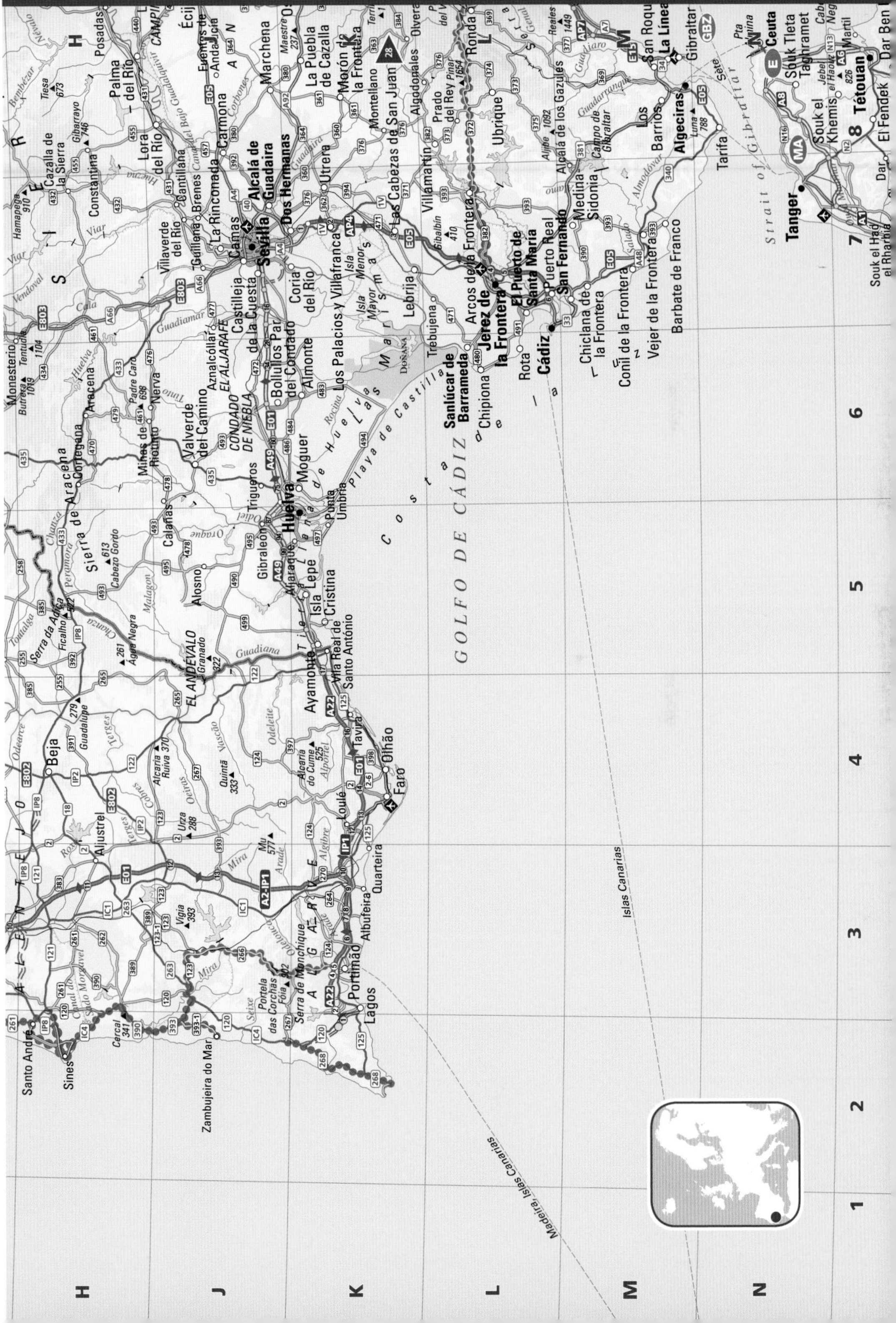

Sevilla
Alcalá de Guadaira
Dos Hermanas
Huelva
Cádiz
Jerez de la Frontera
El Puerto de Santa María
San Fernando
Sanlúcar de Barrameda
Algeciras
Gibraltar
La Línea
San Roque
Ceuta
Tanger
Tétouan
Tarifa
Faro
Olhão
Tavira
Loulé
Portimão
Lagos
Albufeira
Quarteira
Beja
Sines
Santo André
Zambujeira do Mar
Ayamonte
Vila Real de Santo António
Isla Cristina
Lepe
Moguer
Aracena
Carmona
Marchena
Utrera
Ronda
Ubrique
Medina Sidonia
Chiclana de la Frontera
Conil de la Frontera
Vejer de la Frontera
Barbate de Franco
Rota
Chipiona
Lebrija
Arcos de la Frontera
Villamartín
Morón de la Frontera
Osuna
Écija
Posadas
Palma del Río
Lora del Río
Cazalla de la Sierra
Constantina
Valverde del Camino
Almonte
Bollullos Par del Condado
Coria del Río
Los Palacios y Villafranca
Las Cabezas de San Juan
GOLFO DE CÁDIZ
Costa de la Luz
Strait of Gibraltar
Islas Canarias
Madeira, Islas Canarias
A L G A R V E
A L E N T E J O
A N D A L U C I A
Serra de Monchique
Sierra de Aracena
Las Marismas
Playa de Castilla
H
J
K
L
M
N
1
2
3
4
5
6
7
8

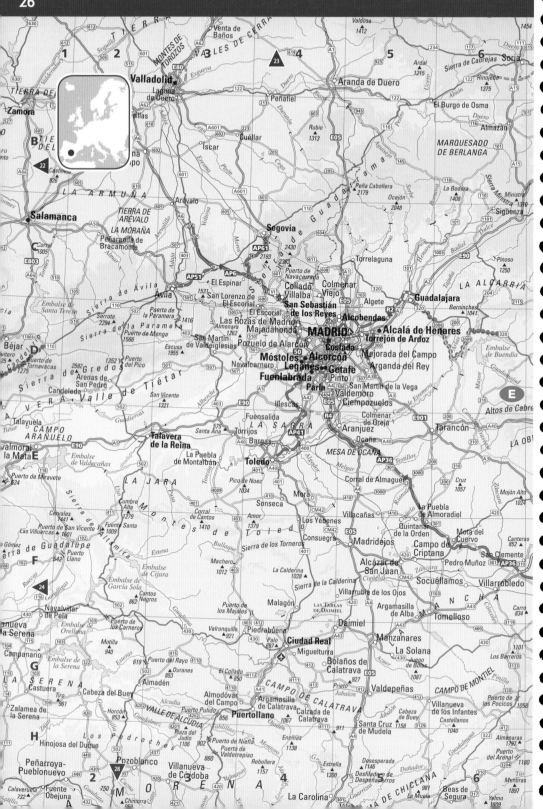

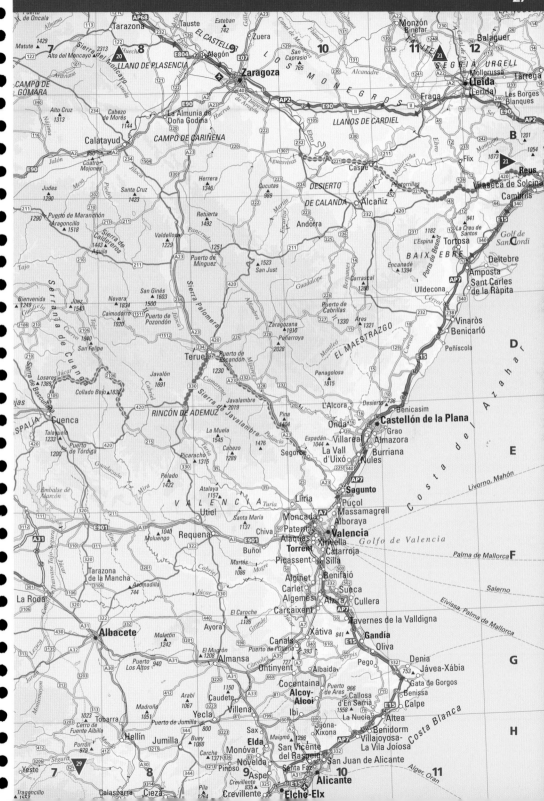

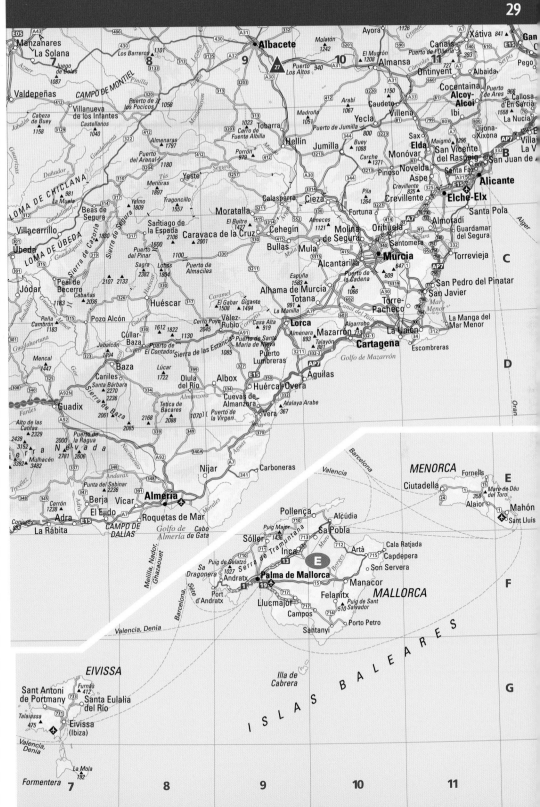

1　2　3　4　5　6

A　B　C　D　E　F　G

△ 32

Pontinia
CIRCEO
Sabaudia
Monte Circeo
541▲
San Felice
Circeo
Terracina
Monte delle Fate
Golfo di
Terracina
Gaeta
Formia
Fondi
Monte Petrella
1533
Aurunca
Sessa
Mondragone
Teano
Vairano
Patenora
Piedimonte
Matese
Guardia
Sanframondi
Sparanise
Caiazzo
Capua
Casèrta
Maddaloni
Montesarchio
Apice
Ariano
Irpino
Mirabella
Eclano
Lioni
Benevento
Monte 1394
Taburno▲
Altavilla
Irpina
Monti d'Avella
1598
Nusco
Avellino

Isole
Ponziane
Isola di Ponza
Grazzanise
Castèl Volturno
Marcianise
Aversa
Lusciano
Giugliano in Campania
Napoli
Pozzuoli
Forio
Ischia
Monte
Epomeo
Isola
d'Ischia
Bacoli
Portici
Torre
del Greco
Caivano
Afragola
Casoria
Vesuvio
Vesuvio
San Giuseppe Vesuviano
Mariglianò
Sarno
Marigliano
Baiano
Torre
Annunziata
Gragnano
Cava
de'Tirreni
Monte
Mai
1807
Baronissi
Salerno
Monte
Cervialto
1809
Monte Picentini

Olbia

Sorrento
Pontecagnano
Faiano
Eboli
Battipaglia

Anacapri
Capri

MARE TIRRENO

Golfo di
Salerno

Albanella
Capaccio

Palermo
Cagliari
Tunis
Valencia
Catania
Messina, Valletta

Agropoli
Castellabate
Vallo della
Stella
1131▲
Monte della
Stella
CILENTO
VALLO DI
Lucania
Ascea

Cagliari
Ustica
Napoli, Salerno
Genova Livorno
Salerno

Isole Lipari
Isola Salina
962▲
Isola
Alicudi
Isola
Filicudi
Isola Lipari
Lipari
Isola Panarea
Isola Vulcano

Capo
Gallo
Capo San Vito
Monte 913
Speziale▲
Terrasini
Capaci 606
Carini
Palermo
Bagheria
Monreale
Partinico
La Pizzuta
1333
Misilmeri
Marineo
Golfo di
Termini Imerese
Cefalù
Termini
Imerese
Castelbuono
Santo Stefano
di Camastra
Capo
d'Orlando
Gioiosa
Marea
Sant'Agata
di Militello
Patti
Tortorici
Villafranca
Tirrena
Milazzo
Barcellona
Pozzo di Gotto
Monti Peloritani

Trapani
Paceco
Erice
Castellammare
del Golfo
Alcamo
San Cipirello
Calatafimi
Salemi
Gibellina Nuova
Mazara
del Vallo
Partanna
Castelvetrano
Campobello
di Mazara
Capo Granitola
Menfi
Sciacca
Isola
Favignana
Marsala
Corleone
Prizzi
Bisacquino
Sambuca di Sicilia
Cammarata
Bivona
Cattabellotta
Ribera
Cianciana
Cattolica
Eraclea
Raffadali
Aragona
Canicattì
Agrigento
Favara
Naro
Porto Empedocle
Campobello
di Licata
Palma di
Montechiaro
Licata

SICILIA

Monreale
Mistretta
Monte
Soro
1847
Randazzo
Troina
Nicosia
Gangi
Petralia
Caltavuturo
Lercara Friddi
Villarosa
Leonforte
Assoro
Enna
Caltanissetta
San Cataldo
Serradifalco
Pietraperzia
Barrafranca
Mazzarino
Sommatino
Ravanusa
Butera
Gela
Acate
Comiso
Vittoria
Ragusa
Santa Croce Camerina
Modica
Scicli
Ispica
Pozzallo
Pachino

Nicosia
Adrano
Regalbuto
Agira
Paternò
Misterbianco
Catania
Piazza
Armerina
Palagonia
Grammichele
Caltagirone
Niscemi
Palazzolo
Acreide
Noto
Rosolini
di Noto
Avola

Linguaglossa
Monte Etna
3323
Zafferana
Giarre
Riposto
Biancavilla
Aci Catena
Aci Castello
Acireale
Fiumefreddo
di Sicilia
Taormina
Santa Teresa
di Riva

Augusta
Melilli
Florida
Siracusa
Canicattini
Bagni

Golfo di
Catania

Golfo di
Augusta

Golfo
di Noto

Pantelleria
Linosa, Lampedusa
Capo Granitola

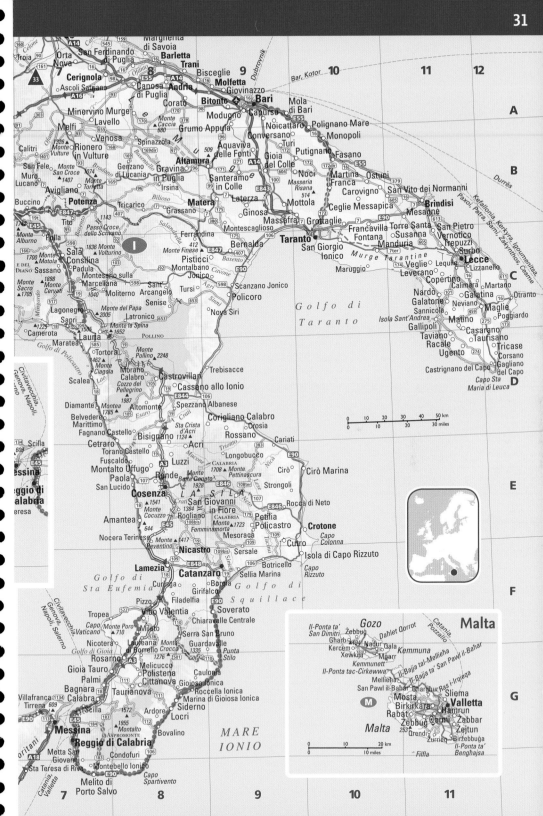

MARE
IONIO

Malta

Gozo

Malta

Golfo di
Taranto

Golfo di
Squillace

Golfo di
Sta Eufemia

1

Isola di Capraia
ARCIPELAGO TOSCANO

Castagneto
Carducci
San
Vincenzo
Campiglia Marittima

646

Colline Metallifere
Poggio di Montieri
1051

Monteroni
d'Arbia

Sinalunga

Cornia

286

2

3

451

Torrita di Siena

Cortona

Umbertide

Gualdo
Tadino

Matelica

6

Poggio di Montieri
1051
441

Massa
Marittimo
Roccastrada

73

Montepulciano

Citta
della Pieve

Montalcino

Chianciano
Terme

220

Monte
Leoni

Castiglione
del Lago

Magione

599

Perugia

448

E45
298

Camerino

Monte
Fieni
1323

Piombino

Follonica

Poggio
Ballone
630

349

223

614

Monte
Amiata
1738

Abbadia San
Salvatore

Marsciano

E35

71

Corciano

Bastia

3bis

Foligno

Nocera
Umbra

Assisi

Spello

Monte
Pennino
1571

Appennino Umbro-Marchigiano

77

E45

Trevi

Monte
Vettore
2476

B

Isola d'Elba
Portoferraio
Monte Capanne
1018

Cima del Monte
516

Castiglione della
Pescaia

Grosseto

G
R
O
S
S
E
T
O

770

Monte Faete

Acquapendente

1107
Monte
Civitella

Orvieto

74

71

Todi

Montefalco

Monte Martano
1094

Spoleto

Sant'Anatolia
di Narco

Monte
Fionchi
1337

Monte
1685

4

ARCIPELAGO TOSCANO

19

415

Albegna

Monti Volsini

E35

Monte Croce
di Serra
994

Amelia

3bis

Terni

260

Monte
Terminillo
2216

Arcipelago Toscano

Barcelona, Toulon

Monte della
Fortezza
645

Poggio
del Leccio

Poggio
della Pagana
498

Monte
Argentario
635

Orbetello

Canino

Tuscania

Montefiascone

204

Offe

Narni

1053
Monte
Cimino

Viterbo

Ombrone

A

Fiora

17

Arrone

578

Monte
Nuria
1888

Reti

Monte Pizzuto
1287

C

Montalto di Castro

Tarquinia

1bis

Vetralla

Mignone

Nepi

311

Castel
Castellana

Rignano
Flaminio

3

Fiano
Romano

Castelnuovo
di Porto

A1dir

Bracciano

Monte
Terminillo

Monterotondo

E35

Guidonia
Monticelio

Subiaco

1623

Monti Si

A24

Aterno

C

Capo Pertusato

19

Bocche di Bonifacio

Santa Teresa
di Gallura

ARCIPELAGO
DE LA MADDALENA

La Maddalena
Palau

Civitavecchia

Santa Marinella

A12

Cerveteri

Ladispoli

E80

Mentana

VATICAN
CITY

ROMA

A24

A1dir

Ciampino

296

E80

A12

A1dir

A1

Frascati

Albano Laziale
Genzano di Roma

Marino

Palestrina

Valmontone

Artena

Velletri

411

Colleferro

E45

Ferentino

D

Marseille

Propriano, Genova

391

Isola
Asinara

Golfo
dell'Asinara

La Nurra

Porto
Torres

464

Monte
Forte

200

291

Sorso

131

Sassari

674

133

Serra
Paoloni

640

200

Castelsardo

134

Anglona

127

692

Tempio
Pausania

Arzachena

911

Monte
Salici

361

125

421

Porto
Cervo

Golfo
Aranci

131

743

127

Olbia

415

Fiumicino,
Salerno

Livorno Piombino

Genova

Civitavecchia

Pomezia

Ardea

148

207

Aprilia

148

Cisterna di Latina

Latina

609

Sezze

1127

Punta
Balastieri

389

199

820

131dcn

M.sa
Pianedda

Maggiore
971

Monte
Lerno
1094

Monte
Senalonga

1076

1019

317

125

Nettuno

Anzio

601

601

156

Pontinia

Circeo

148

Sabaudia

Monte Circeo
541

San Felice
Circeo

E

Alghero

Monte
Mannu
802

292

Ittiri

730

128

Ozieri

Buddusò

Tirso

131bis

597

199

Monte
Grighini
673

Bosa

129

131

292

1200

Macomer

808

Cuccuru su
Pirastru

1259

128bis

914

431dcn

Pico sa
Donna

1050

863

125

Siniscola

1127

Monte
Senes

Nuoro

Oliena

429

895

Dorgali

Isole
Ponziane

Isola di Ponza

Circeo

Orosei

Golfo di
Orosei

SARDEGNA

131dcn

1050

Monte
Pisanu Mele
1463

Punta
Corrasi

Monte su Nuscone
1263

GOLFO DI OROSEI
GENNARGENTU E ASINARA

1595

Punta
La Marmora
1834

389

776

1372

125

1117

Olbia

F

Stagno di Cabras

Cabras

Oristano

Monte
Arci
812

442

Terralba

580

Mogoro

San Gavino
Monreale

197

198

Monte Sta Vittoria
1212

Monte
Codi
849

Monte
Ferru
875

128

1241

Lanusei

Tortoli
Arbatax

Flumendosa

Civitavecchia

Fiumicino

Genova

Arborea

126

Guspini

Monte
Arcuentu
785

197

Sanluri

Serrenti

801

676

589

Villaputzu

MARE
TIRRENO

G

Iglesias

Gonnesa

Isola di
San Pietro

Carloforte

Carbonia

Arbus

Villacidro

1236

Monte
Linas

661

126

196

Villasor

Domusnovas

Samassi

131

Sestu

Serramanna

Monte dei
Sette Fratelli
1023

Selargius

Quartu Sant'Elena

Assemini

723

Monte Orri

Capoterra

Cagliari

Punta
Maxia
1017

195

Villasimius

336

Golfo di
Cagliari

Cagliari

Napoli

Civitavecchia

H

Calasetta

Isola di
Sant'Antioco

271

Sant'Antioco

319

195

Pula

Sarroch

Palermo

Trapani, Tunis

Valencia

Tunis

1

2

3

4

5

6

0 10 20 30 40 50 km
0   10   20   30 miles

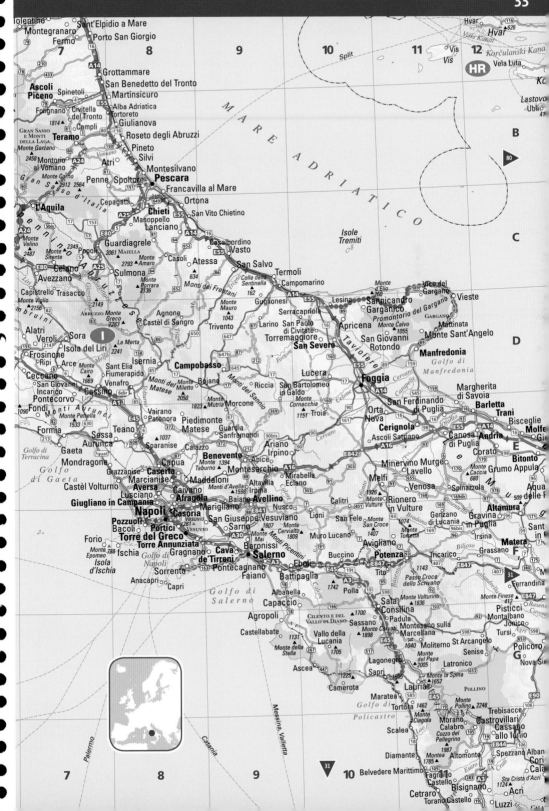

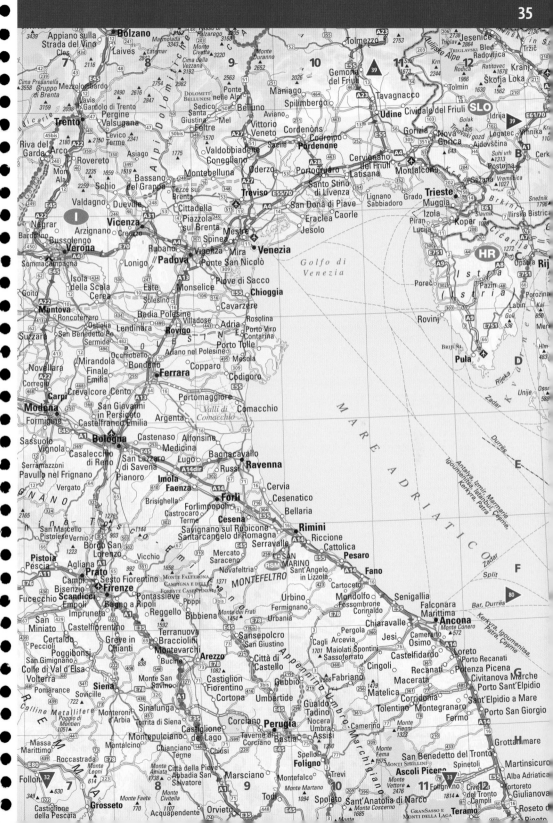

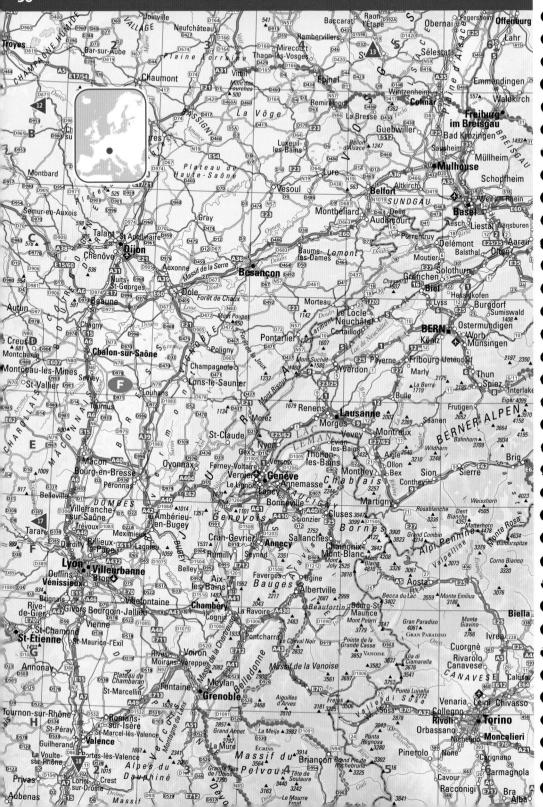

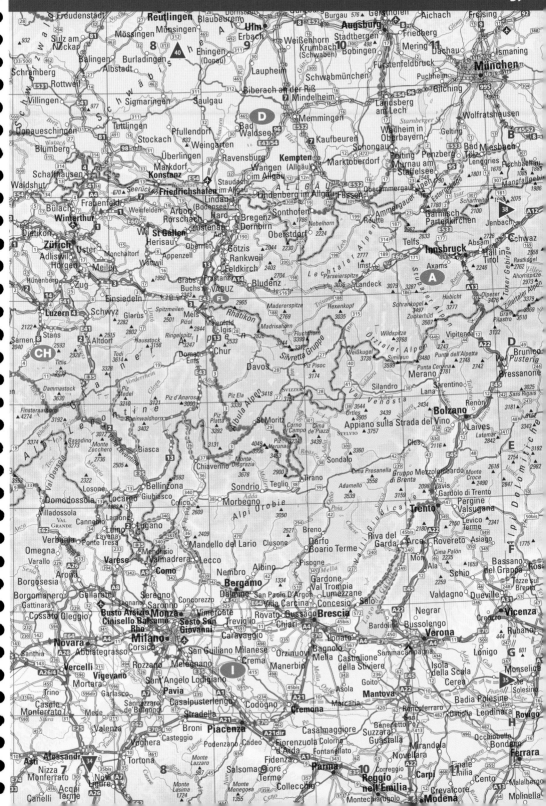

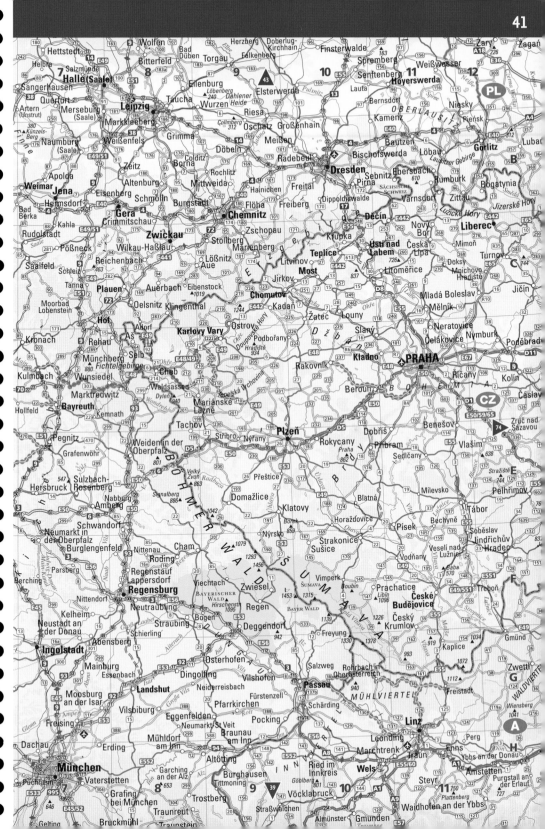

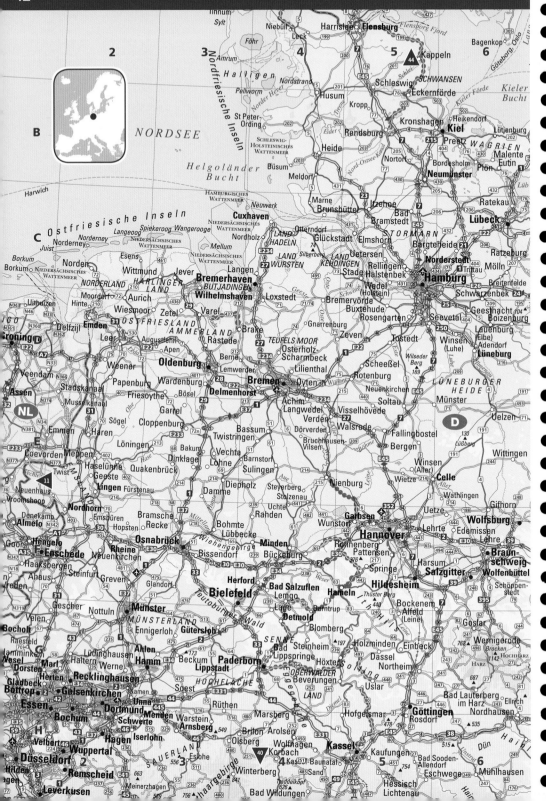

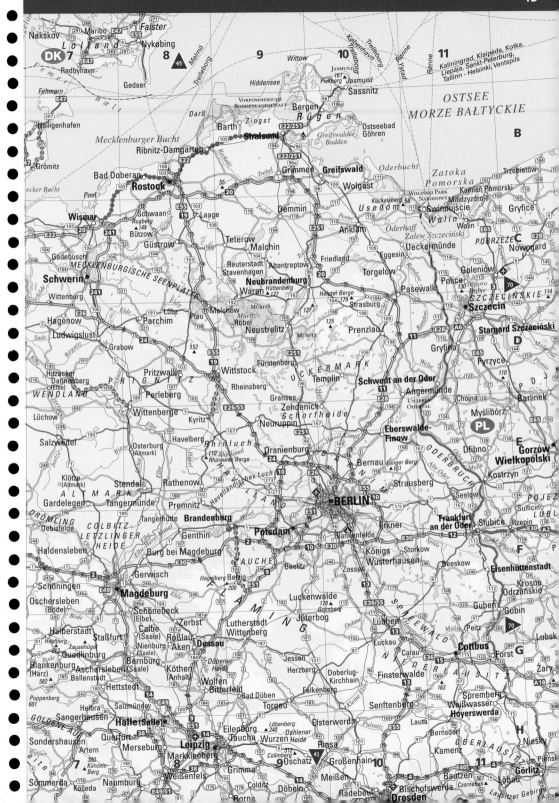

1 2 3 4 5 6

SKAGERRAK

Kristiansand, Bergen, Stavanger
Larvik, Moss, Oslo
Larvik, Moss, Oslo
Oslo
Rönnäng
Marstrand
Kungälv
Surte
Floda
Torslanda
Tuve
Göteborg
Mölndal
Mölnlycke
Kållered
Billdal
Lindome
Kungsbacka

B
Tórshavn, Seyðisfjörður
Hanstholm
Vigsø Bugt
Nørre Vorupør
Skagen
Hirtshals
Tannis Bugt
Ålbæk Bugt
Hirsholmene
Hjørring
Frederikshavn
Sæby
Brønderslev
Blokhus
Byrum
Læsø
Jammerbugten
VENDSYSSEL
Knøsen136
Nørresundby
Aalborg
Varberg

C
THY
Thisted
Limfjorden
Fur
MORS
Nykøbing Mors
Støvring
Aars
HIMMERLAND
Ålborg Bugt
KATTEGAT
Falkenberg
Nissum Bredning
Thyholm
SALLING
Hobro
Anholt

D
Lemvig
Struer
Skive
Viborg
Randers
Grenaa
Holstebro
Hadsten
DJURSLAND
HARSYSSEL
Hover
Hinnerup
Risskov
Mølle
JYLLAND
Herning
Ikast
Silkeborg
Århus
Helgenæs
Ringkøbing
Ringkøbing Fjord
Holmsland Klit

E
DK
Brande
Skanderborg
Tranbjerg
Århus Bugt
Frederiksværk
Helsinge
Skjern
Odder
Alrø
Samsø
Sejerø Bugt
Sejerø
Hillerød
Grindsted
Billund
Horsens
Endelave
Frederikssund
Orø
Varde
Vejle
Juelsminde
Kalundborg
Holbæk
Gladsaxa
Roskilde
Valby

F
Tórshavn, Seyðisfjörður
Esbjerg
Fanø
Fanø Bugt
Ribe
Vejen
Kolding
Fredericia
Hindsholm
Kerteminde
SJÆLLAND
Greve Strand
Køge
Harwich
Mandø
Rødding
Assens
Odense
Fyn
Nyborg
Korsør
Slagelse
Ringsted
Næstved
Rømø
Haderslev
Skælskør
Agersø
Fakse Bugt
Havneby
Lohals
Svendborg
Smålandsfarvandet
Sylt
Aabenraa
Nordborg
Faaborg
Langeland
Vordingborg
Møn
Westerland
Tønder
Als
Tåsinge
Bøgø
Tinnum
Sønderborg
Ærø
Tårs
Feja Femø
Nakskov
Lolland
Nykøbing
Føhr
Harrislee
Flensburg
Flensborg Fjord
Langelands Bælt
Falster
Amrum
D
Kappeln
Rødbyhavn
Gedser
Niebüll
Leck
Halligen
Nordstrand
Schleswig
SCHWANSEN
Femern Bælt
Pellworm
Husum
Eckernförde
Fehmarn
Puttgarden
St Peter-Ording
Kropp
Kieler Bucht
Heiligenhafen
Rendsburg
Kronshagen
Heikendorf
Heiligenhafen
Rostock
Darß
Helgoländer Bucht
Büsum
Meldorf
Heide
Nortorf
Bordesholm
Kiel
Preetz
Lütjenburg
Malente
Futin
Grömitz
Lübeck, Travemünde
WAGRIEN
Mecklenburger Bucht
Ribnitz-Damgarten

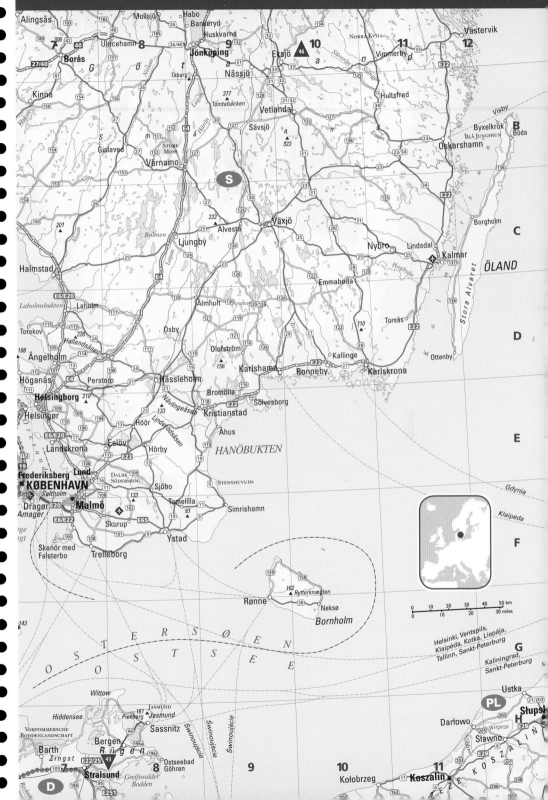

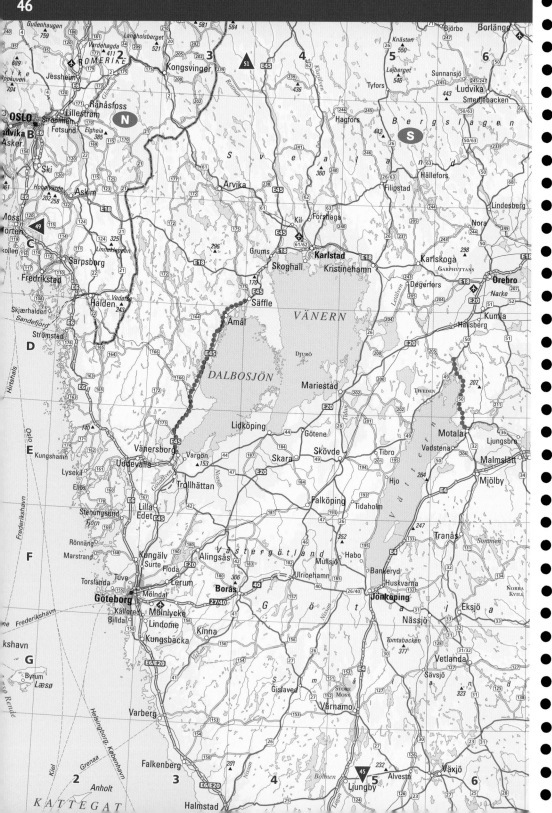

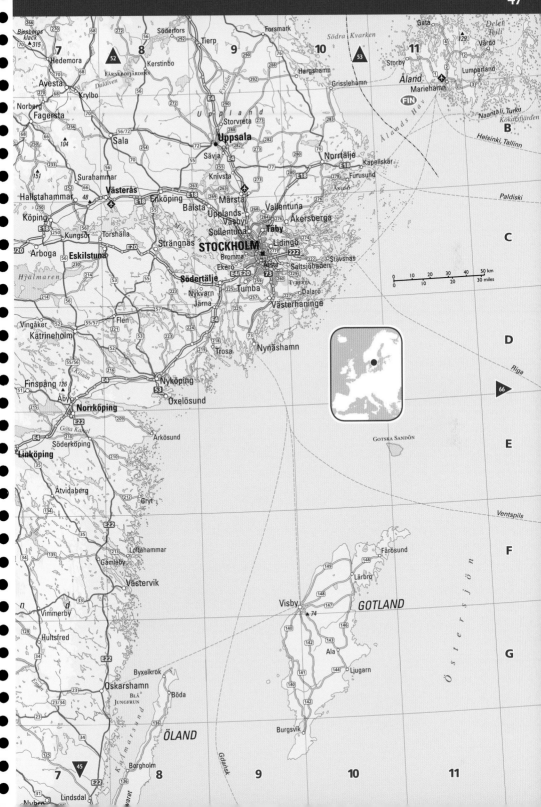

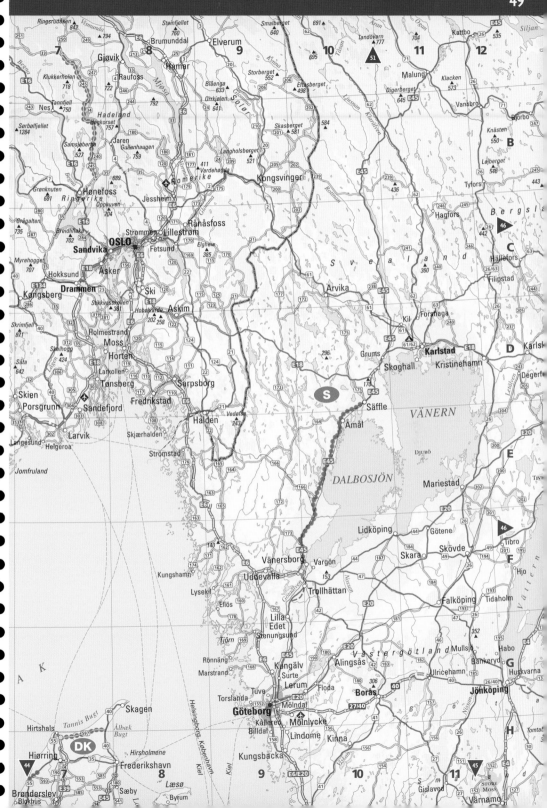

B

C

D

E

F

G

H

1 2 3 4 5 6

0 10 20 30 40 50 km
0 10 20 30 miles

Frøya 716 714
Grandefjæra
Knarrlagsund 714
Sandstad

Veidholmen
Havmyran 713
345 713 Hitra
Smøla 669 Forsnes 714
669 Fonna 722
Korsvoll 680 Omnsfjellet 847

Kristiansund 680 Stabblandet 682 Vinjeøra E39
Hurtigruten Tustna 908 Gråfjellet 1040
70 65 Hjelmen 978
Bud Skalten 663 Averøya 64 Høgfjellet 689 Tindfjellet 1167
664 692 Reinsfjellet 994 670
Gossen NORDMØRE 665 Smisetnebba 1175 Snøfjell 1579 Gjevilvasskamman 1627
Nordøyane Harøya Urfjellet 979 666
Dryna 662 Molde E39 Skåla 1128 62 70 Kråkvasstind 1699
Otrøy 668 660 Sunndalsøra
Blåsjerdingen 661 1069 E39 Åndalsnes 64 70 Slottha 1837 Storskarho 1871
Vigra 658 E39/E136 Storkrymten 1985 Tythøa 1773
Ålesund 61 Spjelkavik Trollvasstinden 1490 63 Kleinegga 1960 Snøhetta 2286 DOVREFJELL
Fosnavåg 827 61 650 Høgstolen 1739 Hånåvålstind 1806 Hjerkinn
697 Urfjellet 1267 60 E136 Bjorli Dovre
Gurskøy SUNNMØRE Kolåstinden 1432 Torvløysa 1851 E136 Lågen Storhe
Stadlandet Ørsta 1630 Storhe 1708 E6
Leikanger 61 652 Volda 655 63 Skarvedalseggen Lora Skarstind 1883 Dombås
Vagsøy 645 620 651 Kvitegga 1717 Sørbarden 1742 Skridulaupen Blåhø 1617 E6
Brurahornet 604 61 Felden 1272 1482 Vollsetskåla 1759 258 1962 1961 Østri Finna 15
Måløy Steinfjellet 616 15 Nordfjordeid Sætrefjellet 1892 15 Lomseggi 2068 Lom 51
Bremangerlandet 681 616 Hornelen 1094 15 Stryn Tverådalskyrkja 2088 Hestbreppiggan 2105 Galdhøpiggen 2470 Glittertinden 2465 Heidalsmuen 1743
Kalvåg Nordfjord Blånibba 1670 60 Høgste Breakulen 1957 Grånosi Liabrekulen 1910 2346 JOTUNHEIMEN 2368 Randsverk 257
Skorpa 310 614 Keipen 1362 Botnafjellet 1572 Snønipa 1827 JOSTEDALSBREEN Kvitå Koll 1775 Hellstusutinden Jotunheimen 51 Ruten 1513
Floro Blånipa 1121 Sandfjellet 1249 Skei Suphellenipa 1734 Såta 1701 Skagastølstindane 2405 Tjornholstinden 2330 Helimdalshø 1843
Stavang Hastein 932 5 Grovabreen 1636 Jostefonni 1815 604 Gaupne Stølsnostind 2073 Eidsbugarden Bitihorn 1607 Skaget 1886
Sunnfjord 1305 609 611 Førde E39 Svartenibba 1151 13 Ingeborgsfjellet 1452 53 Vennisfjellet 1771
Norskehesten Atløy 607 Taget 791 Johannesberg 1448 Leikanger 1173 Berdalseken 1814 E16 51
Askvoll 610 Store Jukleeggi 1921 Sælegga 1137
Pollatind 542 Krakhella 57 55 602 Fresvikbreen 1315 Lærdalsøyri Lærdalselvi E16 Vesleboutnskarvet 1778 VALDRES
Husøy Sula 722 607 Rysjedal Svatjell 877 1660 Blaskavlen 1809 Store Raudbergskarvet 1819 Fågernes
Sløvåg 57 Hope Bjørndalskamden 1402 E16 Liahovden 1763 Hemsedal METUBBA Nystølfjell 1295
Leirvåg Nordhjordland 570 Kvitanosi 1433 Vinje Kaldafjellet 1411 Storskavlen 1729 Blåbergi 1802 Gol Dyna 1212 Blåfjellet 1157
Radøy Fjellbaher 394 569 E16 Voss Raundalselvi Folarskarnuten 1933 70 Hallingdal 7
Alvøy Høgafjellet 869 Skjemmene 1351 572 Ramnabergnutēn 1729 50 Geilo 7 Hallingdalselvi
Tjeldstø Skrámesto 567 Bruravik Bjørdalshuten 1382 Fjellbunutun 1340 Gråfjell
Blomøy 561 Nyborg 13 Norheimsund Søvarnuten 1649 Maurset Synhovd 1438 Bjørkeflåta 40 Uvdalselva 7
Askøy 563 7 Tysse Kinsarvik HARDANGERVIDDA 48 Store Skrekken 1429 Borgsjåbrotet 1484 1045 Solandsfjellet
Bergen 48 1299 49 Solnut 550 1552 HARDANGERVIDDA Røksjæggi 1478 Rollag Eskedalselva
Store Sotra Vik E39 Jondal 552 Hardanger
Hufthamar Øsøyri 7 Varaldsøy 3 Fodnanuten 1454 Odda 4 5 6
Huftarøy Halhjem 48 13 1 2
546

N

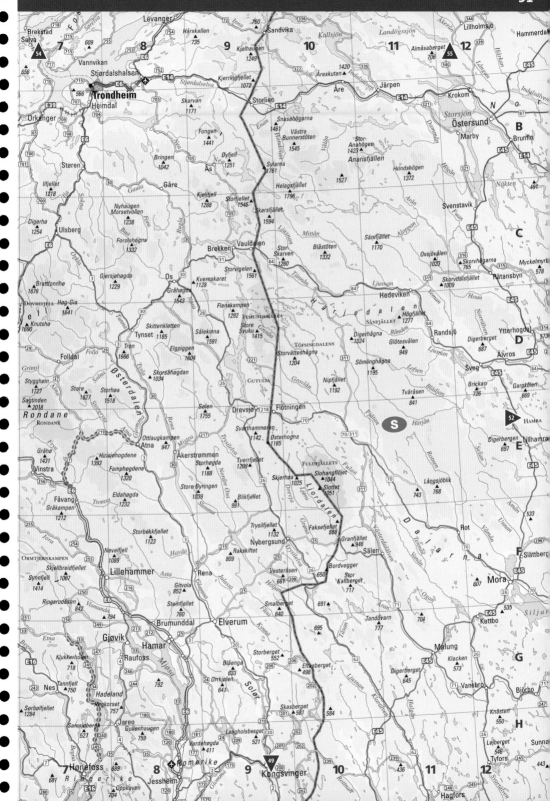

1 2 3 4 5 6

Åreskutan 336 1420
Järpen
E14 54
Krokom
706 340
Längan
Hårkan
344
Storkälen 539
331
Fjällsjöälven
90
Nätraån
348
Ångermanland

N o r r l a n d

Storsjön
Östersund
87
Indalsälven
Överammer
344
Ammerån
Faxälven
55
Björkån
335

Stor-Anåhögen 1423
Anarisfjällen
Marby 321
Brunflo
Ragunda
87
Solleftea
335
Boteå
334
Skuleskogen 338
SKULESKOGEN

1527 B
Hundshögen 1372
Högla
Bleckberget 531
323
Fors
Björnberget 479
331
Viksmon
87
Ullånger
E4

Sårvfjället 1170
Nästen
491
E14
499
320
86
Kälarne
Kramfors
Veda

Svenstavik
Bräcke
Gimån
Hemsjöärna 563
501
Medelpad
Mjällån
331
Härnösand

Oxsjövålen 1023
316
Koberget 570
Tälje
482
320
Indalsälven
Indal
E4

H ä r j e d a l e n
Hedeviken
84
Ljusnan
Vemån
Skorvhögarna 765
Skorvdalsfjället 1009
Rätansbyn
Myckelmyrberget 578
83
550
Holmsjöåsen
86 330
Stöde
Timrå
Alvik
E14 Sundsvall
Sundsvallsbukten

Högfjället 1277 SÅNFJÄLLET
Ljusnan
Randen
314
Fanbyklacken 507
554
305
Ljungan

Digerhågna 1024
Glötesvålen 949
Randsjö
Digerberget 687
84
Ytterhogdal
573
581
Ramsjö
Köln
Årskogen
E4

Sömlinghågna 1195
Löfsen
Ljusnan
Narälven
Älvros
Storberget 627
296
Hasseta
307
Jättendal

D
Tväråsen 841
Härjån
Sveg
Brickan 726
Garpkölen 669
Ängeån
84
Kårböle
83
305
Järnblasten 334

51
Fjällen
Blödan
HAMRA
Los
310
544
Fagerroskölen
Ljusnan
Korskrogen
Ljusdal
84
Delsbo
Hudiksvall
Hornslandet

743 E 768
Långsjöblik
Romen
Digerbergen 697
310
Lillhamra
S
Voxnan
517
Blacksås 457
E4

D a l a r n a
Enån
E45
533
Voxna
301
Bollnäs
H ä l s i n g l a n d
83
Enhammarsfjärden

Sälen
71
70
Rot
Vänman
Unnan
Orrälven
296/301
50
Söderhamn

Västerdalälven
607
Slättberg
Furudal
Halgonberget 497
301
Hälsingeskogen 489
Sibo
272
83
E4

Ösjön
704
Mora
26
70
Siljan
Rättvik
506
80
Lamborn
Kurbergets fab 506
Ödmärden
Testeboån
Hedsjö
303
Hagsta
Gästrikland
272
Kolforsen
Oslättfors
Gävlebukten

Malung
Klacken 573
71
Vansbro
Björbo
Leksand
Gagnef
Falun
293
80
Hofors
302
Valbo
Gävle
Skutskär
E4

Digerberget 645
E45
26
Knästen 550
247
Djuras
Borlänge
266
272
Söderfors
292
Tierp
Forsmark
76

62
Lejberget 546
Tyfors
Sunnansjö
443
Ludvika
50
Hedemora
270
68
184
FÄRNEBOFJÄRDENS
Kerstinbo
290
288

246
245
Hagfors
46
2
Smedjebacken
Avesta
Norberg
Krylbo
Dalälven
Svartån
E4
290
Hargshamn
47

62 360 240
442
26
Bergslagen 68
Fagersta
104
256
56/72
Sala
72
Fyrisån
Storvreta 273
Uppsala
282

BOTTENHAVET

SELKÄMERI

Örnsköldsvik

Norra Kvarken

Norra Gloppet

Östra Gloppet

Björköby

Södra Gloppet

Vaasa (Vasa)

Laihia

Molpe

Nyby

Pörtom

Närpes

Kauhajoki

Kurikka

Kauhava

Alajärvi

Lapua

Ruona

Nurmo

Seinäjoki

Jalasjärvi

Alavus

Virrat

Karvala

Kauhanevan Pohjankankaan

Lauhavuori 230

Parkano

Seitsemisen

Helvetinjärven 211

Kuru

Pohjankangas

Kankaanpää

Hämeenkangas

S A T A K U

FIN

Ylöjärvi

Nokia

Tampere

Pirkkala

Reposaari

Mäntyluoto

Pihlava

Pori

Friitala

Harjavalta

Kokemäki

Eura

Rauma

Vammala

Puurijärven ja Isonsuon

Huittinen

Lempäälä

Toijala

Laitila

Uusikaupunki

Loimaa

Forssa

VARSINAIS-SUOMI

Torronsuon

Liesjärven

Somero

Kustavi

Hakkenpää

Åland

Geta

Storby

Grisslehamn

Mariehamn

Lumparland

Södra Kvarken

Delet Teili

Vårdö

Kihti Skiftet

Stockholm

Stockholm

Naantali

Raisio

Turku (Åbo)

Litteinen

Kaarina

Pargas (Parainen)

Paimio

Salo

Dalsbruk (Taalintehdas)

Bromarv

Karis

Ekenäs (Tammisaari)

SKÄRGÅRDSHAVETS

Hanko (Hangö)

Kökar

Kökarsfjärden

Ålands Hav

EKENÄSKÄRGÅRDS

0 10 20 30 40 50 km
0 10 20 30 miles

1 2 3 4 5 6

B

C

D

E

F

G

H

Meløya
Glomsteet 1288
Ågskaret 1454
Blokktinden 1032
Snøtinden 1594
SALTFJELLET SVARTISEN
Nesøya
Hestmona
Hestmona 568
Jektvik
Kilboghamn
Trænfjorden
Lurøya
Strandtindan 1173
Høgtuva 1268
Snøfjellet 1196
Langvatnet
Løvunden 619
Sjøna
Sjønbotn
Hemnesberget
Nesna
Glein
Levang
Lihødet 842
Toven 991
Hemnesøy
Korgen
Dønna
Dønmannen 838
Engan
Sandnessjøen
Røssvassbukta
Røssvatnet
Tjøtta
Mosjøen
Geittind 1559
Vågsodden
Vefsna
Vega
Trolltinden 797 839
Horn
Anddalsvågen
Trofors
Ivarrud
Bjørgefjellet
Eiteråga
Vennesund
Gutuvikfjellet
Holm
Leka 422
Gutuvikfjellet 594
BØRGEFJELL
Terråk 801
Skatollet 981
Nursfjellet
Drottendalsfjellet 927
Søre Steinfjellet 1008
Mealhkoe 1182
Røyrvik 1160
Vikna 770
Vikna 593 770
606 Kjøringvassfjellet 806
N
Namdalen
Jåavma 1170
Mariafjellet 793
Geisnes
Abelvær 768 769
Salfjella 759
757
Heimdalshaugen 1150
Skorovatn
Portfjellet 838
Skorva 665
776
775
Nesåpiggen 988
Sanddøla
Eidet
Tommervikfjellet 446
648
Skogmo
760
Vestre Brandsfjellet 1072
Lauvsnes
Namsos 540
Geitfjellet 872
Formofoss
Lura
GRESSÅMOEN
Osen
Reinsjøfjellet 726
Langnesfjellet 775
Finnhúva 995
765
Kjerringheia 540
Finnvollheia 675
Sprova
Snåsavatnet
Imsa
Imsdalsfjellet 941
Blåfjellshatten 1332
Harsvik
Storfjellet 664
Steinkjer 762
Brannheiklumpen 818
Mahkene 1266
Åfjord
720
761
759
Løysmundhatten 1090
Ansätten 1091
Tarva
715
710
Verdalsøra
72
757
Sandfjellet 1248
Mjölkvattsfjellet
Åkersjön
Frøya
Brekstad
Grandefjæra
Knarrlagsund
Selva 609
Levanger
Hårskallen 735
Skäckerfjällen
Hårskallen 1035
Sandvika
Landögssjön
Hitra
Sandstad 656
Vannvikan
Stjørdalshalsen
Kjølhaugen 1249
Almåsaberget 706
Forsnes
Kristiansund, Ålesund Bergen
566
Trondheim
Heimdal
Kjerringfjellet 1072
Åreskutan 1420
Järpen
Fonna 722
Omnsfjellet 847
Orkanger
Skarven 1171
S1
Storlien
Åre
Vinjeøra
Gråfjellet 1040
Fongen 1441
Snøsahögarna 1461

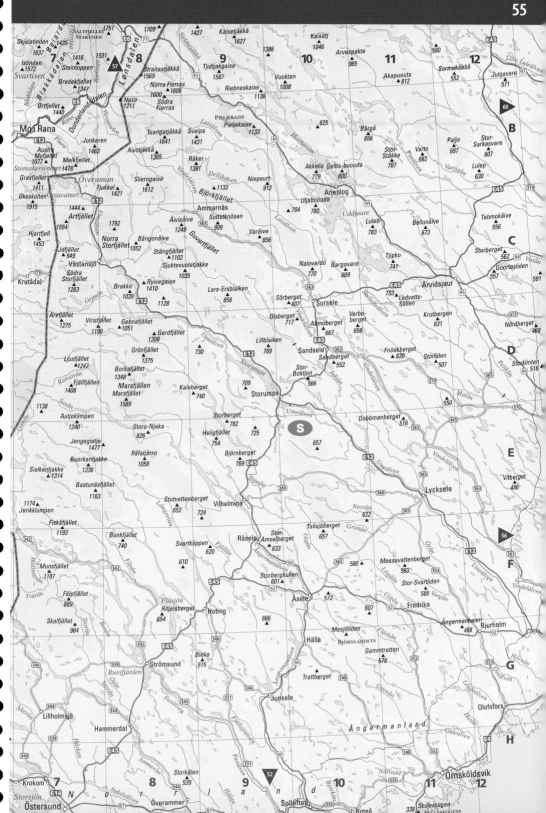

Skjelatinden 1637
Istinden 1572
SALTFJELLET SVARTISEN 1751
Bejard
1435
1416
Steintoppen
1531
57
8
Bredekfjellet 1347
1709
Straitastjåkkå 1569
1427
Kaisetjåkkå 1627
9
Tjidtjakgaise 1587
1386
Kaisatj 1046
Arvespakte 965
11
580
12
Sarmekåbbå 552
Lilla Luleälven
97
Jutsavare 571

Svartisen
Bjakkådalen
E6
77
Lønsdalen
95
Vuoktan 1008
Riebneskaise 1136
Akapuouta 812
60
B

Ørtfjellet 1440
E6
Nasa 1211
Norra Fierras 1606
1600
Södra Fierras
PIELJEKAISE
Pieljekaise 1133
825
Bårgå 856
Stor-Stäkke 787
Palja 697
Varto 682
Stor-Sarkasvare 607

Mo I Rana
E12
Austre Mofjellet 1077
Junkeren 1463
Melkfjellet 1478
Tsangatjåkkå 1641
Svaipa 1431
Aivotjåkkå 1365
Laisälven
Hornavan
Akkelis Galtis-buouda 779 800
Lulep 630
374

Storeakersvatnet
Grasfjellet 1411
Överuman
Slierogaise 1612
Räker 1381
Dellikälven
Niepsurt 912
Arjeplog
E45

Øksskolten 1915
Grasvatnet
Tjukkel 1421
E12
Björkfjället
Uljabuouda 780
704
95
Uddjaure
Luleb 783
Bellunåive 673
Tabmokåive 556
C

Artfjället 1444
1554
1792
Ämmarnäs
Suttsknösen
363
Aivisåive
909
Varåive 856
Nalovardo 770
Gargovare 669
Tjipko 741
Storberget 562
94
Vistån 591
Guortesliden 557

Hjartfjell 1453
Norra Storfjället 1052
Bångonåive
Stångfjället 1102
Guvertfjället
Sjuktevuoletjakke 1035
363
E45
Arvidsjaur
Ledvatts-fjällen
733
95
373
Nördberget 469

Jofjället 949
Västansjö
Södra Storfjället 1263
Brakko 1039
Ryivegaise 1410
1128
E12
Lars-Ersblaiken 1133
858
Sörberget 407
Sorsele
Olsberget 717
Åhmoberget 667
Verbo-berget 656
Krutbergen 631
Stocklinten 516

Krutådal
73
Arefjället 1275
Virisfjället 1190
Gebnafjället 1051
Gardfjället 1308
Umeälven
Lillblaiken 789
E12
Sandsele
363
Sandberget 552
Fnöskberget 620
Störliden 507
95
365
Petikån

Ljusfjället 1247
Grönfjället 1375
730
Storuman
709
Stor-Boktjon 566
Jeltan
Vindelälven
370
Malån
516

Ransarån
Borkafjället 1348
Fjällfjällen 1408
Saxån
Marsfjället 1589
Kalvberget 740
Storuman
Umeälven
550
S
Dobbmanberget 516
363
365
E

1138
Gejmån
Autjoklimpen 1240
Storberget 782
Heligfjället 754
725
657
E12
Umeälven
Vindelälven
Lycksele
363
Vitberget 486

Stora-Njaka 826
Jengegietje 1477
Råfatjärro 1058
Björnberget 769
E45
Volmån
360
Norrån 622
360
365
56

Buorkantjakke 1236
Sielkentjakke 1314
Bastunäsfjället 1163
Stutvattenberget 652
Vilhelmina
724
Tallsjöberget 657
Granån
E12
363
F

1174 Jerikklumpen
Fiskåfjället 1193
Bunkfjället 740
Svartklippen 620
610
Råsele
Ångermanälven
Stor-Amselberget 633
90
365
580
Mossavattenberget 583
Stor-Svartliden 589
353
Vargan
Umeälven
Vindelälven

342
Munsfjället 1187
342
E45
Storbergskullen 601
92
Åsele 572
607
92
Fredrika
Gideån
Ängermanälven 488
Bjurholm
92
Hörnån

Tvärån
Fälpfjället 889
Skalfjället 964
Flåsjön
Ritjelsberget 654
Hoting
666
Mesjöliden
BJÖRNLANDETS
Gammtratten 578
352
353
Oreälven
G

340
339
342
346
Bieka 515
331
Hälla
Trattberget 348
Österån
Olofsfors
E4

344
Lillholmsjö
344
Strömsund
Russfjärden
Faxälven
Junsele
346
Ängermanälven
90
Ängermanland
Gideälven
H

340
339
E45
Hammerdal
Härkan
Ammerån
Storkälen 539
331
Fjällsjöälven
52
90
Näträn
338
SKULESKOGENS
Örnsköldsvik

Krokom 7
E14
Östersund
Storsjön
87
Överammer
8
344
9
87
Sollefteå
10
335
Boteå
11
335
12
N o r r l a n d
Indalsälven
Faxälven
Fjällsjöälven

apuouta 331
812

Särmekåbbå 552

Jutsavare 571 2

Stora Luleälven

Lilla Luleälven 97

Vuottarauto 474

468 417

E10

Ängesån

Kalixälven

21

932

3

4 60

5

Tornedalen

Torniojoki

932

6

Naustapuouta 636

Luottåive 603

Rätneälven

Stor-Lappberget 263

98

392

930

930

E8

929

62

FIN

Varto 882

Palja 697

Stor-Sarkasvare 607

E45

Piteälven

Kårjisån

Luleälven

391

231

398

99

21

E8

927

4

E75

B

Lulep 630

Vitberget 594

97

356

E10

E4

Kukasjäkk

Sangisälven

926

Junkerkölen 348

673 Harrejaureliden 647

Tabmokåive 556

Bellunåive

374

Enstakaberget 440

Boden 383

Kalix 398

E4

Haparanda

Tornio

Kemi

Storberget 562

Nattberget 458

94

356

97

E45

E8 E75

95

Guortesliden 557

Vistån

591

Byskeälven

330

Älvsbyn 247

Gammelstaden

94

Luleå

HAPARANDA SKÄRGÅRD

PERÄMEREN

Arvidsjaur

C

95

374

E4

Krutbergen 631

S

Stor-Flötuberget 426

373

Piteå

Kallfjärden

Nördberget 469

Storliden 507

55

Skellefteälven

Malån

365

Pettikån

Storklinten 516

95

370

Byskeälven

Åbyälven

E4

550 D

365

370

Kågeälven

B O T T E N V I K E N

P E R Ä M E R I

cksele

Vindelälven

363

Vitberget 486

Stor-Blåbergsliden 374

Skellefteå

Byreälven

364

Raahe

E

Risån

Sikån

E12

365

364

E4

Kalajoki

7840

787

787 786

353

Umeälven

Vindelälven

363

Sävarån

E4

E8

7730

774

7720

27

Ylivieska

155

Ångermanbalen 488

Bjurholm

92

E12

Umeå

Hörnån

775

86

63

62

Pirttiharju

63

353

Öreälven

Holmsund

Kokkola (Karleby)

13

28

757

63

FIN

G

Lögdeälven

Husån

Olofsfors

E4

Västra Kvarken

Yttrefjärden

Jakobstad (Pietarsaari)

749

748

747

7450

63

775

sköldsvik

Norra Kvarken

Merenkurkku

Norra Gloppet

Östra Gloppet

7270

741

68

750

751

7320

19

738

751

13

Björköby

7240

7300

741

7370

2

3

Södra Gloppet

Vaasa (Vasa)

8

E8

718

718

8

725

711

E12

717

7210

723

4

64

68

5

733

Kauhava

711

16

6

Alajärvi

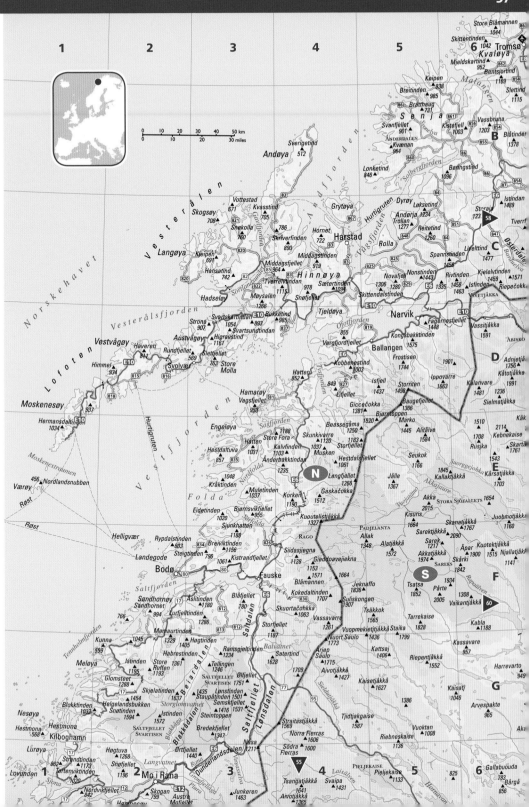

Store Blåmannen 1044

Skittentinden 1042 Tromsø
Kvaløya

Mjeldskartind 952
Bentsjortind 1169

Keipen
Breitinden 938

985
Matangen
Bråtthaug 731

Slettind 1115

Svanfjellet 901
Senja
Kistefjell 1003
Vassbruna 1203
Blåtinder 1378

ANDERDALEN
Kvænan 964

Lønketind 846
Bøningstind 1096

1 2 3 4 5 6

0 10 20 30 40 50 km
0 10 20 30 miles

Sverigetind

Andøya 512

Vesterålen

Vottestad
Skogsøy 671 Kvasstind 705
Snøkolla 760 786
Hornet 722

Dyrøy
Grytøya

Løksetind
Andørja 1234
Trollan 1277
Reitetind 1260

Istindan 1489
Storaja 123. 58
Tverrf

Hurtigruten

Langøya
Kleipeh 691
Skriverfinden 890
Harstad
Middagstinden 919
Rolla
Spannstinden 1458
Livelttind 1477
Østerdale

Hansatind 742
Middagsfjellet 964
Tverrelvindan 1115
Hinnøya
Sætertinden 978
1094

Novafjell 1306
Nonstinden 1443
Rivtinden 1280
Kjelelvtinden 1459
Isfinden 1463
Riepečokk

Hadseløy
Møysalen 1266
Snøfjellet
Tjeldøya
Skittendalstinden

Narvik
Fagernesfjellet 1448
Vassitjåkka 1591
ABISKO

Vesterålsfjorden
Svartskartindan 1054
Strona 907
Bukketind 985
Svartsundtindan 893
837
Ofotfjorden 855
Kongsbakktinden

Vestvågøy
Haveren 811
Austvågøy
Rundfjellet 569
Higravstind 1161
Slettfjellet 763
Vargfjordtinden 1327
Ballangen 1575
Frostisen 1744
1901

Adnjetjå 1756
Kåtotjåkka 1991

Himmel 934
Svolvær
Store Molla
Hatten 852
Kobbenestind 1003
Isfjell 1437
Storriten 1498
Ippovarre 1663
Kålanvare 1481
1236

Lofoten

Moskenesøy
Hermansdalen 1034
Hamarøy
Vågsfjellet 953
Liljfellet 849
Giccečokka 1381
Baugefjellet 1366
1510
2114
Käk

Moskenesstraumen
456 Nordlandsnubben
Værøy
Røst
Engeløya
Store Fora 1188
Skunkivarre 1250
Beassegåma 1520
Marko 1445
Bjørntoppen
Alitåive 1584
1708
Rusjka
Kebnekaise
1543
Skartå 1761

Hatten 1037
Kalvfinden 103 A
Store Fora 1120
Musken
Storfjellet 1183
Hestdalsfjellet 1061
Seukok 1166
1845
Kallaktjåkkå

Kårsatjåkka 1703

Hestdaltuva 857
Ånderbakktindan 1235
1048

N
Langfjellet 1266
Jålle 1367
Suorggjohka

Akkajaure

Folda
Kråktinden
Muletinden 1037
Korken 1190
Gaskačokka 1512
Akka 2015
STORA SJÖFALLETS
1654

Eidetinden 1020
Bjørnsvikfjellet 955
Kisuris 1664
Juobmotjåkkå 1160

Helligvær
Rypdalstinden 803
Breiviktinden 1156
Sjunkhatten 1188
RAGO
Kuoutelistjåkkå 1327
PADJELANTA
Allak
Skanatjåkkå 1767
Sarektjåkkå 2090

Landegode
Steigtinden 796
Kistrandfjellet 1061
Siidasjiegna 1128
Gieddoavejiekna 1153
1348
Alatjåkkå 1572
Sarek 1217
Åpar 1900
Kuotektjåkkå 1515
Njallatjåkkå 1141

Bodø
Fauske
Blåmannen
Kokedaltinden 1707
Jeknaffo 1836
Suliskongen 1907
Akkatjåkkå 1974
Skårki 1842
SAREKS

Saltfjorden
Sandhornøy
Sandhornet 994
Aslitinden 180
Blåfjellet 780
Skuortačohkka 1063
Tsåkkok 1565
Tsatsa 1852
Pårte 2005
1934
Vaikantjåkkå 60

766
Lurfjelltinden 1266
Vassavare 1261
Vuopmekietitjåkkå Staika
Nuort Saulo 1773
Tarrekaise 1828
Kabla 1188

Tennholmtraumen
Kunna 559
Memaurtinden
Høgtinden 1329 1405
Storfjellet 1187
Arjep Saulo 1715
Kattsaj 1406
Kassavare 957

Meløya
Istinden 1195
Store Ruffen 1193
Habrestinden 1234
Ramsgjeltinden
Sætertind 1628
Aivotjåkkå 1427
1709
Riepentjåkkå 1552
Harrevarto 949

Glomsteet 1288
Telingen 1246
Ølfjellet 1531
Kaisetjåkkå 1627
Kaisatj 1046

Skjelatinden 1454
SALTFJELLET SVARTISEN 1751
Lønstinden 1435
Staupåtinden 1507
Semskfjellet 1416
1386
Arvespakte 965

Blokktinden 1032
Helgelandsbukken 1637
Snøtinden 1594
Istinden
Steintoppen
Tjidtjakgaise 1587
Vuokta 1008

Nesøya
Hestmona 568
Kilboghamn
SALTFJELLET SVARTISEN
Bredekfjellet 1347
Straitastjåkkå 1569
Norra Fierras 1606
Riebneskaise 1136

Lurøya
Høgtuva 1268
Ørtfjellet 1440
Nasa 1211
Södra Fierras 1600
Pieljekaise 55
PIELJEKAISE
Pieljekaise 1133
Gallabuouda 793
Bårgå 856

Lovünden 962
Strandtinden 1173
Snøfjellet 1196
Langvatnet
Dunderlandsdalen
Mo i Rana
Tsangatjåkkå 1641
Aivotjåkkå
Svaipa 1431
Laisälven
825

Nordvikfjellet 942
Skogan 799
Austra
Junkeren 1463

1   2   3   4   5   6

B

0 10 20 30 40 50 km
0 10 20 30 miles

NORDISHAVET

C

Hammerfest
Kvaløya
Svartfjellet
630

580

Sørøya
Vatnafjellet
882   656

Lopphavet   Hasvik

Sørøysundet

Seiland
1079   985

Skinnfjellet
710

94

Nord-Kvaløy

Fugløya
Fugløykallen
753

Arnøya
1168

Kvænangen

Eliassen
939 949
Stjernøya

Stjernsundet

Øksfjord

E6

Middagsfjellet
1312
1071   1066 1304

Liv'luvarri
958

Alta
740

Alángen
737

Vanna
Vanntindan
1033

Nevernesfjellet
1181   1041

Fjelltindnasen
882

Navgastat
713

883

Rebbenesøy

Skjervøy

Lassefjellet
1166

Stuora
Hal'di
1149

E6

Svartevasstind
876

Hansnes

Reinøy
Reinskartind
863

Kågen
1098

Retisfjorden

Gierdoidvarri
810

93

Gæv'dni
672

Ringvassøy

Istind
953

Uløya
866

Blåind
1142

E6

Nubivarri
841

Fiesjárri

D

Grøtsundet

Ullsfjorden

Tverrbakktind
1390

Vaggastinden
1398

Rieppesgai'sa
1337

N

Vir'dnečåk'ka
590

Store Blåmannen
1044

Ullstind
1094

Stortind
1512

Bæssetindan
1312

865

Badojokka

Skittentinden
1042

Kvaløya
952

Tromsø Tromsdalen
Tromsdalstind
862   1238

Fornesfjellet
1478

Nordmannviktind
1336

Bæccæhal'di
1326

1301

Cuonjaoai'vi
1089

Čáravárri
887

Mjeldskartind

91

E8

Lavangsdalen

Sennedaltfjellet
1385

Isfjellet
1375

Mållejus
975

E Senja 861

Kistefjell
1003

856

Slettind
1115

Bardfjorde

Balfjorde

Bentsjortind
1169   858

Jiehkkevarri
1833

Lakselvtindan
1617

868

E6

 Čiččenvárri
1312

Reisdalen

Reisa

Bråtinden
985

ANDERDALEN

86   854

Blåtinden
1378

858

E8

Piggtind
1505

Henriktind
1219

E6/8

Manndalen

Skibotndalen

Skibotnelva

Rássanibba
1252

Halti
1328

860   855   87

Lille
Russetind
1527

Mannfjellet
1533

Goahterássa
1371

E8

Vuoskuvarri
527

Kolberghjorden

Børingstind
1096 84

86

Stormauken
854   857
1249

Møselva

Dividalen

Baras
1419

Kåhperusvaarat
1144

Saana
1025

Jollanoaivi
1029

Rommaenov

Bas'tevarri
658

yrøy

84

Storaia
1237

Istindan
1489

Langfjelltind
1504

Rostadalen

Rostaelva

Moskkugáisi
1523

942

93

etetind
1260

851

87

Barduelva

Kjerkestinden
1677

1271

Peeravaara
933

Konkamaalven

491

Spannstinden
1456

47

Livelttind
1477

Njumis
1713

Jerta
1428

Ropi
945

Torisono

Urtivaara
633

onstingen
1443

Rivtinden
1458

E6

Østerdalen

Kjelelvtinden
1571

ØVRE DIVIDAL

Kistefjell
1633

Paltäive
915

21

Tarju
735

Tarjantovaara
591

Jierstivaara
647

E6

57

VAVETJÅKKA

Råkkunbårri
1659

Tsåktso
1119

Rostonsjåkå

Rastoelva

21

Ruutusoive
842

Jietajoki

Lainiojoki

93

Vassitjåkka
1591

ABISKO

Tuoptejåkkah
1604

Måissavarri
1022

Roopi
799

E45

99

21

Pebpki

956

G

den

E10

S

Torneträsk

Vittangivaara

93

Pyhäkero
711

901

ippovarre
1663

E10

Råkisvare
985

Puollanáive
796

60

E8

Outtakka
723

957

Kalanvare
1481

Kåtotjåkka
1991

Lulep-
Patsajåkel
782

Vittangivaara
836

PALLAS JA OUNASTUNTURIN
KANSALLISPUISTO

H

Rassepautastjåkka
1750

Råppe
1014

Nunasvaara
580

Taivaskero
807

1510

Kebnekaise
2114

Vista-sjokka

Leavvosjohka

612

Haiju
551

Merasjoki

21

Keimiötunturi
610

Rusjka
1708

Skartåive
1761

2

1017

3

Kiruna

Vittangiälven

4

Rautusakara

E45

5

99

6

79

laktjåkka

1543

Piedjastjåkka

627

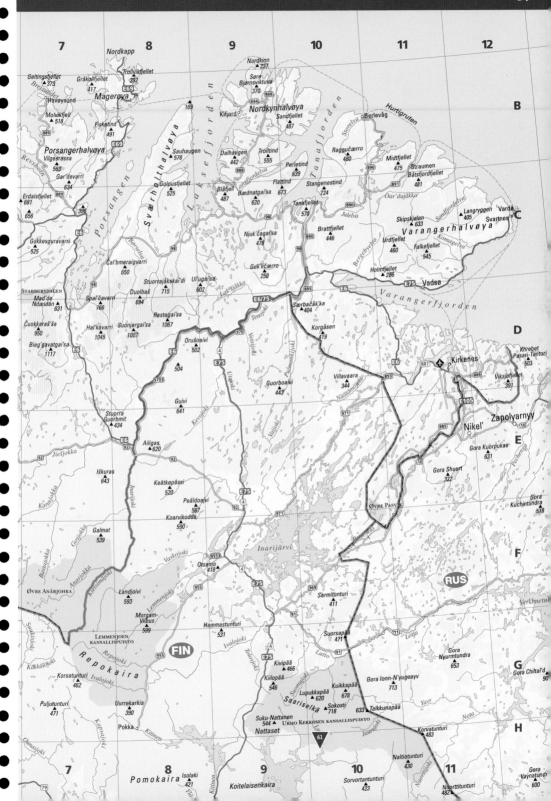

7　　8　　9　　10　　11　　12

Nordkapp

B

Geitingsfjellet 373
Gråkollfjellet 417
Trollvikfjellet 392
Nordkinn 237
Søre Bjørnsviktuva 370
Nordkynhalvøya
Berlevåg
Hurtigruten

Breivikeidet
Havøysund
Magerøya
E69
169
Kifjord
Sandfjellet 487
Storelva

Molvikfjell 518
Fisketind 491
Sauhaugen 578
Dalhaugen 442
Trolltind 555
Ragguč́œrro 480
Midtfjellet 475
Straumen
Båtsfjordfjellet 481

Porsangerhalvøya
Vilgesrassa 563
E69
Golpusfjellet 525
Blåfjell 487
Bædnatgai'sa 620
Perletind 639
Flattind 673
Stangenestind 724
Oar'dujåkk

Gar'devarri 634
Njuk'čagal'sa 478
Tanafjellet 570
Skipskjølen 633
Langryggen 405
Vardø
Svartnes C

Erdalsfjellet 681
656
E6
Brattfjellet 446
Varangerhalvøya
Falkefjellet 545

Gukkesguravarri 525
Čal'bmeraigvarri 650
Guk'kč́œrro 250
Urdtfjellet 460
Holmfjellet 285
E75
Vadsø

STABBURSDALEN
Mad'de Ndæidan 631
Spal'čavarri 766
Duolbaš 694
Stuorrajåkskai'di 715
Ul'ugai'sa 602
Varangerfjorden
E6

Čuokkaraš'sa 950
Hal'kavarri 1045
Suonjergai'sa 1007
Restegai'sa 1067
Sǽrbačåk'ka 404
Korgåsen 419
E6/75

Bieg'gavatgai'sa 1117
E6
Orušoaivi 502
Villavaara 344
Kirkenes
Khrebet Pasari-Tunturi 503

504
Guorboaivi 443
Viksjøfjellet 391
E105

Stuorra Guorbmit 434
Gulvi 641
Nikel'
Zapolyarnyy

Ailigas 620
E6
Gora Kuørpukas 631

Iškuras 643
Keätkepåssi 520
Gora Shuort 322
Gora Kuchintundra 578

Peäldoaivi 567
Koarvikodds 590
ØVRE PASVIK

Galmat 539
Otsamo 418
Inarijärvi
RUS

ØVRE ANÁRJOKKA
Lándjoivi 593
Sarmitunturi 411

Morgam-Viibus 599
Hammastunturi 531
Suorsapää 471
Gora Nyurmtundra 653

LEMMENJOEN KANSALLISPUISTO
FIN
Repokaira
Kivipää 466
Gora Chiltal'd 90

Korsatunturi 462
Kiilopää 546
Lupukkapää 620
Kuikkapää 678
Gora Ionn-N'yugoayv 713
Talkkunapää

Puljutunturi 471
Uurrekarkia 390
Sariselkä
Sokosti 718
633
Korvatunturi 483

Pokka
Suku-Nattanen 544
URHO KEKKOSEN KANSALLISPUISTO
Nattaset
61
Naltiotunturi 430

7　　8　　9　　10　　11

Pomokaira
Isolaki 421
Koitelaisenkaira
Sorvortantunturi 423
Nuorttitunturi 482
Gora Vaynatundr 600

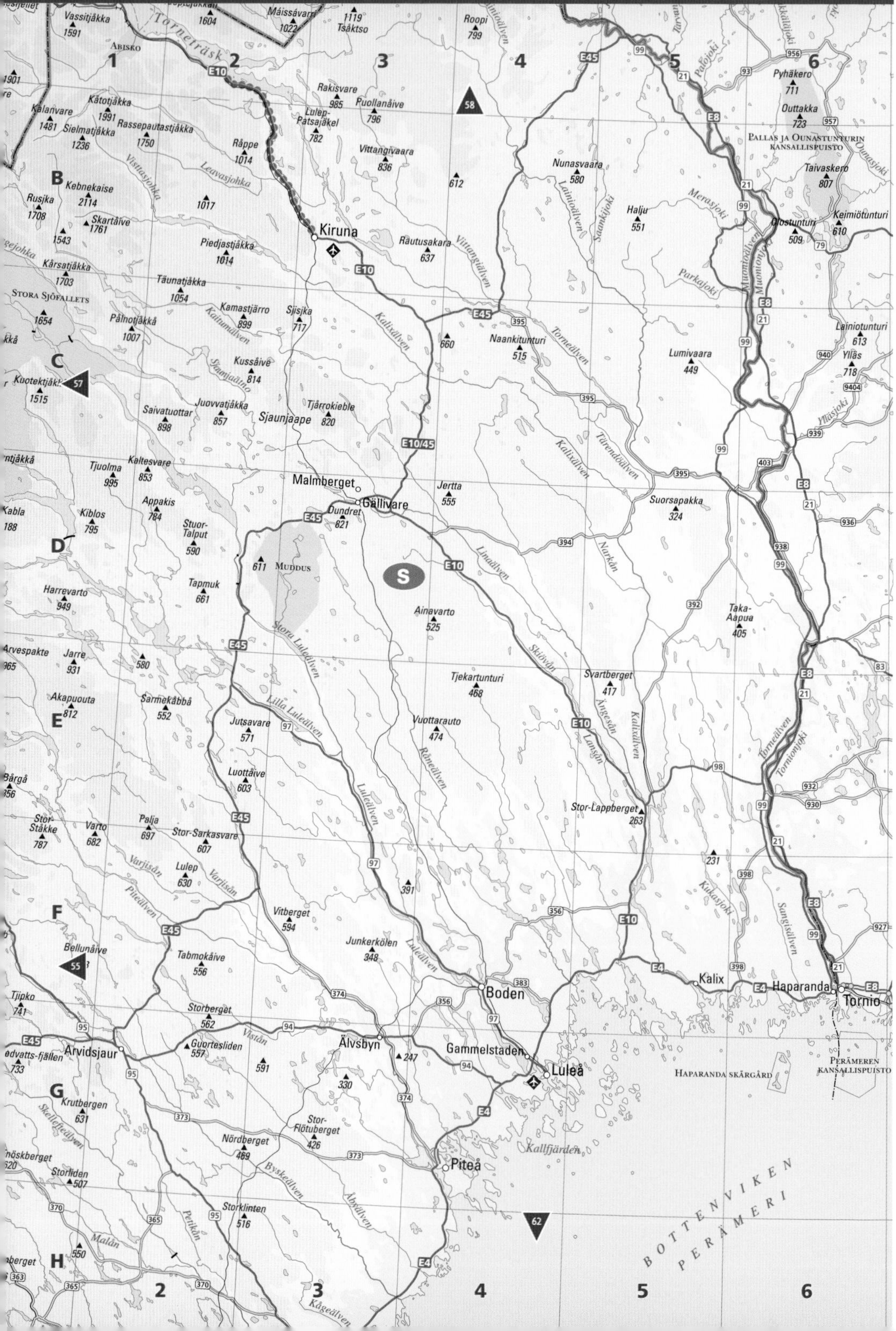

Vassitjåkka 1591
Máissávarre 1022
1119 Tsåktso
Roopi 799
956
93 Pyhäkero 711
6
Torneträsk
1604

ABISKO 1
E10 2
3
4
E45
99 21 5
E8
Outtakka 723 957

Kalanvare 1481
Kåtotjåkka 1991
Rassepautastjåkka 1750
Rakisvare 985
Puollanåive 796
58
612
Nunasvaara 580
PALLAS JA OUNASTUNTURIN KANSALLISPUISTO
Taivaskero 807

1901
Sielmatjåkka 1236
Lulep Patsajåkel 782
Råppe 1014
Vittangivaara 836
Menasjoki
Halju 551
Olostunturi 509
Keimiötunturi 610
79

B
Rusjka 1708
Kebnekaise 2114
Skartåive 1761
1017
Kiruna
E10
Räutusakara 637
21
Parkaloki
21

1543
Kårsatjåkka 1703
Piedjastjåkka 1014
Täunatjåkka 1054
E45 395
Naankitunturi 515
Tornedalven
Lumivaara 449
940
Yllås 718
9404

STORA SJÖFALLETS 1654
Pålnotjåkkå 1007
Kamastjärro 899
Sjisjka 717
660
395
Lainiotunturi 613
939

C 57
Kuotektjåkk 1515
Kussåive 814
Juovvatjåkka 857
Sjaunjaape
Tjårrokieble 820
E10/45
395
403
E8
936

ntjåkkå
Tjuolma 995
Kaltesvare 853
Malmberget
Jertta 555
99
Suorsapakka 324
938

Kabla 188
Kiblos 795
Appakis 784
Gällivare
Dundret 821
E45
S
E10
394
Taka-Aapua 405
99

D
Harrevarto 949
Stuor-Talput 590
611 MUDDUS
Tapmuk 661
Ainavarto 525
392
83

Arvespakte 365
Jarre 931
580
Tjekartunturi 468
Svartberget 417
E8 21

Akapuouta 812
Sarmekåbbå 552
Jutsavare 571
Vuottarauto 476
E10
98

E
Bárgá 856
Luottåive 603
Stor-Lappberget 263
932
930

Stor Ståkke 787
Varto 682
Palja 697
Stor-Sarkasvare 607
E45
231
E8 99

Lulep 630
Vitberget 594
Junkerkölen 348
356
E10
398
927

F
Bellunåive 55
Tabmokåive 556
374
Boden
383
Kalix
398
Haparanda
Tornio
21 E8

Tjipko 741
Storberget 562
94
Älvsbyn
356
97
E4

E45
Arvidsjaur
Guortesliden 557
591
247
Gammelstaden
94
Luleå
HAPARANDA SKÄRGÅRD
PERÄMEREN KANSALLISPUISTO

G
Krutbergen 631
373
330
374

Nördbergen 469
Stor-Flötuberget 426
373
Piteå
Kallfjärden

Storliden 507
Storklinten 516
62

H 550
365
95
BOTTENVIKEN PERÄMERI

1 2 3 4 5 6

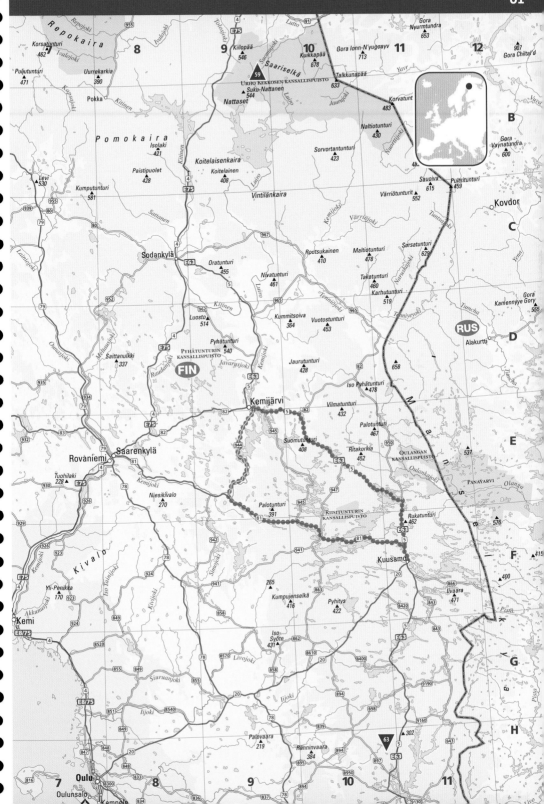

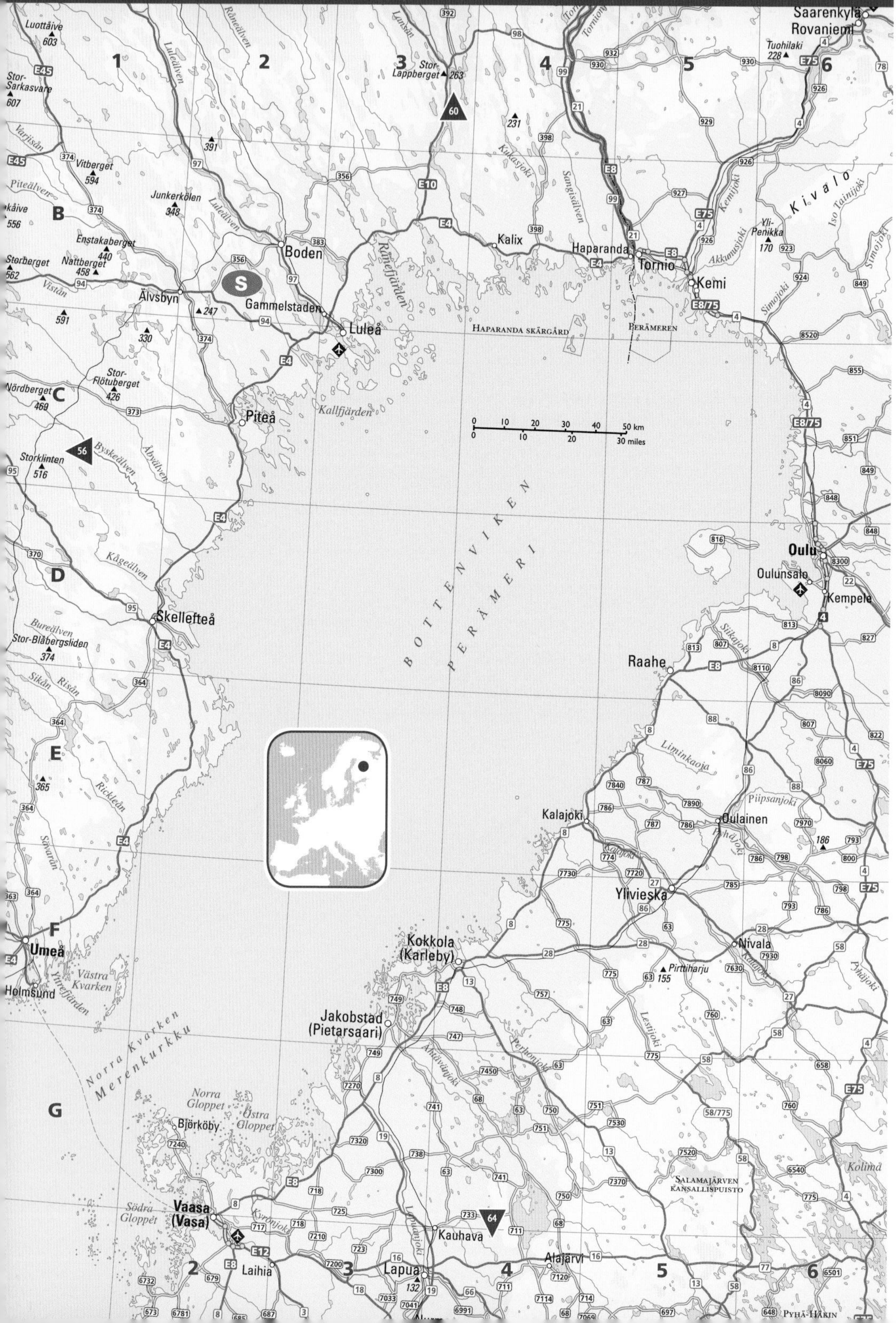

Luottåive 603

Stor-Sarkasvare 607

1

2

3 Stor-Lappberget ▲263

Råneälven

Lansan 392

98

Torneälven

Tornionjoki

932

930

99

4

5

Saarenkylä
Rovaniemi

Tuohilaki 228 ▲

E75

6

78

926

▲ 60

231 ▲

21

398

929

E45

374 Vitberget 594

97

356

E10

99

99

927

E75

Kalixälven

Kemijoki

Kivalo

Iso Tainijoki

Piteälven

kåive 556

B

374

Junkerkölen 348

Luleälven

E4

Kalix

398

E8

E75

Yli-Penikka 170

923

924

Enstakaberget 440

Boden

383

Haparanda

21

926

Simojoki

Storberget 562

Nattberget 458

94

356

Råneälven

Tornio

E8

Kemi

924

849

Vistån

97

S

Älvsbyn

591

▲247

Gammelstaden

94

Luleå

E4

HAPARANDA SKÄRGÅRD

PERÄMEREN

E8/75

330

374

C

Nordberget 469

Stor-Flötuberget 426

373

Piteå

Kallfjärden

0   10   20   30   40   50 km
0   10   20   30 miles

8520

855

D

Storklinten 516

56

95

Byskeälven

Åbyälven

E4

848

848

816

Oulu

E8/75

849

851

8300

370

Kågeälven

95

Skellefteå

E4

Oulunsalo

22

Kempele

813

827

Bureälven

Stor-Blåbergsliden 374

364

Sikån

Risån

364

Raahe

E8

813

807

8110

86

8090

807

Liminkaoja

E

365

Rickleån

364

8060

822

E75

7840

787

86

Piipsanjoki

Kalajoki

7890

7970

186

793

800

364

E4

774

787

786

Oulainen

786

798

E75

Sävarån

363

364

7730

7720

27

785

793

786

Ylivieska

798

E75

Umeå

F

E4

86

28

793

786

Holmsund

Västra Kvarken

Ytterfjärden

Kokkola
(Karleby)

775

28

28

Nivala

7930

58

7630

E75

63

Pirttiharju 155

760

Norra Kvarken

Merenkurkku

Jakobstad
(Pietarsaari)

E8

13

748

757

63

Lestijoki

Perhonjoki

775

658

747

749

7450

750

751

58/775

760

G

Norra Gloppet

Östra Gloppet

7270

741

68

750

7530

751

13

6540

Kolima

Björköby

7240

7320

19

SALAMAJÄRVEN KANSALLISPUISTO

775

Södra Gloppet

Vaasa
(Vasa)

8

Kyröjoki

718

7300

63

741

7370

7520

775

2

E12

7210

725

Lappajoki

733

64

68

711

5

6

6501

Laihia

E8

679

7200

Lapua

18

Kauhava

16

77

58

6732

687

7033

132

19

66

711

714

68

7041

697

648

PYHÄ-HÄKIN

673

6781

8

685

6991

714

7044

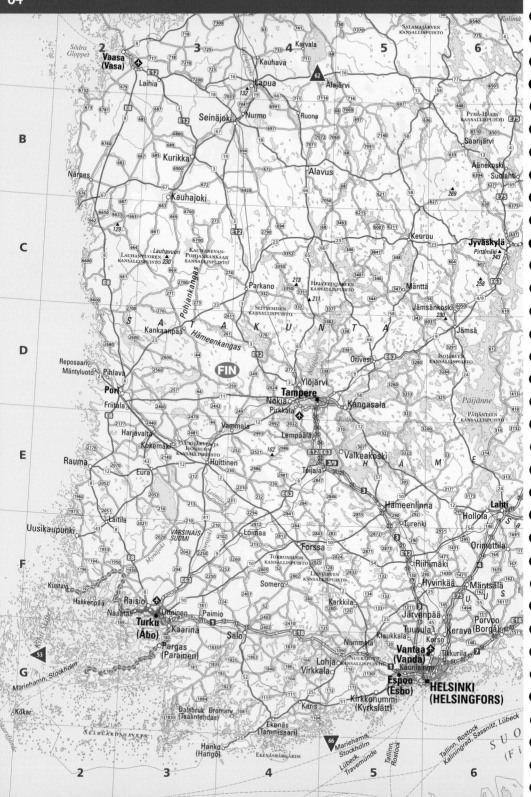

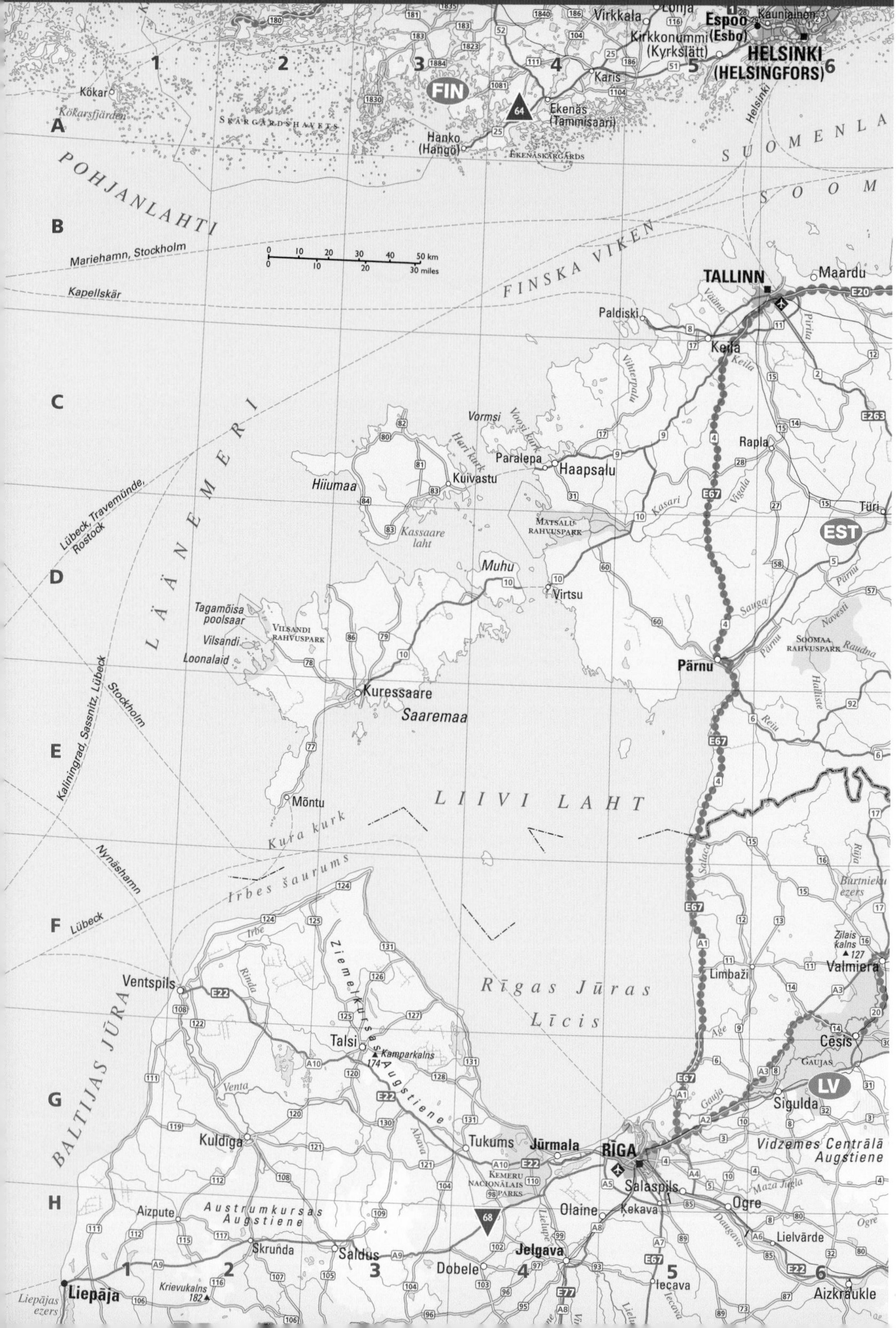

1   2   3   FIN   4   5   6

Virkkala   Lohja   Espoo   Kauniainen
(Esbo)   HELSINKI
Kökar   Kirkkonummi   (HELSINGFORS)
(Kyrkslätt)   Karis   Helsinki
Kökarsfjärden   SKÄRGÅRDSHAVET   64   Ekenäs   Maardu

POHJANLAHTI

A   Hanko   (Tammisaari)
(Hangö)   EKENÄSSKÄRGÅRD   SUOMENLA

FINSKA VIKEN   SOOM

B   Mariehamn, Stockholm   TALLINN   Maardu
0   10   20   30   40   50 km   E20
0   10   20   30 miles
Kapellskär   Paldiski   Vääna   Pirita
Keila   Keila   E263

C   Vormsi   Vangl kurk   Rapla   EST
Paralepa   Haapsalu   Rapla   Türi
Hiiumaa   Kuivastu   Kasari   E67   Pärnu
Hari kurk   MATSALU   Sauga
RAHVUSPARK   SOOMAA   RAHVUSPARK

Lübeck, Travemünde,
Rostock   Kassaare   Muhu   Pärnu   Navesti   Raudna
laht   Virtsu   Hädiste

D   Tagamõisa   VILSANDI   Pärnu
poolsaar   RAHVUSPARK   Reiu
Vilsandi   86   79   E67
Loonalaid   78   10
Kuressaare   Saaremaa

E   Mõntu   LIIVI LAHT   E67
Kura kurk   Salaca
Nynäshamn   Irbes šaurums   124   Burtnieki
ezers

F   Lübeck   124   125   Zilais kalns   Valmiera
Irbe   131   A1   127   Cēsis
Ventspils   E22   126   Limbaži   GAUJAS
Rinda   125   127   Aģe   A3
Talsi   Kamparkalns   131   Gauja   Sigulda   LV
A10   174   128   E67   Vidzemes Centrālā
Kuldīga   120   130   A1   Augstiene
121   131   Tukums   Jūrmala   RĪGA   Mazā Jugla
112   108   121   104   KEMERU   A10   Salaspils   Ogre
NACIONĀLAIS   110   A5   Daugava   Lielvārde
PARKS   68   Olaine   Ķekava   A7
Aizpute   Austrumkursas   109   102   Jelgava   Pļeçava   Aizkraukle
Augstiene   Skrunda   Saldus   A9   Dobele   97   E77   E22
Liepāja   Krievukalns   116   105   104   103   96   93   95   87

BALTIJAS JŪRA

LĀNEMERI

Rīgas Jūras
Līcis

Liepājas
ezers   182

ITÄISEN SUOMENLAHDEN KANSALLISPUISTO

Zelenogorsk
Serlolovo
Pesochnyy
Sestroretsk
Pargolovo
Kuz'm
A123
N
7 8 9 10 11 12
Kronshtadt
Lebyazh'ye
Sankt-Peterburg
(St Petersburg)
M18
FINSKIY ZALIV
65
Sosnovyy
Bor
Petrodvorets
Metallostroy
D
E L A H T
A120
Pushkin
Kolp
A121
Pavlovsk
Kommunar
LAHEMAA RAHVUSPARK
Kunda
Loobu
Selja
Kunu
Narva laht
Narvskiy zaliv
Volosovo
Vyritsa
E20
Gatchina
B
Siverskiy
Kohtla-
Järve
Sillamäe
A121
M11
Kingisepp
A120
E20
Narva
Ivangorod
Rakvere
Kiviõli
Jõhvi
Ahtme
Luga
E95
Tapa
Pandivere
kõrgustik
Kellavere
155
Narvskoye
Vdkhr.
Oz. Vyal'ye
M20
C
Slantsy
Emumägi
166
Peipsi
järv
Ozero
Chudskoye
Oredezh
Palde
Pihkva
Luga
Põltsamaa
Gdov
Jõgeva
RUS
D
E263
Tartu
Zhelcha
Strugi-
Krasnyye
200
E95
Viljandi
Võrtsjärv
Sakala
kõrgustik
Rutu
mägi
144
Elva
Chernaya
Pskovskoye
ozero
Sol'tsy
E
E264
Kuutse
mägi
217
Põlva
Otepää
kõrgustik
Võru
Piusa
Pechory
Pskov
Dno
Polonka
Porkhov
Belka
F
Valka
Valga
KARULA
RAHVUSPARK
Suur Munamägi
318
E77
Cherekha
Shelon'
Dedovichi
Seda
Abula
Gauja
Delinkalns
271
Alüksnes
Sudomskiye
Vysoty
293
Smiltene
Alüksne
Ostrov
G
E77
A2
Gauja
Gulbene
Balvi
E262
E95
Pushkinskiye
Gory
Novorzhev
Bezhanitsy
Gaizinkalns
311
Madona
Pytalovo
A116
Bezhanitskaya Vozvyshennost'
338
Loknya
H
Krasnogorodskoye
Opochka
M20
Jēkabpils
E22
Ludza
Rēzekne
E22
A12

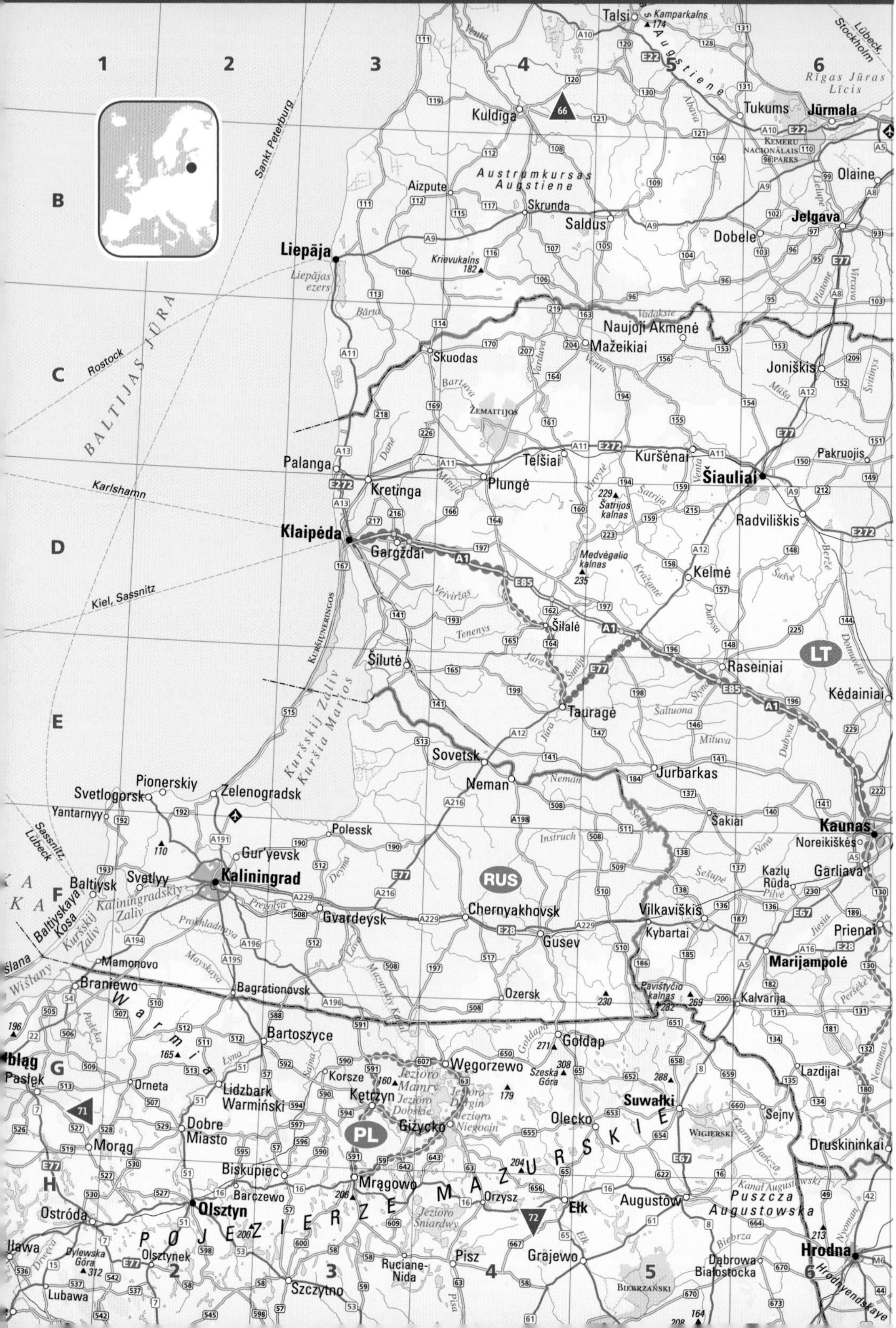

1 2 3 4 5 6

B

Sankt Peterburg

BALTIJAS JŪRA

Rostock

Karlshamn

Kiel, Sassnitz

Sassnitz, Lübeck

Lübeck, Stockholm

Rīgas Jūras Līcis

Talsi · Kamparkalns
174
Augstiene

Kuldīga 66

Austrumkursas Augstiene

Tukums Jūrmala

KEMERU NACIONĀLAIS PARKS

Olaine

Aizpute Skrunda Saldus Dobele Jelgava

Liepāja

Liepājas ezers

Bārta

Krievukalns 182

Naujoji Akmenė

Skuodas Mažeikiai Joniškis

Bartuva ŽEMAITIJOS

Palanga Telšiai Kuršėnai Pakruojis

Kretinga Plungė Šiauliai

Klaipėda Šatrijos kalnas 229 Radviliškis

Gargždai A1 Medvėgalio kalnas 235 Kelmė

KURŠIŲ NERINGOS

Šilalė A1 Kėdainiai

Šilutė Raseiniai

KURŠIŲ ZALIV / KURŠIA MARIOS

Tauragė

Sovetsk

Neman Jurbarkas

Pionerskiy Zelenogradsk Kaunas

Svetlogorsk Noreikiškės

Yantarnyy Polessk Sakiai

Gur'yevsk Kazlų Rūda Garliava

Baltiysk Svetlyy Kaliningrad Chernyakhovsk Vilkaviškis

Gvardeysk Prienai

Gusev Kybartai

Marijampolė

Mamonovo Ozersk Kalvarija

Braniewo Bagrationovsk Pavištyčio kalnas 292

Bartoszyce Goldap Lazdijai

bląg Korsze Węgorzewo Suwałki Sejny

Pasłęk Lidzbark Warmiński Olecko

Orneta 71 Kętrzyn Druskininkai

Dobre Miasto Giżycko WIGIERSKI

Morąg Biskupiec PUSZCZA AUGUSTOWSKA

Ostróda Mrągowo Ełk 72 Augustów

Olsztyn Orzysz

Iława Bylewska Góra 312 Pisz Grajewo Dąbrowa Białostocka Hrodna

Lubawa Ruciane-Nida Szczytno BIEBRZAŃSKI Hrodzyenskaye

POJEZIERZE MAZURSKIE

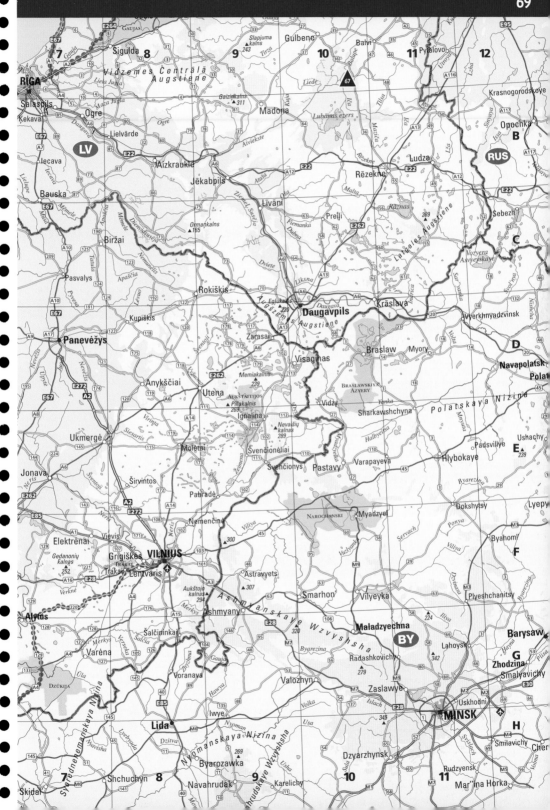

1   2   3   4   5   6

København
Lübeck   Ystad   Rønne   Rønne   Klaipėda, Kaliningrad, Sankt-Peterburg
Trelleborg

Wittow
Hiddensee   JASMUND   Ustka   21/203
VORPOMMERSCHE   Piekberg 161   Jasmund
BODDENLANDSCHAFT   Jasmund   Słupsk   203
Bergen   196a   Sassnitz   Darłowo   Wieprza   210   KOSZALIN   Słupia
Zingst   Rügen   196   Sławno   205   207   208
B 2/251   30   196   Ostseebad   203
105   Göhren   OSTSEE   Koszalin   MORZE BAŁTYCKIE
Stralsund   Greifswalder   96   Kołobrzeg   11   226
194   Bodden   104   163   Radew   207
22/251   Grimmen   Ryck   Oderbucht   Trzebiatów   162   Karlino   167   168   200   232   Miastko
96   109   Greifswald   Zatoka   102   103   Białogard   167   169   207   203
Demmin   Wolgast   Pomorska   Gryfice   E28   Parsęta   202   Czarne   202
E251   Peene   Kamień Pomorski   105   162   169   171   M   201
Anklam   Usedom   110   Międzyzdroje   106   107   163   Parsęta   Czarne
Reuterstadt   Świnoujście   Wolin   E65   108   Świdwin   Pobrzeże   151   202   Szczecinek   Debrzno
Stavenhagen   Friedland   Eggesin   Wolin   111   152   Połczyn   169   219   172   188
104   Torgelow   POBRZEŻE   Nowogard   147   Zdrój   151   Czaplinek   Złotów
96   20   114   112   Rega   145   Łobez   150   211   POJ
Neubrandenburg   115   Goleniów   148   Drawsko   Jastrowie   KRA
43   179   Police   130   144   Pomorskie   177   Piła   242
MÜRITZ   Helene   Strasburg   130   Dąbie   114   Złocieniec   207   207   190
Neustrelitz   Berge   Szczecin   SZCZECIŃSKIE   142   Wałcz   Trzcianka   191
Prenzlau   A6   E28   120   144   Stargard Szczeciński   11   188   Chodzież   192
Fürstenberg   UCKERMARK   Gryfino   Pyrzyce   155   Choszczno   DRAWIEŃSKI   Czarnków   Wągrowiec   195
Rheinsberg   Templin   11   31   110   Barlinek   118   Wieleń   Noteć   182   Rogoźno   196
Gransee   Schwedt an der Oder   122   53   Krzyż   181   Oborniki   187
Zehdenick   E28   Chojna   26   Myślibórz   Strzelce   Wielkopolski   Drezdenko   Murowana   153
Schorfheide   Angermünde   126   130   Krajeńskie   157   Wronki   184   306   Goślina   E261
Eberswalde-   Dębno   Gorzów   Puszcza   Szamotuły   Poznań   Swarzędz   42
Finow   Wriezen   Langer Berg   Wielkopolski   158   Sieraków   Międzychód   307   Buk   E30
Bernau   Myśla   Skwierzyna   Pniewy   Nowy Tomyśl   E30   A2   Luboń   E30
BERLIN   10   Strausberg   Seelow   Kostrzyn   POJEZIERZE   Międzyrzecz   137   Opalenica   104   Kórnik   431
Potsdam   Erkner   D   1/5   LUBUSKIE   Międzyrzecz   302   Mosina   435
E51   Blankenfelde   Frankfurt   Słubice   Rzepin   A2   Świebodzin   304   Grodzisk   Środa   E261
Königs   an der Oder   12   134   E65   Wielkopolski   308   309   Wielkopolska
43   Wusterhausen   Storkow   112   Puszczykowo   Wolsztyn   312   Kościan   Śrem   436
Zossen   Beeskow   246   138   Sulechów   314   Śmigiel
Luckenwalde   13   SPREEWALD   Eisenhüttenstadt   226   Śmigiel   432
Golßen   178   Krosno   112   Odrą   Sulechów   Śmigiel   Leszno   Gostyń
E36/55   Odrzańskie   Zielona Góra   279   Wschowa   432   34
Jüterbog   Guben   Gubin   286   322   Góra   E261
G   102   Malxe   Peitz   285   Bóbr   Nowa Sól   315   Lubsko   Kożuchów   Rawicz
Herzberg   Vetschau   Cottbus   112   283   291   Głogów   324   Milicz
Falkenberg   E36   15   Forst   Żary   Żagań   228   Góra   Orla   15
183   Weißwasser   350   Szprotawa   A18   Przemków   205   Żmigród
Elsterwerda   Hoyerswerda   226   300   Polkowice   E65   292   Scinawa   340
Riesa   101   Bernsdorf   74   Chocianów   36   Lubin   Wołów   Brzeg   Trzebnica
Großenhain   97   Niesky   351   296   Bolesławiec   A4   Chojnów   338   340   Dolny   342
Meißen   Kamenz   Pieńsk   372   A4   297   E36/40   Legnica   341

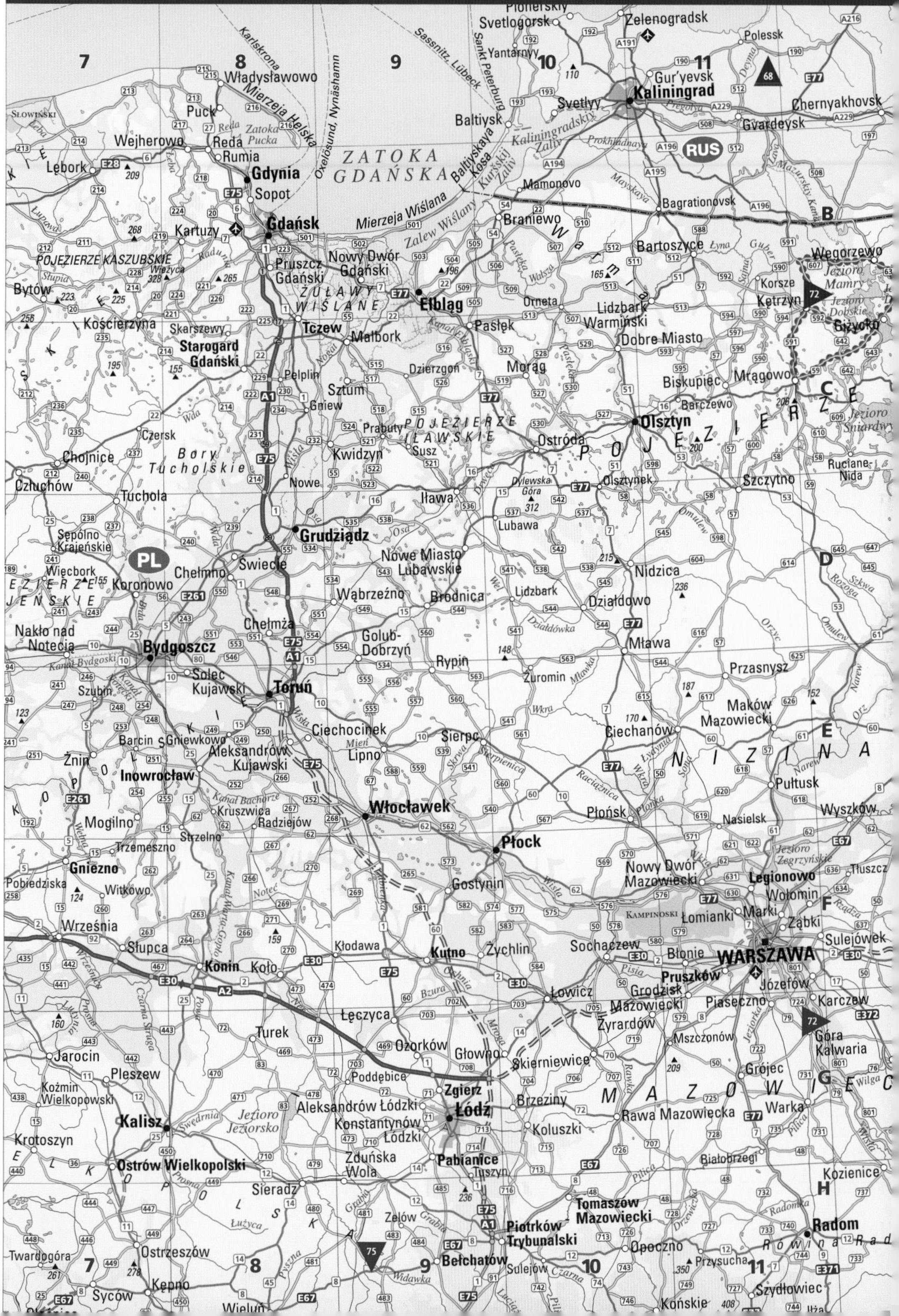

Svetlogorsk
Zelenogradsk
Polessk
Yantarnyy
Gur'yevsk
Kaliningrad
Chernyakhovsk
Svetlyy
Baltiysk
Gvardeysk
RUS
Mamonovo
Bagrationovsk
Braniewo
Bartoszyce
Węgorzewo
Korsze
Kętrzyn
Giżycko
Elbląg
Pasłęk
Orneta
Lidzbark Warmiński
Dobre Miasto
Morąg
Biskupiec
Mrągowo
Barczewo
Olsztyn
Ostróda
Olsztynek
Szczytno
Ruciane-Nida
Iława
Lubawa
Nidzica
Działdowo
Lidzbark
Mława
Przasnysz
Maków Mazowiecki
Ciechanów
Pułtusk
Wyszków
Płońsk
Nasielsk
Nowy Dwór Mazowiecki
Legionowo
Wołomin
Tłuszcz
Łomianki
Marki
Ząbki
Sulejówek
WARSZAWA
Józefów
Karczew
Piaseczno
Pruszków
Błonie
Grodzisk Mazowiecki
Żyrardów
Sochaczew
Łowicz
Mszczonów
Góra Kalwaria
Grójec
Warka
Rawa Mazowiecka
Białobrzegi
Kozienice
Radom
Przysucha
Szydłowiec
Końskie
Opoczno
Tomaszów Mazowiecki
Piotrków Trybunalski
Bełchatów
Sulejów
Skierniewice
Brzeziny
Koluszki
Łódź
Zgierz
Aleksandrów Łódzki
Konstantynów Łódzki
Pabianice
Tuszyn
Zduńska Wola
Zelów
Sieradz
Głowno
Ozorków
Łęczyca
Kutno
Żychlin
Gostynin
Płock
Włocławek
Kłodawa
Koło
Konin
Turek
Poddębice
Słupca
Września
Witkowo
Gniezno
Pobiedziska
Trzemeszno
Mogilno
Strzelno
Kruszwica
Radziejów
Inowrocław
Żnin
Barcin
Gniewkowo
Aleksandrów Kujawski
Ciechocinek
Lipno
Sierpc
Toruń
Solec Kujawski
Bydgoszcz
Szubin
Nakło nad Notecią
Koronowo
Więcbork
Sępólno Krajeńskie
Chełmno
Świecie
Chełmża
Golub-Dobrzyń
Rypin
Żuromin
Wąbrzeźno
Brodnica
Nowe Miasto Lubawskie
Grudziądz
Nowe
Kwidzyn
Susz
Prabuty
Sztum
Gniew
Pelplin
Dzierzgoń
Malbork
Tczew
Starogard Gdański
Skarszewy
Kościerzyna
Czersk
Chojnice
Człuchów
Tuchola
Bytów
Kartuzy
Pruszcz Gdański
Nowy Dwór Gdański
Gdańsk
Sopot
Gdynia
Rumia
Reda
Wejherowo
Puck
Władysławowo
Lębork
Jarocin
Pleszew
Koźmin Wielkopolski
Krotoszyn
Kalisz
Ostrów Wielkopolski
Ostrzeszów
Kępno
Syców
Twardogóra
Wieluń
PL
ZATOKA GDAŃSKA
Mierzeja Helska
Mierzeja Wiślana
Zalew Wiślany
Kaliningradskiy Zaliv
Baltiyskaya Kosa
Kurshskiy Zaliv
POJEZIERZE KASZUBSKIE
ŻUŁAWY WIŚLANE
POJEZIERZE IŁAWSKIE
Bory Tucholskie
NIZINA
MAZOWIECKA
KAMPINOSKI
Karlskrona
Oxelösund, Nynäshamn
Sassnitz, Lübeck
Sankt Peterburg
Wisła
Jezioro Jeziorsko
Jezioro Zegrzyńskie
Jezioro Mamry
Jezioro Śniardwy

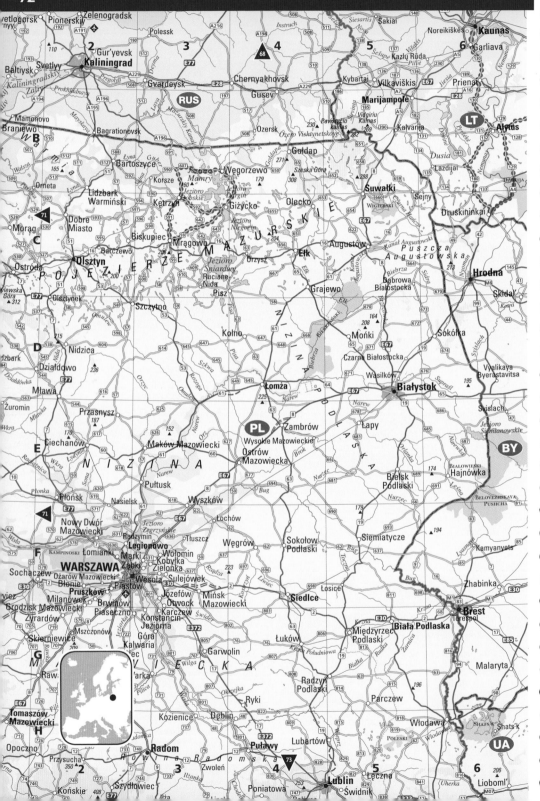

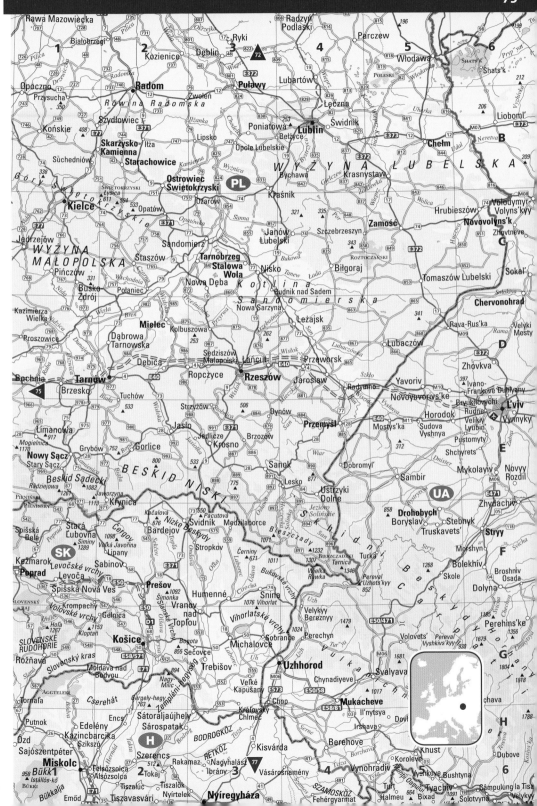

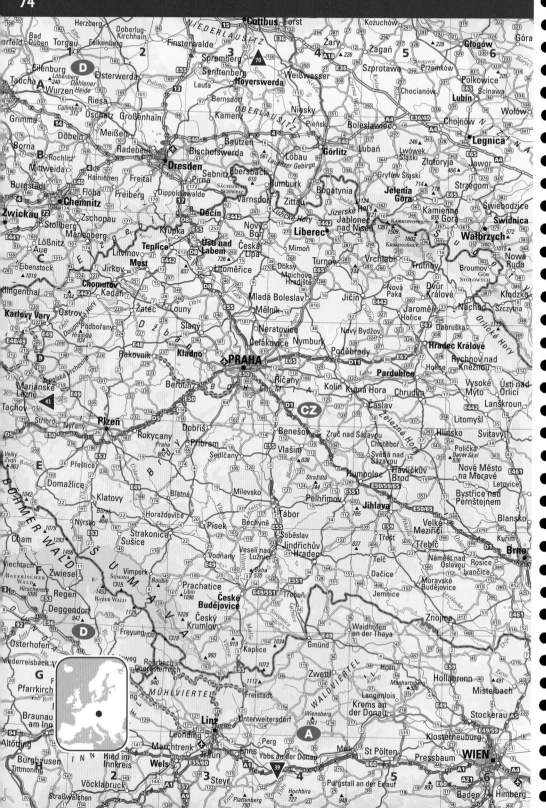

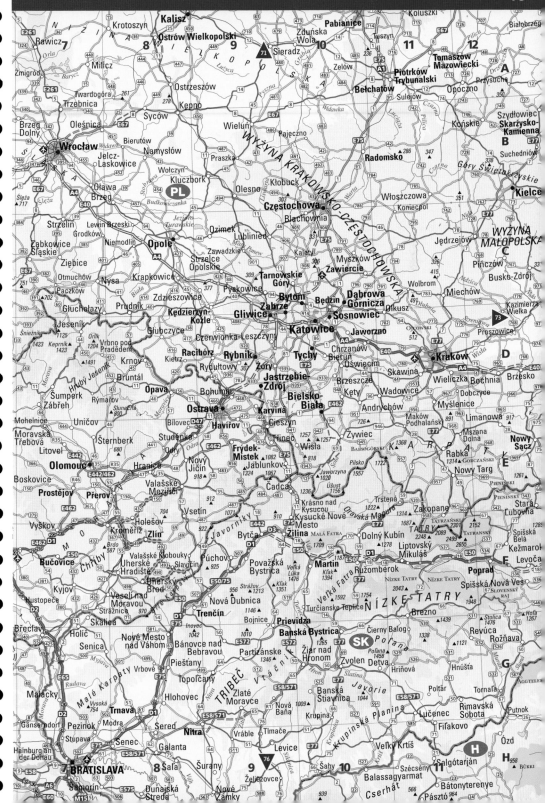

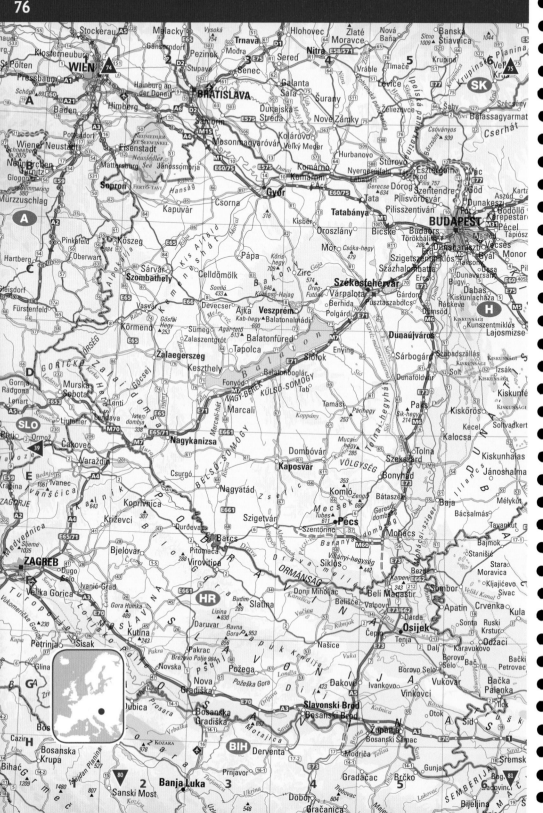

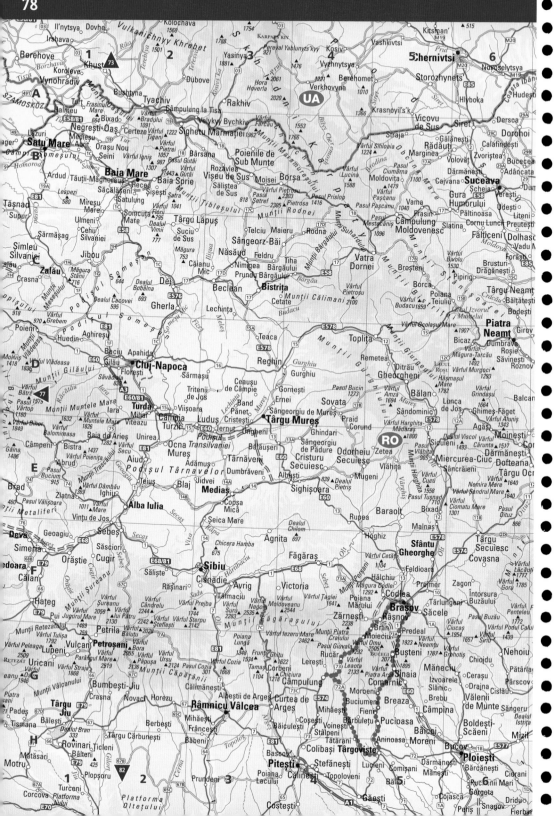

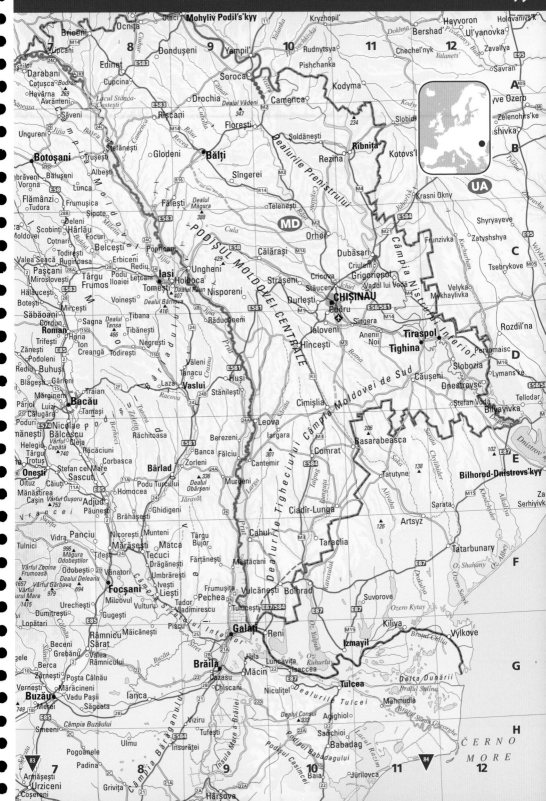

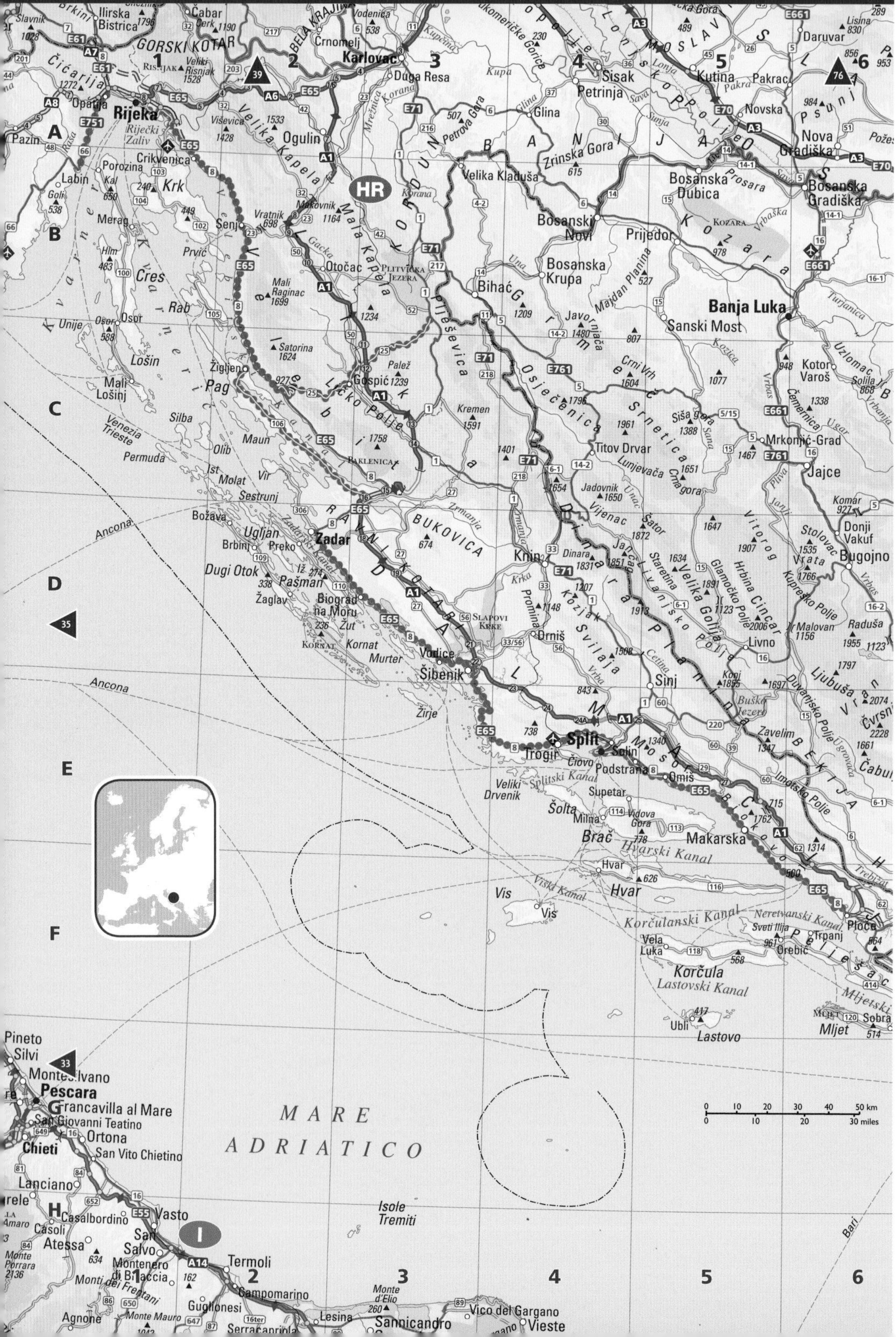

MARE ADRIATICO

GORSKI KOTAR

HR

BANIJA

MOSLAVINA

Rijeka
Karlovac
Sisak
Petrinja
Kutina
Pakrac
Novska
Nova Gradiška
Bosanska Gradiška

Opatija
Pazin
Labin
Krk
Senj
Crikvenica
Ogulin
Duga Resa
Glina
Velika Kladuša
Bosanska Dubica
Bosanski Novi
Prijedor
Banja Luka
Sanski Most

Cres
Lošinj
Mali Lošinj
Rab
Pag
Žigljen
Otočac
Plitvička Jezera
Bihać
Bosanska Krupa
Kozara
Titov Drvar
Mrkonjić-Grad
Jajce

Zadar
Biograd na Moru
Pašman
Dugi Otok
Žut
Kornat
Murter
Vodice
Šibenik
Žirje
Knin
Dinara
Drniš
Sinj
Livno
Bugojno
Donji Vakuf

Split
Trogir
Solin
Podstrana
Omiš
Supetar
Šolta
Milna
Brač
Makarska
Hvar
Vis
Korčula
Vela Luka
Orebić
Ploče
Lastovo
Mljet
Sobra

MARE ADRIATICO

Pineto
Silvi
Montesilvano
Pescara
Francavilla al Mare
San Giovanni Teatino
Ortona
Chieti
Lanciano
San Vito Chietino
Casalbordino
Vasto
Termoli
Campomarino
Guglionesi
Lesina
Vieste

BUKOVICA

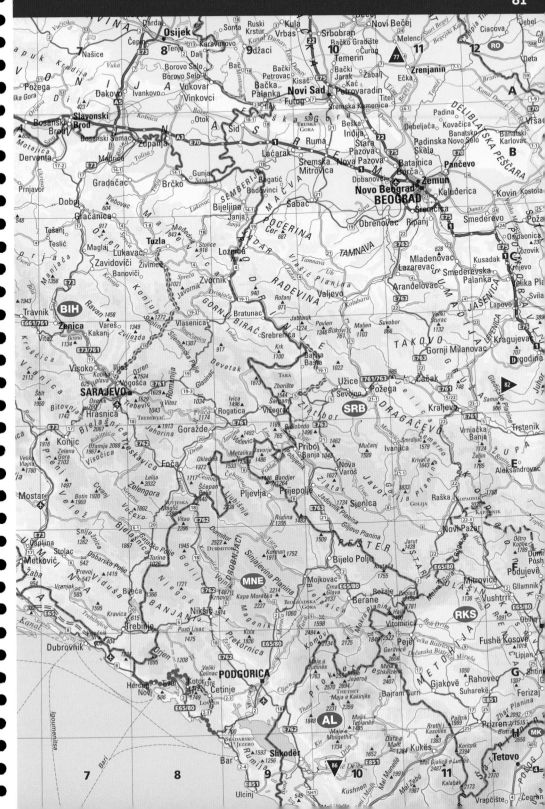

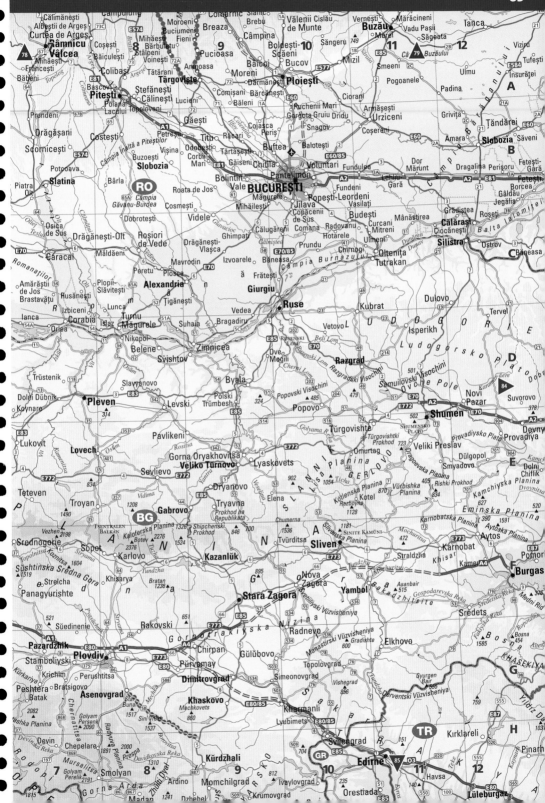

RO

BG

TR

Buzău · Vadu Pașii · Mărăcineni · Măgura · Săgeata · Ianca · Chiscani · Niculițel · **Tulcea** · Brațul Sulina · Delta Dunării

Mizil · Smeeni · Pogoanele · Ulmu · Insurăței · Viziru · Tufești · Dealul Consul · Agighiol · Mahmudia · Brațul Sfântu Gheorghe

Ciorani · Armășești · Padina · Podișul Babadagului · Sarichioi · **Babadag** · Lacul Razim

Dridu · Urziceni · Coșereni · Grivița · **Tăndărei** · Săveni · Făcăeni · Cogealac · Podișul Casimcei · Jurilovca · Baia · Lacul Sinoie

Fundulea · Dor Mărunt · Dragalina · Perișoru · Fetești-Gară · Borcea · Nicolae Bălcescu · Hârșova · Topolog · **Sloboziа** · Bordușani

Fundeni · Vasilați · Lehliu Gară · **Fetești** · Gâldău · Jegălia · Roseți · Mircea Vodă · Cernavodă · Mihail Kogălniceanu · Castelu · Ovidiu · **Năvodari** · Lumina

Budești · Curcani · Mânăstirea · Grădiștea · Ciocănești · **Călărași** · Medgidia · Basarabi · **Constanța**

Radovanu · Hotarele · Mitreni · Ulmeni · Dunărea · **Silistra** · Ostrov · Băneasa · Cobadin · Valu lui Traian · Cumpăna · Techirghiol

Chirnogi · Oltenița · Tutrakan · Dunav · Topraisar · Eforie · Tuzla

Kubrat · Dulovo · Podișul Negru Vodă · Negru Vodă · **Mangalia**

Vetovo · Isperikh · Tervel · General Toshevo · Kavarna

Razgrad · Samuilovski Visochini · Ovche Pole · **Dobrich** · Balchik

Türgovishte · Novi Pazar · Suvorovo · Zlatni Pyasütsi

Shumen · Provadiysko Plato · Deviня · **Varna** · Galata

Veliki Preslav · Provadiya · Dülgopol · Smyadovo · Dolni Chiflik

Omurtag · Vürbishka Planina · Rishki Prokhod · Kamchiya

Kotel · Razboyna · Eminska Planina · Karnobatska Planina · Dvoynitsa

Sliven · Grebenets · Aytos · Karnobat · Khisar

Yambol · Straldzha · Asanbair · Kameno · **Burgas** · Pomorie

Sredets · Elkhovo · Gradishte · Bosna · Papiya

KHASENIYATA · Rezovska Reka · Demirköy

Kırklareli · Pınarhisar · Vize

Edirne · Havsa · Babaeski · Saray · Lüleburgaz

ČERNO MORE

0 10 20 30 40 50 km
0 10 20 30 miles

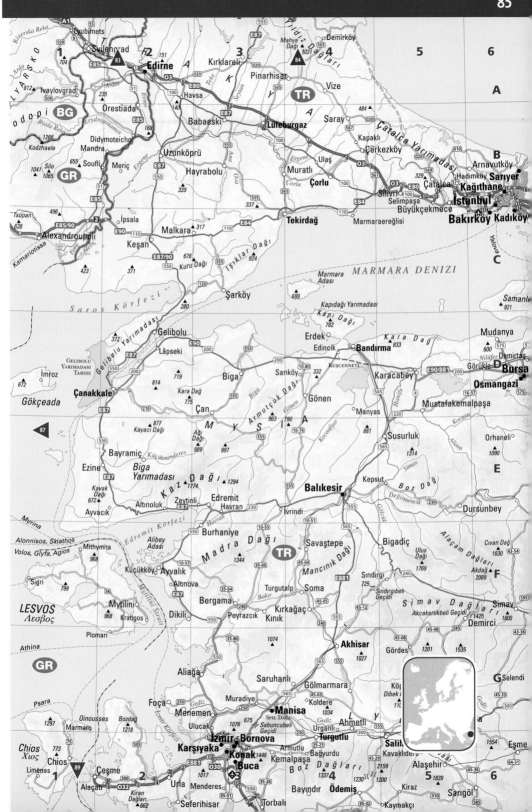

Bar
Ulcinj
Rumija 1593
Mbilqethit 1734
Mali Munellë 1991
Liqeni i Vaut të Dejes
Liqeni i Shkodrës 1256
Shkodër
Kukës 1383
E851
81
SH1
545
Kushnen
Mali i Velës
Bunë
Gjiri i Drinit
Lezhë
2394
Komnik 2487
Mal Gjalicë e Lumës
Kalabak
2770
Tetovo 4
Polog
Bistra 2650 405
Crna
SLAVISTA
Kriva Palanka
Osogovske
Kumanovo
E871
Aračinov 5 1
Dorce Petrov
Kratovo 1670
Probištip
Kočani
82
Dyče Pole
206
105
Stip 997
Radoviš
E65

Vrapčište
Čegrane
Suva Gora
SKOPJE
TORBEŠIJA
Kitka 1569
Sveti Nikole
201

Lures 2764
Mal Dejë 2246
Peshkopi
Mali i Velivarit 2374
Bukovik
Gostivar
E65
PORECE
Jakupica 2540
Solunska Glava 2163
MK
Veles
663
Klepa 1149
Babuna Planina
E75

Burrel
Bulqizë
Debar
Bistra 2102
Kičevo
Brod
Busheva Planina Musica 1791
Prilep
Dren Planina 1549
E75
Negotino 1
Kavadarci
106

Fushe Kruje
Mamuras
Maja e Liqenit 1723
Krujë 1268
Mali i Gamtit 2020
Maja e Dhoksit 1873
2273
Ilinska Planina
Crna Reka 1909
Kruševo
Demir Hisar 1999
1472
Seleckа Planina
1886
2182

Durrës
Shijak
Kamëz 1612
TIRANË
AL
Librazhd
Struga
204
E65
E852
Ohridsko Ezero
Ohrid Resen
Plakenska Planina
Prespansko Ezero
Pelister 2610
Baba Planina
Bitola
E65
Crna
MARIOVO
2524
Aridaia
Edessa Giannitsa
Krya Vrysi
E86

Kavajë
Peqin
Cërrik
Elbasan
Gramsh
Pogradec
Psarades 2334 2156
Prespes
E86
Florina
Limni Vegoritida
Naousa 2052
Alexandreia
E90
Veroia
2

Lushnjë
Berat
Korçë
E86
Bilisht
Kastoria
Ptolemaida
A27
Siniatsiko 1259
Kozani
E65
1804

Fier
Patos
Ballsh
Poliçan
Çorovodë
Ersekë 2503
Grámmos
Argos Orestiko
Vourinos 1866
Siatista
Grevena
2194
E65

Vlorë
Sazan
Selenicë
Memaliaj
Tepelenë
Përmet
Mal Nëmerçkë
Smolikas 2637
Aoos
Vorela Pindos
Vikos-Aoou
Ethnikos Drymos Pindou 2177
E90
Chasia
Elassona
906
Ampelonas
Tyrnavos

Gjirokastër
Delvinë
Sarandë
Mal Kazanje
E853
Ioannina
Ιωάννινα
E951
Kalampaka
GR
Trikala
E92
Larisa
Λάρισα

Kerkyra
Κέρκυρα
goumenitsa
E90/92
Tomaros 1974
Kerovouni 1614
2393
Palamas
E65
Karditsa
Sofades
Farsala
1011
Kastania

Palaiokastritsa
Ano Lefkimmi
Parga
Paxoi
E55
E951
Arta
Acheloos
Vatou
Loutra Smokovou
Fourna
2042
984

Preveza
Amvrakikos Kolpos
Techniti Limni Kremaston
Karpenisi
E952
Lamia
Ethnikos Drymos Oitis
2152

Lefkada
Λευκάς
Ithaki
Elati 1158
88
Agrinio
Angelokastro
Thermo
Limni Trichonida
Amfissa
E55/951
Voreies Echinades

A   B   C   D   E   F   G   H
2   3   4   5   6

Plan Osogo
Beltok 1524
Rujen 2252
Delčevo
Čavka 1538
Vinica Trabotivište
Lisec 1754
Vica Planina
Berovo
MALEŠEVO
Kadiytsa 1924
Markovi Kladentsi 1523
Ogražden
Strumica
Strumičko Polje
Valandovo
Bogdanci
Gevgelija
Polykastro
Koufalia
Sindos Evosmos
Ampelokipoi Polichni
Kalamaria
Thessaloniki
Θεσσαλονίκη
Mesimeri
Katerini
Litochoro
Thermaïkos Kolpos
Agiokampos
Nea Ionia
Volos
Pagasitikos Kolpos
Almyros
Platanias
Atalanti
ETHNIKOS DRYMOS PARNASSOU
Parnassos 2457
Orchomenos
Apoximeni
Nea Artaki
Chalkida

2729
Musala 2925
Slavov Vrükh
Slavov Vrükh 2306
Alabak
Pazardzhik
Stamboliyski
Peshtera
Plovdiv
Pürvomay
Gülübovo
Simeon
Dimitrovgrad
Blagoevgrad
Yakoruda
Velingrad
Rakitovo
Bratsigovo
Asenovgrad
Khaskovo
Lyubin
Razlog
Bansko
Batashka Planina
Batak
Chernatitsa
Golyam Persenk 2090
Radiuva Planina
Sini Vrükh
Mechkovets 860
Star Bünar
Kh
Kürdzhali
Iva
Ko
Sandanski
Orelek
Gotse Delchev
Mursalitsa
Golyam Perelik 2191
Smolyan
Gorna Arda
Ardino Momchilgrad
Madan
Dzhebel
Nedelino
Zlatograd
Krumovgrad
B
Petrich
Slavyanka 2212
Orvilos
Exochi
Nestos
RHODOPE MOUNTAINS
Iztochni Rodopi
Sidirokastro
Falakro
Drama
Xanthi
Komotini
C
Serres
Nigrita
Strymonas
Chrysoupoli
Keramoti
Paralia Avdiron
Agios Charalampos
Alexandroupoli
Kilkis
Lagkadas
Pangaio
Kavala
Κάβαλα
Thasos
Thasos Θάσος
Kamariotissa
Fengari 1600
Samothraki
D
Polygyros
Ouranoupoli
Kolpos Agiou Orous
Athos 2033
Gökçeada
Thrakiko Pelagos
Kolpos Kassandras
Sithonia
Kassandra
Skopia 430
Myrina
Limnos Λήμνος
E
Agios Efstratios
Agios Efstratios
Mytilini
F
Voreies Sporades
Βόρειοι Σποράδες
Gioura
Kyra Panagia
Skiathos
Glossa
Alonnisos
Peristera
Chora
Skopelos
Skyros
Linaria
Kochylas 792
Xiro 991
Pyxaria 1343
Kymi
Psachna
Voreios Evvoikos Kolpos
Psara
Antipsara
LES

E79 E85 E80/85 E90 E75 E92 E75/92 A25

BG

7 8 9 10 11 12
B
C
D
E
F
G
H
7 8 9 10 11

0 10 20 30 40 50 km
0 10 20 30 miles

Map Labels

LEFKADA
Λευκας
Lefkada
E55/952
507
1589
Elati
1158
2
3
750
Akarnanika
893
38
Karpenisi
1924
Agrinio
2101
4
Lamia
Oiti
77
Xiro
991
ETHNIKOS
DRYMOS OITIS
2152
5
E75
1
6
Voreios Evvoïkos
Angelokastro
930
602
Limni
Trichonida
Thermo
1734
2510
E65
1372
Atalanti
E75
Voreies
Echinades
806
5
E55/951
Ithaki
Achelo
Moryos
27
E65
Amfissa
ETHNIKOS
DRYMOS
PARNASSOU
Parnassos
2457
1080
Orchomenos
Apoxirameni
Limni
Kopaidas
1

B
1131
Sami
Argostoli
1628
KEFALLONIA
Κεφαλληνία
ETHNIKOS
DRYMOS
AINOU
Mesolongi
1039
Patraïkos Kolpos
Nafpaktos
Trikorfo
1545
E65
48
Livadeia
1748
Paralia
Saranti
1409
E962
3
Thiva
Asopos

Patra
Πατρα
E65
Aigio
8A
1926
Korinthiakos Kolpos
1208
8A
Kiato
Loutraki
Korinthos
Κόρινθος
1351
Megara
8
A
E94
Salamina
Σαλαμίνα

Kyllini
Vrachionas
756
Porthmos Zakynthou
966
2224
Selinountas
Ladonas
2341
Kyllini
2376
GR
872
E65
7
Aigina
1199
743
Salamina
Sar

C
ZAKYNTHOS
Ζακυνθος
Zakynthos
9
Amaliada
798
1446
1616
7
Aigina
Ermioni
1251

Pyrgos
E55
74
Alfeios
Ladonas
1366
1981
Argos
Nafplio
113
P   e   l   o   p   o   n   n   i   s   o   s
Πελοπόννησος

Kyparissiakos
Kolpos
Nedas
1419
Tripoli
1274
E55
7
976
Argolikos Kolpos

Thessaloniki
Chios
Kuşadası Körfezi
515
Kuşadası
604
9A
1254
E961
1935
Parnonas
Leonidio
Spetses
Spetses

D
Karlovasi
1153
Samos
Sazlı
Söke
Davutlar
1237
Özbaşı
1224
9
E55/65
1852
1839
Sparti
1327
Paralia
1433
Pythagoreio
Samos
Σαμοσ
DILEK YARIMADASI
MILLI PARKI
Sarıkemer
TR
İlbira Dağı
Gargalianoi
Messini
1359
82
Taygetos
Fournoi
Agathonisi
Yenihisar
1083
525
Lykodimo
958
2404
516
E961
916
1125
Gytheio

Patmos
Arkoi
Leipsoi
Farmakonisi

E
Leros
326
Lakki
Güllük Körfezi
330
879
Mani
916
86
Monemvasia
Peiraias
Telendos
678
Bodrum
Yaran Dağı
4215
716

Kalymnos
Kalymnos
Pserimos
Kos
846
89
Gökova Körfezi
Lakonikos
Kolpos
Neapoli
772
Agia Pelagia

F
Kefalos
426
Gyali
Kos
Κωσ
748
400
Reşadiye Yarımadası
Datça
1144
Hisarönü Körfezi
507
KYTHIRA
Κυθηρα
Astypalaia
698
Nisyros
616
Symi
Kythira

Astypalaia
Syrna
Dodekanisos
Δωδεκανησος
GR
851
Tilos
Rodos
Trianta
Ancona, Bari, Brindisi

G
Peiraias
Alimia
Chalki
593
Chalki
798
Attavyros
1215
95
0 10 20 30 40 50 km
0   10   20   30 miles
378
Kissamos

Monolithos
Skiadi
563
458
Lindos
RODOS
Ροδος
Kattavia
213
Saria
630

Iraklio, Sitelia, Agios, Nikolaos
Steno Karpathou
718

2
3
4
5
6

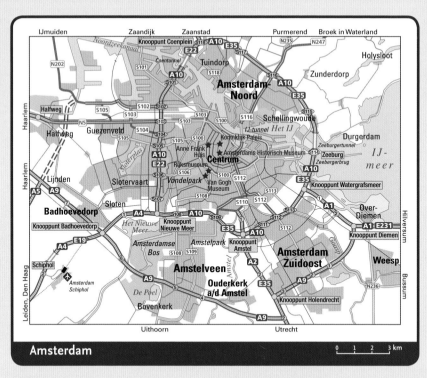

Amsterdam

0 1 2 3 km

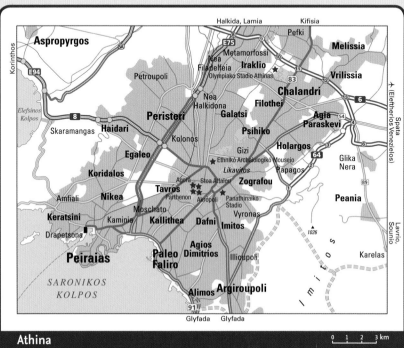

Athina

0 1 2 3 km

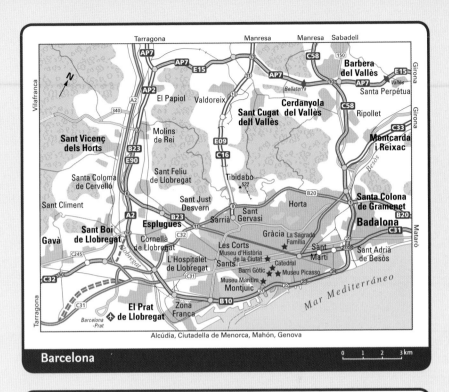

Barcelona

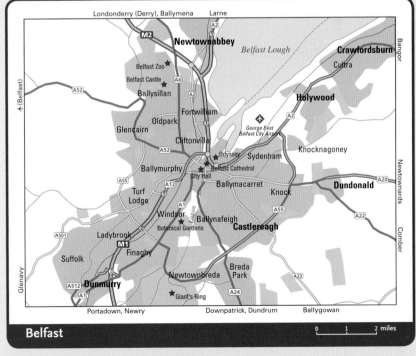

Belfast

Berlin

0   5   10 km

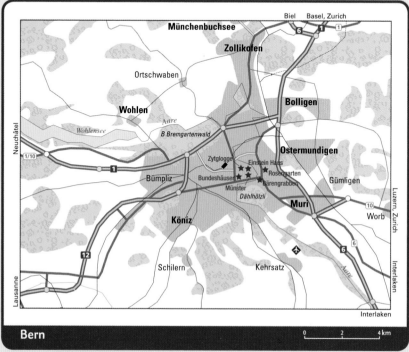

Bern

0   2   4 km

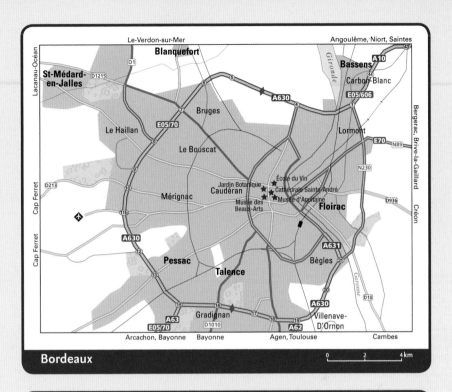

Bordeaux

Le-Verdon-sur-Mer

Angoulême, Niort, Saintes

Lacanau-Océan

Blanquefort

D1

Gironde

Bassens

A10

**St-Médard-
en-Jalles**

D1215

Carbon-Blanc

E05/606

Bergerac, Brive-la-Gaillard

Bruges

E05/70

A630

Lormont

E70

N89

Le Haillan

Le Bouscat

Cap Ferret

N230

Cap Ferret

D213

École du Vin

Jardin Botanique

Cathédrale Sainte-André

Créon

Mérignac

Cauderan

Musée d'Aquitaine

D936

Musée des
Beaux-Arts

Floirac

A630

A631

Pessac

Bègles

Garonne

Talence

A630

Villenave-
D'Ornon

D10

A63

Gradignan

D1010

A62

E05/70

Arcachon, Bayonne

Bayonne

Agen, Toulouse

Cambes

0   2   4 km

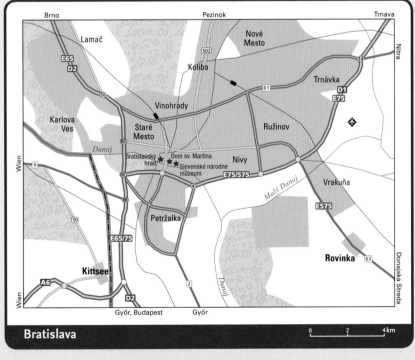

Bratislava

Brno

Pezinok

Trnava

Lamač

**Nové
Mesto**

502

E65

D2

Koliba

Nitra

E1

Vinohrady

61

Trnávka

D1

E75

**Karlova
Ves**

Dunaj

**Staré
Mesto**

Ružinov

9

Bratislavský
hrad

Dom sv. Martina

Nivy

Wien

Slovenské národne
múzeum

E75/575

Malý Dunaj

Vrakuňa

E575

Petržalka

Dunaj

E65/75

Rovinka

63

Donajská Streda

Kittsee

A6

2

Wien

D2

Győr, Budapest

Győr

0   2   4 km

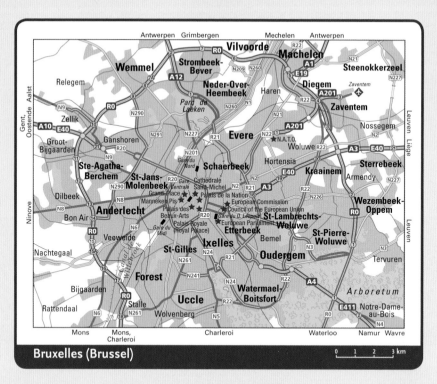

Bruxelles (Brussel)

0 1 2 3 km

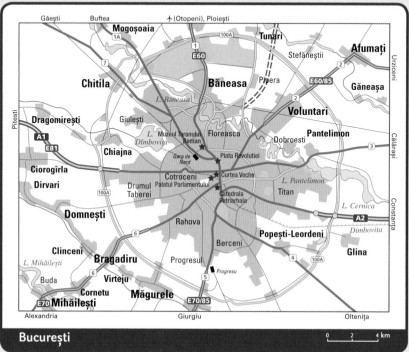

Bucureşti

0 2 4 km

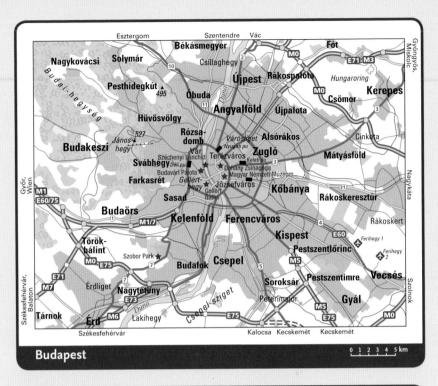

Budapest

0 1 2 3 4 5 km

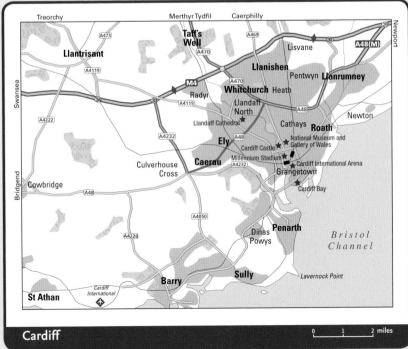

Cardiff

0 1 2 miles

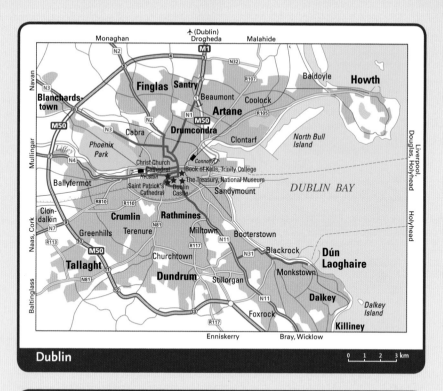

Dublin

0 1 2 3 km

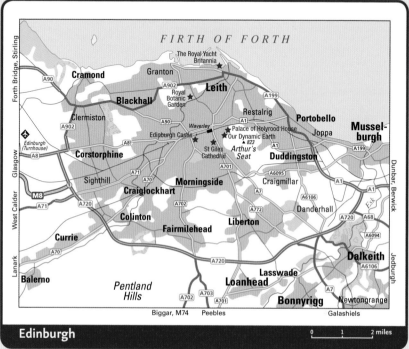

Edinburgh

0 1 2 miles

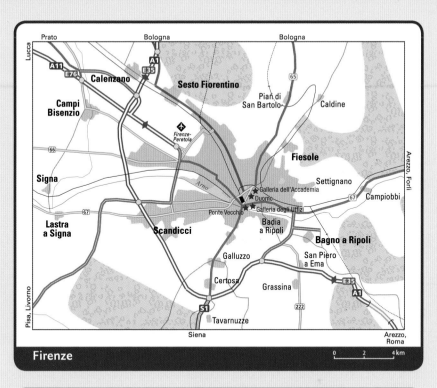

Firenze

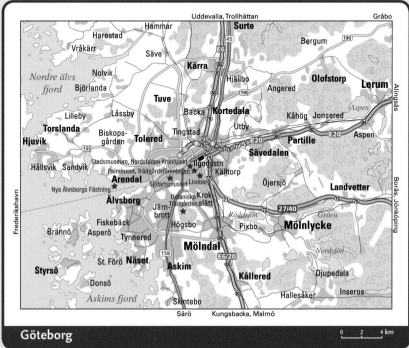

Göteborg

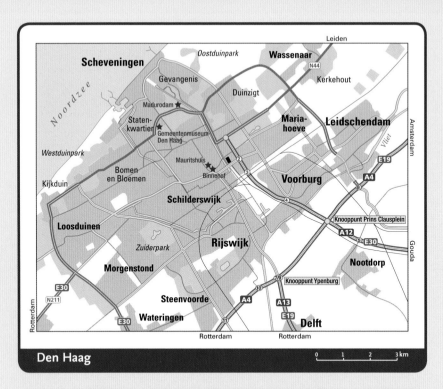

Den Haag

0 1 2 3 km

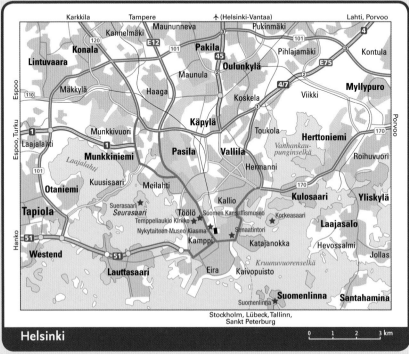

Helsinki

0 1 2 3 km

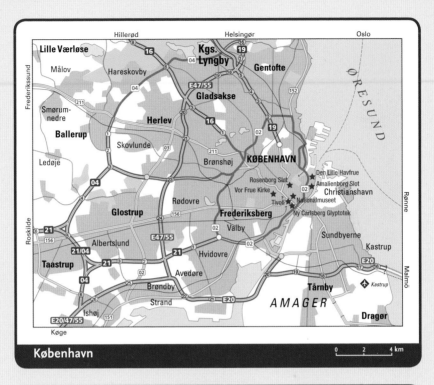

København

0   2   4 km

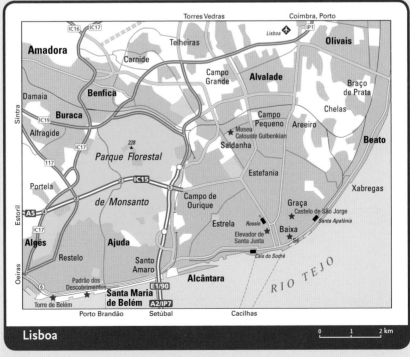

Lisboa

0   1   2 km

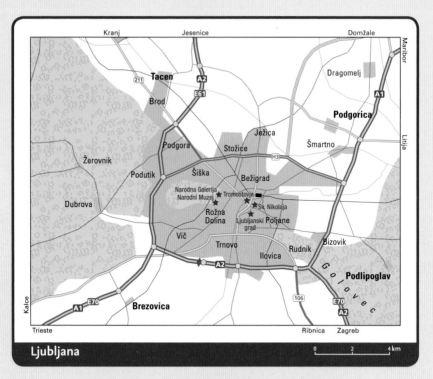

Ljubljana

0   2   4 km

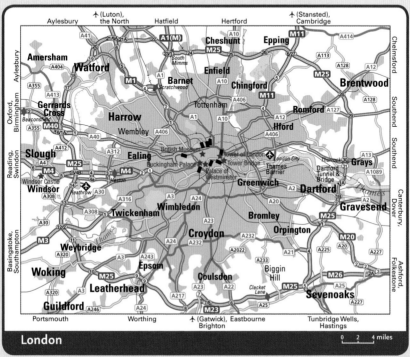

London

0   2   4 miles

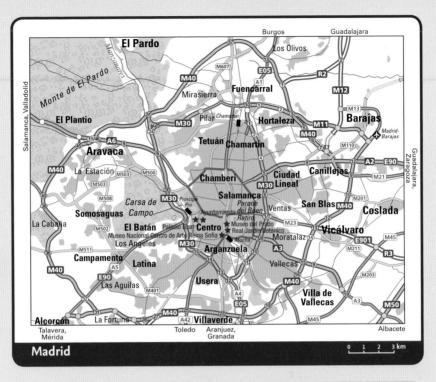

Madrid

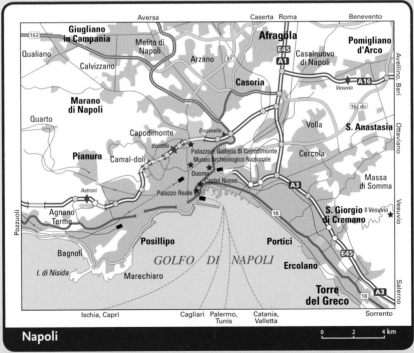

Napoli

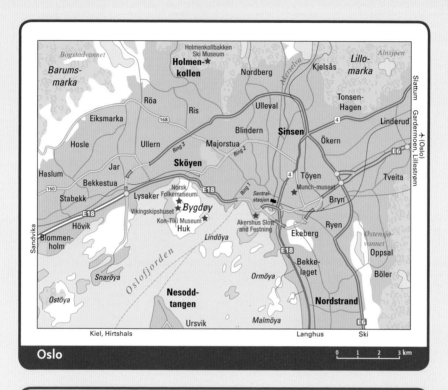

Oslo

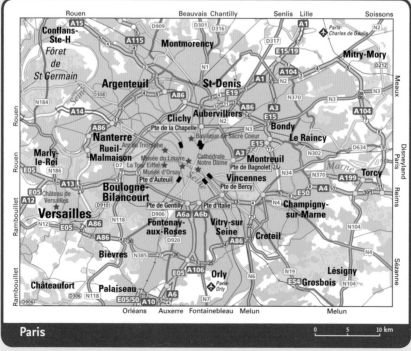

Paris

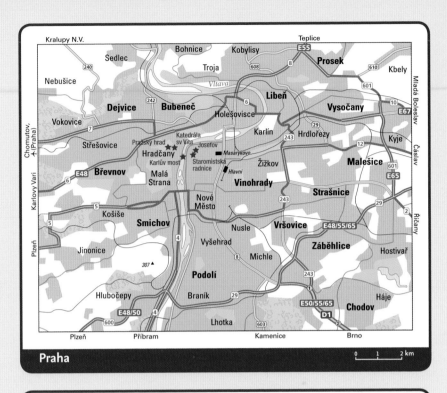

Praha

0 1 2 km

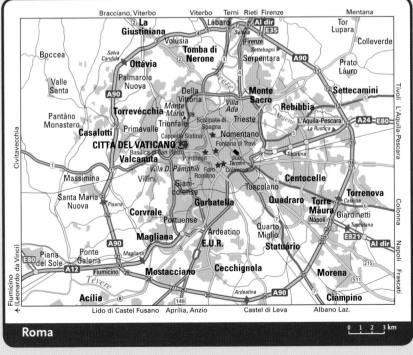

Roma

0 1 2 3 km

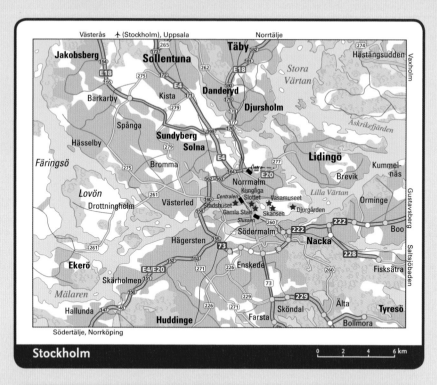

Stockholm

0   2   4   6 km

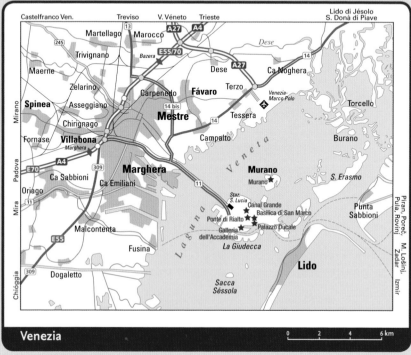

Venezia

0   2   4   6 km

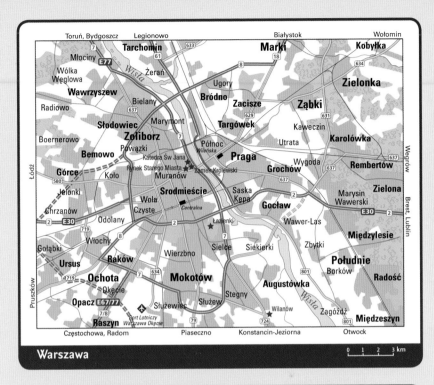

Warszawa

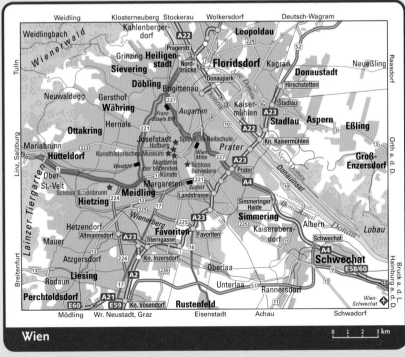

Wien

Index

The index contains a selection of the major towns and cities found on the reference map section of the atlas.
All indexed entries have a page and grid reference.

Entries which have a ☐ symbol instead of a grid reference are located on small insets within the appropriate page.

A	Austria		IRL	Ireland
AL	Albania		IS	Iceland
AND	Andorra		L	Luxembourg
B	Belgium		LT	Lithuania
BG	Bulgaria		LV	Latvia
BIH	Bosnia-Herzogovina		M	Malta
BY	Belarus		MA	Morocco
CH	Switzerland		MC	Monaco
CZ	Czech Republic		MD	Moldova
D	Germany		MK	Macedonia (F.Y.R.O.M.)
DK	Denmark		MNE	Montenegro
E	Spain		N	Norway
EST	Estonia		NL	Netherlands
F	France		P	Portugal
FIN	Finland		PL	Poland
FL	Liechtenstein		RKS	Kosovo
FO	Faroe Islands		RO	Romania
GB	United Kingdom		RSM	San Marino
GBG	Guernsey		RUS	Russian Federation
GBJ	Jersey		S	Sweden
GBM	Isle of Man		SK	Slovakia
GBZ	Gibraltar		SLO	Slovenia
GR	Greece		SRB	Serbia
H	Hungary		TR	Turkey
HR	Croatia		UA	Ukraine
I	Italy			

A

Aabenraa	DK	44 G3
Aachen	D	11 G8
Aalborg	DK	44 C4
Aalen	D	38 A3
Aalst	B	10 F5
Aalten	NL	11 D8
Äänekoski	FIN	64 B6
Aarau	CH	13 G10
Aars	DK	44 C3
Abádszalók	H	77 C8
A Baiuca	E	22 B2
Abarán	E	29 B10
Abbadia San Salvatore	I	32 B4
Abbeville	F	9 G12
Abelvær	N	54 E4
Abensberg	D	38 A5
Aberdare	GB	8 D4
Aberdeen	GB	3 E8
Abergavenny	GB	8 D5
Abergwaun	GB	8 D2
Abertawe	GB	8 D4
Abertillery	GB	8 D5
Aberystwyth	GB	8 C3
Abingdon	GB	9 D7
Åbo	FIN	53 G11
Abony	H	77 C7
Abrantes	P	24 D3
Abrud	RO	77 E12
Absam	A	37 C11
Abtenau	A	39 D7
Åby	S	47 D7
A Cañiza	E	22 D3
A Carreira	E	22 B3
Acate	I	30 G5
Accrington	GB	5 F7
Acerra	I	30 B5
Aceuchal	E	24 F6
Acharnes	GR	89 B7
Achern	D	13 D10
Aci Castello	I	30 F6
Aci Catena	I	30 F6
Acireale	I	30 F6
Aci Sant'Antonio	I	30 F6
A Coruña	E	22 B3
Acquapendente	I	32 B4
Acquedolci	I	30 E5
Acqui Terme	I	19 B11
Acri	I	31 E8
Ács	H	76 B4
Ada	SRB	77 F7
Adamas	GR	89 E8
Adămuş	RO	78 E3
Adâncata	RO	78 B6
Adendorf	D	42 D6
Adjud	RO	79 E8
Adorf	D	41 C8
Adra	E	29 E7
Adrano	I	30 F5
Adunaţii-Copăceni	RO	83 C10
Aesch	CH	13 G10
A Estrada	E	22 C2
Åfjord	N	54 G3
A Fonsagrada	E	22 B5
Afragola	I	30 B5
Afumaţi	RO	83 B10
A Gándara de Altea	E	22 B3
Agăş	RO	78 D6

Agde	F	18 E2
Agen	F	16 F6
Aghireşu	RO	77 D12
Agia Marina	GR	89 B8
Agia Pelagia	GR	88 F6
Agighiol	RO	79 G10
Agios Charalampos	GR	87 C12
Agios Dimitrios	GR	89 C7
Agios Efstratios	GR	87 F11
Agios Nikolaos	GR	89 G11
Agira	I	30 F5
Agliana	I	35 F7
Agnita	RO	78 F3
Agnone	I	33 D8
Agolada	E	22 C3
Agrigento	I	30 F3
Agrinio	GR	86 H5
Agropoli	I	30 C6
Ågskaret	N	57 G2
A Guarda	E	22 E2
Aguilar de Campóo	E	23 C9
Aguilar de la Frontera	E	28 D4
Águilas	E	29 D10
Ahaus	D	11 D9
Ahlen	D	11 E10
Ahmetli	TR	85 G4
Ahrensburg	D	42 C6
Ahtme	EST	67 B9
Åhus	S	45 E9
Aichach	D	38 B4
Aidone	I	30 F5
Aigina	GR	88 C7
Aigio	GR	88 B4
Aigle	CH	36 E5
Aigues-Mortes	F	17 H11
Ailly-sur-Somme	F	12 B3
Aire-sur-l'Adour	F	16 G4
Aiud	RO	78 E2
Aix-en-Provence	F	18 D6
Aix-les-Bains	F	36 F3
Aizenay	F	16 A2
Aizkraukle	LV	69 B8
Aizpute	LV	66 H2
Ajaccio	F	19 H10
Ajdovščina	SLO	35 B12
Ajka	H	76 C3
Åkarp	S	45 E8
Aken	D	43 G8
Åkersberga	S	47 C10
Åkerstrømmen	N	51 E8
Akhisar	TR	85 G4
Åkrehamn	N	48 D2
Ala	S	47 G10
Alaçatı	TR	89 B11
Alagón	E	20 E5
Alaior	E	29 E11
Alajärvi	FIN	53 B12
Alakurtti	RUS	61 D12
Alaquàs	E	27 F10
Alaşehir	TR	85 H5
Alassio	I	19 C10
Alatri	I	33 D7
Alavus	FIN	53 C12
Alba	I	19 B10
Alba Adriatica	I	33 B8
Albacete	E	27 G7
Albaida	E	27 G10
Alba Iulia	RO	78 E2
Albanella	I	30 C6
Albano Laziale	I	32 D5

Albaville	I	34 B4
Albenga	I	19 C10
Albert	F	12 B3
Albertirsa	H	77 C7
Albertville	F	36 F4
Albeşti	RO	78 E4
Albeşti	RO	79 B7
Albeştii de Argeş	RO	78 G3
Albi	F	17 G8
Albino	I	34 B5
Albisola Superiore	I	19 C11
Alboraya	E	27 F10
Albox	E	29 D9
Albstadt	D	13 E12
Albufeira	P	25 K3
Alburquerque	E	24 E5
Alcalá de Guadaira	E	25 J7
Alcalá de Henares	E	23 H11
Alcalá de los Gazules	E	25 M7
Alcalá la Real	E	28 D6
Alcamo	I	30 E2
Alcañiz	E	20 G6
Alcantarilla	E	29 C10
Alcaudete	E	28 D5
Alcázar de San Juan	E	26 F5
Alcester	GB	8 C7
Alcobaça	P	24 D2
Alcobendas	E	23 H10
Alcorcón	E	23 H10
Alcoy-Alcoi	E	27 G10
Alcúdia	E	29 E10
Aldershot	GB	9 E8
Aleksandrovac	SRB	81 E12
Aleksandrów Kujawski	PL	71 E8
Aleksandrów Łódzki	PL	71 G9
Aleksinac	SRB	82 D2
Alençon	F	15 E9
Alès	F	17 G11
Aleşd	RO	77 C11
Alessandria	I	19 A11
Alessandria della Rocca	I	30 F3
Alessano	I	31 D12
Ålesund	N	50 C3
Alexandreia	GR	86 D6
Alexandria	RO	83 C9
Alexandria	GB	2 G5
Alexandroupoli	GR	85 C1
Alezio	I	31 C11
Alfaro	E	20 D3
Alfeld (Leine)	D	42 G5
Alfreton	GB	5 G9
Algeciras	E	25 M8
Algemesí	E	27 F10
Algete	E	23 G11
Alghero	I	32 E1
Alginet	E	27 F10
Algodonales	E	25 L8
Algorta	E	20 B1
Alhama de Granada	E	28 E6
Alhama de Murcia	E	29 C10
Alhaurín de la Torre	E	28 F5
Aliağa	TR	85 G3
Alicante	E	27 H10
Alingsås	S	46 F3
Aljaraque	E	25 K5
Aljustrel	P	25 H3
Alkmaar	NL	10 C6
Allariz	E	22 D4
Allevard	F	36 G4
Alliste	I	31 D11

Alloa	GB	2	G6	Amesbury	GB	9	E7	Anzegem	B	10	F4
Allonnes	F	15	F9	Amfissa	GR	88	A5	Anzin	F	10	G4
Almada	P	24	F2	Amiens	F	12	B2	Anzio	I	32	D5
Almadén	E	26	G2	Amilly	F	12	F3	Aosta	I	34	B1
Almansa	E	27	G9	Ammanford	GB	8	D4	Apahida	RO	78	D2
Almazán	E	20	F2	Ammarnäs	S	55	C9	Apatin	SRB	76	F5
Almazora	E	27	E10	Amorebieta	E	20	B2	Apeldoorn	NL	11	D7
Almeirim	P	24	E3	Åmot	N	48	D5	Apen	D	11	B10
Almelo	NL	11	C8	Ampelokipoi	GR	87	D7	Apice	I	30	A6
Almendralejo	E	24	F6	Ampelonas	GR	86	F6	Apolda	D	41	B7
Almería	E	29	E8	Amposta	E	21	G7	Appenzell	CH	37	C8
Älmhult	S	45	D9	Amsterdam	NL	10	C6	Appiano sulla Strada del Vino	I	37	E11
Almodóvar del Campo	E	26	G4	Amurrio	E	20	C1	Apricena	I	33	D10
Almonte	E	25	K6	Anacapri	I	30	B5	Aprilia	I	32	D5
Almoradí	E	29	C11	Anafi	GR	89	F10	Apt	F	18	D5
Almuñécar	E	28	E6	Anagni	I	32	D6	Aquaviva delle Fonti	I	31	B9
Almünster	A	39	C8	Anan'yiv	UA	79	B12	Aracena	E	25	H6
Almyros	GR	87	G7	Ancenis	F	15	G7	Aračinovo	MK	82	G2
Alness	GB	2	D5	An Cóbh	IRL	7	N4	Arad	RO	77	E9
Alnwick	GB	5	C8	Ancona	I	35	G11	Aradeo	I	31	C11
Álora	E	28	E4	Åndalsnes	N	50	C4	Aragona	I	30	F3
Alós d'Ensil	E	21	C8	Anddalsvågen	N	54	C5	A Ramallosa	E	22	C2
Alosno	E	25	J5	Andernos-les-Bains	F	16	E3	Aranda de Duero	E	23	E10
Alost	B	10	F5	Andoain	E	20	B3	Aranđelovac	SRB	81	C11
Alsfeld	D	11	G12	Andorra	E	20	G6	Aranjuez	E	26	E5
Alsózsolca	H	77	A9	Andorra la Vella	AND	21	C7	Arbatax	I	32	F4
Alta	N	58	D6	Andover	GB	9	E7	Arboga	S	47	C7
Ålta	S	47	C9	Andrano	I	31	D12	Arbon	CH	37	C8
Altamura	I	31	B9	Andratx	E	29	F9	Arbroath	GB	3	F7
Altavilla Irpina	I	30	B6	Andria	I	31	A8	Arbus	I	32	G2
Altavilla Silentina	I	30	B6	Andrychów	PL	75	D10	Arcachon	F	16	F3
Altdorf	CH	13	H11	Andújar	E	28	C5	Arce	I	33	D7
Altea	E	27	G10	Anenii Noi	MD	79	D11	Arcevia	I	35	G10
Altenburg	D	41	B8	Ängelholm	S	45	D7	Archidona	E	28	E5
Altenkirchen (Westerwald)	D	11	G10	Angelokastro	GR	88	A3	Arco	I	35	B7
Altentreptow	D	43	C9	Angermünde	D	43	D10	Arcos de la Frontera	E	25	L7
Althofen	A	39	E9	Angers	F	15	G8	Arcozelo	P	22	F2
Altınoluk	TR	85	E2	Anglès	E	18	G1	Ardea	I	32	D5
Altınova	TR	85	F2	Anglet	F	16	H2	Ardino	BG	87	B11
Altkirch	F	13	F9	Angoulême	F	16	D5	Ardore	I	31	G8
Altofonte	I	30	E3	Angri	I	30	B5	Ardres	F	9	F12
Altomonte	I	31	D8	Anguillara Sabazia	I	32	C5	Ardrossan	GB	4	B4
Alton	GB	9	E8	Anif	A	39	C7	Ardud	RO	77	B12
Altopascio	I	35	F6	Anina	RO	77	G10	Ardvasar	GB	2	E3
Altötting	D	38	B6	Aninoasa	RO	78	H5	Åre	S	51	A10
Alüksne	LV	67	F8	Anjalankoski	FIN	65	F7	Arenas de San Pedro	E	26	D2
Alverca	P	24	E2	Anklam	D	43	C10	Arendal	N	48	F6
Alvesta	S	45	C9	Anlaby	GB	5	F10	Arenys de Mar	E	21	F11
Alvik	S	52	C5	An Muileann gCearr	IRL	4	F1	Arenzano	I	19	B11
Älvros	S	51	D12	Annan	GB	4	D6	Ares	F	16	E3
Älvsbyn	S	56	C3	Anna Paulowna	NL	10	B6	Arévalo	E	23	G9
Alytus	LT	69	G7	An Nás	IRL	4	G2	Arezzo	I	35	G8
Alzey	D	13	B11	Annecy	F	36	F4	Argamasilla de Alba	E	26	F5
Alzira	E	27	F10	Annemasse	F	36	E4	Argamasilla de Calatrava	E	26	G4
Amadora	P	24	F2	Annonay	F	17	D12	Arganda del Rey	E	26	D5
Åmål	S	46	D3	Ano Lefkimmi	GR	86	F2	Argelès-sur-Mer	F	18	F2
Amalfi	I	30	B5	Anould	F	13	E9	Argenta	I	35	E8
Amaliada	GR	88	C3	Ans	B	11	G7	Argentan	F	15	D8
Amantea	I	31	E8	Ansbach	D	40	E5	Argenteuil	F	12	D2
Amara	RO	83	B12	Ansó	E	20	C5	Argenton-sur-Creuse	F	17	B7
Amarante	P	22	F3	An tAonach	IRL	7	K4	Argetoaia	RO	82	B5
Amărăştii de Jos	RO	83	C7	Antequera	E	28	E5	Argos	GR	88	C5
Amberg	D	41	E7	Antibes	F	19	D8	Argos Orestiko	GR	86	D4
Ambérieu-en-Bugey	F	36	F3	An tInbhear Mór	IRL	4	H3	Argostoli	GR	88	B2
Ambert	F	17	D11	Antony	F	12	D2	Århus	DK	44	D4
Amble	GB	5	C8	Antrim	GB	4	D2	Ariano Irpino	I	30	A6
Amboise	F	15	G10	Antwerpen	B	10	F5	Ariano nel Polesine	I	35	D9
Amelia	I	32	B5	An Uaimh	IRL	4	F2	Ariccia	I	32	D5
Amersfoort	NL	11	D7	Anvers	B	10	F5	Arizgoiti	E	20	B2
Amersham	GB	9	D8	Anykščiai	LT	69	D8	Arjeplog	S	55	B10

Place	Country	No.	Grid
Arjona	E	28	C5
Arklow	IRL	4	H3
Arkösund	S	47	E8
Arles	F	17	H12
Arlon	B	13	B7
Armagh	GB	4	E2
Armăşeşti	RO	83	B11
Armilla	E	28	E6
Armutlu	TR	85	H4
Arnage	F	15	F9
Arnavutköy	TR	85	B6
Arnedo	E	20	D3
Arnhem	NL	11	D7
Arnoldstein	A	39	F8
Arnsberg	D	11	E10
Arnstadt	D	40	B6
Arolsen	D	11	E12
Arona	I	34	B3
Arpino	I	33	D7
Arras	F	10	H3
Arrasate	E	20	C2
Arriondas	E	23	B8
Arroyo de la Luz	E	24	D6
Arsta	S	47	C9
Arsvågen	N	48	D2
Arta	GR	86	G4
Artà	E	29	F10
Artena	I	32	D6
Artern (Unstrut)	D	41	A6
Artsyz	UA	79	F11
A Rúa	E	22	D5
Arvidsjaur	S	55	C12
Arvika	S	46	B3
Arzachena	I	32	D3
Arzúa	E	22	C3
Aš	CZ	41	D8
Ås	N	51	B9
Ascea	I	30	C6
Aschaffenburg	D	13	B12
Aschersleben	D	43	G7
Ascoli Piceno	I	33	B7
Ascoli Satriano	I	31	A7
Åsele	S	55	F10
Asenovgrad	BG	83	G8
Åseral	N	48	E4
A Serra de Outes	E	22	C2
Ashby de la Zouch	GB	5	H8
Ashford	GB	9	E10
Ashington	GB	5	C8
Ashmyany	BY	69	F9
Asiago	I	35	B8
Asilah	MA	28	H2
Asker	N	49	C7
Askim	N	46	C2
Askvoll	N	50	F1
Aspe	E	27	H9
Aspropyrgos	GR	89	C7
Assemini	I	32	G2
Assen	NL	11	B8
Assens	DK	44	F4
Assisi	I	32	A5
Assoro	I	30	F5
Asti	I	19	A10
Astillero	E	23	B10
Aston	GB	8	C6
Astorga	E	22	D6
Åstorp	S	45	D7
Astravyets	BY	69	F9
Aszód	H	76	B6
Atalanti	GR	87	H7
Atessa	I	33	C8
Athens	GR	89	C7
Atherstone	GB	9	C7
Athina	GR	89	C7
Athlone	IRL	7	J5
Athy	IRL	4	H2
Atna	N	51	E8
Atri	I	33	B8
Atripalda	I	30	B6
Attleborough	GB	9	C11
Åtvidaberg	S	47	E7
Au	CH	37	C9
Aubagne	F	18	E6
Aubange	B	13	B7
Aubenas	F	17	F12
Aubigny-sur-Nère	F	12	G2
Auch	F	16	H5
Audierne	F	14	E2
Audincourt	F	13	G9
Aue	D	41	C9
Auerbach	D	41	C8
Augsburg	D	38	B4
Augusta	I	30	F6
Augustfehn	D	11	B10
Augustów	PL	68	H5
Aulla	I	34	E5
Aulnoye-Aymeries	F	10	H4
Aulus-les-Bains	F	21	C9
Auray	F	14	F4
Aurec-sur-Loire	F	17	D11
Aureilhan	F	21	B7
Aurich	D	11	A10
Aurillac	F	17	E9
Auriol	F	18	E6
Auterive	F	21	B9
Autun	F	12	H5
Auxerre	F	12	F4
Auxonne	F	13	G7
Avallon	F	12	F5
Avanca	P	22	G2
Aveiro	P	22	G2
Avella	I	30	B5
Avellino	I	30	B6
Aversa	I	30	B5
Avesnes-sur-Helpe	F	10	H5
Avesta	S	47	A7
Avetrano	I	31	C11
Avezzano	I	33	C7
Aviano	I	35	B10
Avigliano	I	31	B7
Avignon	F	18	C5
Ávila	E	23	G9
Avilés	E	23	B7
Avlonas	GR	89	B7
Avola	I	30	G6
Avonmouth	GB	8	E5
Avrämeni	RO	79	A7
Avranches	F	15	D7
Avrig	RO	78	F3
Avrillé	F	15	F8
Axams	A	37	C11
Ayamonte	E	25	K5
Aylesbury	GB	9	D8
Aylsham	GB	9	B11
Ayora	E	27	G9
Ayr	GB	4	C4
Aytos	BG	83	F12
Aytré	F	16	C3
Ayvacık	TR	85	E2
Ayvalık	TR	85	F2
Azanja	SRB	81	C12
Azkoitia	E	20	B2
Aznalcóllar	E	25	J7
Azuaga	E	24	G8

B

Place	Country	No.	Grid
Babadag	RO	79	H10
Babaeski	TR	85	B3
Băbeni	RO	78	H3
Bač	SRB	76	G6
Bacău	RO	79	D7
Baccarat	F	13	E9
Baciu	RO	78	D2
Bačka Palanka	SRB	76	G6
Bačka Topola	SRB	77	F7
Bački Jarak	SRB	77	G7
Bački Petrovac	SRB	77	G7
Bačko Gradište	SRB	77	F7
Bacoli	I	30	B4
Bácsalmás	H	76	E6
Badajoz	E	24	F5
Badalona	E	21	F10
Bad Aussee	A	39	D8
Bad Berka	D	41	B6
Bad Bramstedt	D	42	C5
Bad Doberan	D	43	B8
Bad Düben	D	43	G9
Baden	A	39	C12
Baden-Baden	D	13	D11
Badgastein	A	39	E7
Bad Goisern	A	39	D8
Bad Hersfeld	D	40	B4
Bad Hofgastein	A	39	E7
Badia Polesine	I	35	D8
Bad Ischl	A	39	C8
Bad Kissingen	D	40	D5
Bad Krozingen	D	13	F10
Bad Lauterberg im Harz	D	42	G6
Bad Münstereifel	D	11	G9
Bad Neustadt an der Saale	D	40	C5
Badovinci	SRB	81	B9
Bad Salzuflen	D	11	D11
Bad Salzungen	D	40	B5
Bad Sooden-Allendorf	D	40	B5
Bad Waldsee	D	37	B9
Bad Wildungen	D	11	F12
Bad Windsheim	D	40	E5
Baena	E	28	D5
Baeza	E	28	C6
Bagheria	I	30	E3
Bagnacavallo	I	35	E9
Bagnara Calabra	I	31	G7
Bagnères-de-Bigorre	F	21	C7
Bagno a Ripoli	I	35	F8
Bagno di Romagna	I	35	F9
Bagnolo Mella	I	34	C6
Bagnols-sur-Cèze	F	17	G12
Bagrationovsk	RUS	68	G2
Bagshot	GB	9	E8
Bağyurdu	TR	85	H4
Baia	RO	84	B5
Baia de Aramă	RO	77	H12
Baia de Arieş	RO	78	E1
Baia Mare	RO	78	B2
Baiano	I	30	B5
Baia Sprie	RO	78	B2
Băicoi	RO	78	G5
Băiculeşti	RO	78	G3

B

Baile Átha Cliath	IRL	4	G2
Baile Átha Luain	IRL	7	J5
Băile Herculane	RO	77	H11
Bailén	E	28	C6
Băileşti	RO	82	C5
Baillargues	F	17	H11
Bailleul	F	10	G3
Bain-de-Bretagne	F	14	F6
Baiona	E	22	D2
Baja	H	76	E5
Bajina Bašta	SRB	81	D10
Bajmok	SRB	76	F6
Bajram Curri	AL	81	G10
Bakırköy	TR	85	C6
Bakum	D	11	C11
Balaguer	E	21	E8
Bălan	RO	78	D5
Balassagyarmat	H	76	A6
Balatonalmádi	H	76	C4
Balatonboglár	H	76	D3
Balatonfüred	H	76	D4
Bălăuşeri	RO	78	E3
Balbriggan	IRL	4	F3
Balcani	RO	79	D7
Bălceşti	RO	82	B6
Balchik	BG	84	D4
Băleni	RO	78	H5
Băleşti	RO	78	G1
Balestrate	I	30	E2
Balıkesir	TR	85	E4
Balingen	D	13	E12
Balkány	H	77	B10
Ballainvilliers	F	12	D2
Ballangen	N	57	D5
Ballenstedt	D	43	G7
Ballerup	DK	44	E7
Ballina	IRL	6	G3
Ballinasloe	IRL	7	J4
Ballsh	AL	86	D2
Ballycastle	GB	4	C2
Ballyclare	GB	4	D3
Ballymena	GB	4	D2
Ballymoney	GB	4	C2
Ballynahinch	GB	4	E3
Balmaseda	E	20	B1
Balmazújváros	H	77	B9
Baloteşti	RO	83	B10
Balş	RO	82	B6
Bålsta	S	47	C9
Balsthal	CH	13	G10
Balta	UA	79	B12
Bălţăteşti	RO	78	C6
Bălteni	RO	78	H1
Bălţi	MD	79	B9
Baltiysk	RUS	68	F1
Băluşeni	RO	79	B7
Balvi	LV	67	G9
Bamberg	D	40	D6
Banatski Karlovac	SRB	77	G9
Banatsko Novo Selo	SRB	77	H8
Banbridge	GB	4	E2
Banbury	GB	9	D7
Banca	RO	79	E9
Banchory	GB	3	E7
Band	RO	78	D3
Bandırma	TR	85	D4
Băneasa	RO	83	C10
Băneasa	RO	84	C3
Bangor	GB	4	D3
Bangor	GB	4	G5
Banja	SRB	81	E9
Banja Luka	BIH	80	B5
Bankeryd	S	46	F5
Bankya	BG	82	F5
Bánovce nad Bebravou	SK	75	G9
Banovići	BIH	81	C8
Banská Bystrica	SK	75	G10
Banská Štiavnica	SK	75	G10
Bansko	BG	82	G5
Banyoles	E	18	G1
Bar	MNE	81	H9
Barakaldo	E	20	B1
Barañain	E	20	C4
Baraolt	RO	78	E5
Barbastro	E	21	E7
Barbate de Franco	E	25	M7
Barberá del Vallès	E	21	F10
Barberino di Mugello	I	35	F7
Bărbuleţu	RO	78	G4
Barcelona	E	21	F10
Barcellona Pozzo di Gotto	I	30	E6
Barcin	PL	71	E7
Barcs	H	76	F3
Barczewo	PL	68	H2
Bardejov	SK	73	F2
Barentin	F	15	B10
Barfleur	F	15	B7
Barga	I	34	F6
Bargas	E	26	E4
Bargoed	GB	8	D5
Bargteheide	D	42	C6
Bari	I	31	A9
Bârla	RO	83	B8
Bârlad	RO	79	E8
Bar-le-Duc	F	12	D6
Barletta	I	33	E11
Barlinek	PL	70	E4
Barnard Castle	GB	5	D8
Barnoldswick	GB	5	E6
Barnsley	GB	5	F8
Barnstaple	GB	8	F3
Barnstorf	D	11	C11
Barntrup	D	11	D12
Baronissi	I	30	B6
Barr	F	13	E10
Barrafranca	I	30	F4
Barreiro	P	24	F2
Barrhead	GB	2	H5
Barrow-in-Furness	GB	4	E6
Barry	GB	8	E5
Bârsana	RO	78	B3
Bar-sur-Aube	F	12	E6
Barth	D	43	B9
Barton-upon-Humber	GB	5	F10
Bartoszyce	PL	68	G3
Basarabeasca	MD	79	E11
Basarabi	RO	84	C4
Basauri	E	23	B12
Bascov	RO	78	H4
Basel	CH	13	F10
Basildon	GB	9	E10
Basingstoke	GB	9	E8
Bassano del Grappa	I	35	B8
Basse-Goulaine	F	14	G6
Bassens	F	16	E4
Bassum	D	11	B11
Bastia	F	19	E12
Bastia	I	32	A5
Batajnica	SRB	77	H8
Batak	BG	83	G7
Batăr	RO	77	D10
Bátaszék	H	76	E5
Bath	GB	8	E6
Bathgate	GB	2	G6
Bátonyterenye	H	77	B7
Battenberg (Eder)	D	40	B3
Battipaglia	I	30	B6
Battle	GB	9	F10
Battonya	H	77	E9
Baume-les-Dames	F	13	G8
Baunatal	D	11	F12
Bauska	LV	69	B7
Bavay	F	10	H4
Bayeux	F	15	C7
Bayonne	F	16	H2
Bayramiç	TR	85	E2
Bayreuth	D	41	D7
Bayston Hill	GB	8	B5
Baza	E	29	D8
Béal an Átha	IRL	6	G3
Béal Átha na Sluaighe	IRL	7	J4
Beasain	E	20	C3
Beas de Segura	E	29	B7
Beaucaire	F	17	G12
Beaumont-lès-Valence	F	18	B5
Beaune	F	12	G6
Beaupréau	F	15	G7
Beauvais	F	12	C2
Bebington	GB	5	G6
Bebra	D	40	B4
Beccles	GB	9	C11
Bečej	SRB	77	F7
Beceni	RO	79	G7
Bechyně	CZ	41	F11
Beclean	RO	78	C3
Bédarieux	F	17	H10
Bédarrides	F	18	C5
Bedford	GB	9	C9
Bedlington	GB	5	C8
Będzin	PL	75	C10
Beelitz	D	43	F9
Beernem	B	10	F4
Beeskow	D	43	F11
Begles	F	16	E4
Beith	GB	2	H5
Beiuş	RO	77	D11
Beja	P	25	H4
Béjar	E	23	H7
Békés	H	77	D9
Békéscsaba	H	77	D9
Bela Crkva	SRB	77	H10
Bela Palanka	SRB	82	E3
Belceşti	RO	79	C7
Bełchatów	PL	71	H9
Belene	BG	83	D8
Belfast	GB	4	D3
Belfort	F	13	F9
Belgrade	SRB	81	B11
Beli Manastir	HR	76	F5
Belišće	HR	76	F5
Bellac	F	16	C6
Bellaria	I	35	F9
Belleville	F	17	C12
Belley	F	36	F3
Bellinzona	CH	34	A4
Bellizzi	I	30	B6
Belluno	I	35	B9
Belmont	GB	3	B12
Belogradchik	BG	82	D4

Name	Country	Col1	Col2
Belovo	BG	82	G6
Belpasso	I	30	F6
Belper	GB	5	G8
Belvedere Marittimo	I	31	D7
Belzig	D	43	F9
Bełżyce	PL	73	B3
Bembibre	E	22	C2
Bembibre	E	22	C6
Benalmádena	E	28	F5
Benavente	P	24	E2
Benavente	E	23	E7
Benešov	CZ	41	E11
Benevento	I	30	A6
Benfeld	F	13	E10
Benicarló	E	21	H7
Benicasim	E	27	E11
Benidorm	E	27	H10
Benifaió	E	27	F10
Benissa	E	27	G11
Benson	GB	9	D8
Beograd	SRB	81	B11
Berane	MNE	81	F10
Berat	AL	86	D2
Berbeşti	RO	78	G2
Berca	RO	79	G7
Berceni	RO	78	H6
Berching	D	41	F7
Berck	F	9	G11
Berehomet	UA	78	A5
Berehove	UA	73	H4
Berettyóújfalu	H	77	C10
Berezeni	RO	79	E9
Berga	E	21	D9
Bergama	TR	85	F3
Bergamo	I	34	C5
Bergara	E	20	B2
Bergen	D	42	E5
Bergen	D	43	B10
Bergen	NL	10	C6
Bergen	N	48	B2
Bergerac	F	16	E5
Bergues	F	10	F2
Berhida	H	76	C4
Beringen	B	10	F6
Berja	E	29	E7
Berkovitsa	BG	82	E5
Berlevåg	N	59	B10
Berlin	D	43	E10
Bermeo	E	20	B2
Bern	CH	13	H10
Bernalda	I	31	C9
Bernau	D	43	E10
Bernay	F	15	C9
Bernburg (Saale)	D	43	G8
Berne	D	11	B11
Bernsdorf	D	41	A10
Beroun	CZ	41	D10
Berovo	MK	82	H4
Berre-l'Étang	F	18	D5
Berriozar	E	20	C4
Bertamirans	E	22	C2
Bertinoro	I	35	F9
Berwick-upon-Tweed	GB	3	H8
Besançon	F	13	G8
Beška	SRB	77	G7
Betanzos	E	22	B3
Béthune	F	10	G3
Bettembourg	L	13	B8
Betton	F	14	E6
Betzdorf	D	11	G10
Beverley	GB	5	F10
Beverwijk	NL	10	C6
Bewdley	GB	8	G8
Bex	CH	36	E5
Bexhill	GB	9	F10
Bezdan	SRB	76	F5
Bezhanitsy	RUS	67	G12
Béziers	F	18	E2
Biała Podlaska	PL	72	G5
Białobrzegi	PL	71	G11
Białogard	PL	70	C5
Białystok	PL	72	D5
Biancavilla	I	30	F5
Biarritz	F	16	H2
Biasca	CH	37	E8
Bibbiena	I	35	G8
Biberach an der Riß	D	37	B9
Bicaz	RO	78	D6
Bicester	GB	9	D8
Bicske	H	76	B5
Bideford	GB	8	F3
Biel	CH	13	G9
Bielefeld	D	11	D11
Biella	I	34	C2
Bielsko-Biała	PL	75	D10
Bielsk Podlaski	PL	72	E5
Bieruń	PL	75	D10
Bierutów	PL	75	B8
Biga	TR	85	D3
Bigadiç	TR	85	F5
Biganos	F	16	F3
Biggleswade	GB	9	D9
Biguglia	F	19	E12
Bihać	BIH	80	B3
Biharia	RO	77	C10
Bijeljina	BIH	81	B9
Bijelo Polje	MNE	81	F10
Bilbao	E	20	B1
Bilbo	E	20	B1
Bileća	BIH	81	F8
Biled	RO	77	F9
Biłgoraj	PL	73	C4
Bilisht	AL	86	D4
Billabona	E	20	B3
Billdal	S	44	B6
Billère	F	20	B6
Billingham	GB	5	D9
Billingshurst	GB	9	F9
Billund	DK	44	E3
Bílovec	CZ	75	E8
Bilyayivka	UA	79	E12
Binefar	E	21	E7
Bingen	D	37	A8
Binic	F	14	D4
Biograd na Moru	HR	80	D3
Birchington	GB	9	E11
Birkenfeld	D	13	B9
Birkenhead	GB	5	G6
Birkerød	DK	44	E7
Birkirkara	M	31	❐
Birmingham	GB	8	C7
Birsay	GB	3	E9
Biržai	LT	69	C7
Bisacquino	I	30	E3
Biscarrosse	F	16	F3
Bisceglie	I	31	A9
Bischofswerda	D	41	B11
Bishop Auckland	GB	5	D8
Bishop's Cleeve	GB	8	D6
Bishop's Stortford	GB	9	D9
Bishop's Waltham	GB	9	F7
Bisignano	I	31	D8
Biskupiec	PL	68	H3
Bistra	RO	77	E12
Bistriţa	RO	78	C3
Bitburg	D	13	B8
Bitche	F	13	C10
Bitetto	I	31	A9
Bitola	MK	86	C5
Bitonto	I	31	A9
Bitterfeld	D	43	G8
Bivona	I	30	F3
Bixad	RO	78	B1
Bixad	RO	78	E5
Bjärred	S	45	E7
Bjelovar	HR	76	F2
Bjerringbro	DK	44	D3
Björbo	S	52	G2
Bjørkeflåta	N	48	B5
Björköby	FIN	53	A10
Bjorli	N	50	D5
Bjurholm	S	55	G12
Bjuv	S	45	E7
Blachownia	PL	75	C10
Blackburn	GB	5	F7
Blackpool	GB	4	F6
Blaenavon	GB	8	D5
Blăgeşti	RO	79	D7
Blagoevgrad	BG	82	G5
Blain	F	14	G6
Blairgowrie	GB	2	F6
Blaj	RO	78	E2
Blandford Forum	GB	8	F6
Blanes	E	21	E11
Blankenberge	B	10	E3
Blankenburg (Harz)	D	43	G7
Blankenfelde	D	43	F10
Blanquefort	F	16	E3
Blansko	CZ	74	E6
Blatná	CZ	41	E10
Bled	SLO	39	F9
Blejoi	RO	78	H6
Bléré	F	15	G10
Blois	F	15	F10
Blokhus	DK	44	B3
Blomberg	D	11	D12
Błonie	PL	71	F11
Bludenz	A	37	C9
Blumberg	D	13	F11
Blyth	GB	5	C8
Bobingen	D	37	A10
Boborás	E	22	D3
Bobovdol	BG	82	F5
Bochnia	PL	73	D1
Bocholt	D	11	D8
Bochum	D	11	E9
Bockenem	D	42	F6
Bocşa	RO	77	G10
Böda	S	45	B12
Boden	S	56	B4
Bodeşti	RO	78	C6
Bodmin	GB	8	G2
Bodø	N	57	F2
Bodrum	TR	88	E3
Boën	F	17	C11
Bogatić	SRB	81	H6
Bogatynia	PL	41	B12
Bogdanci	MK	87	C7
Bognor Regis	GB	9	F8
Bohmte	D	11	C11

B

B

Bohumín	CZ	75	D9
Bois-Guillaume	F	15	C10
Boizenburg	D	42	D6
Bojano	I	33	D8
Bojnice	SK	75	G9
Bolaños de Calatrava	E	26	G4
Bolbec	F	15	B9
Boldeşti-Scăeni	RO	78	G6
Bolekhiv	UA	73	F6
Bolesławiec	PL	74	B5
Bolhrad	UA	79	F10
Bolintin-Deal	RO	83	B9
Bolintin-Vale	RO	83	B9
Bollène	F	18	C4
Bollnäs	S	52	E4
Bollullos Par del Condado	E	25	J6
Bologna	I	35	E8
Bolsover	GB	5	G9
Bolton	GB	5	F7
Bolzano	I	37	E11
Bompas	F	18	F1
Bondeno	I	35	D8
Bo'ness	GB	2	G6
Bonn	D	11	G9
Bonneville	F	36	F4
Bonyhád	H	76	E5
Boo	S	47	C9
Bootle	GB	5	G7
Boppard	D	11	H10
Bor	SRB	82	C3
Borås	S	45	A7
Borca	RO	78	C5
Borcea	RO	84	B3
Bordeaux	F	16	E4
Bordesholm	D	42	B5
Bordighera	I	19	D9
Borduşani	RO	84	B3
Borgholm	S	45	C12
Borgia	I	31	F9
Borgo	F	19	E12
Borgomanero	I	34	C3
Borgo San Dalmazzo	I	19	C9
Borgo San Lorenzo	I	35	F8
Borgosesia	I	34	B2
Borgo Val di Taro	I	34	E5
Borhaug	N	48	F3
Borken	D	11	D9
Borkum	D	42	C1
Borlänge	S	52	G3
Borna	D	41	B8
Bornova	TR	85	H3
Borovo Selo	HR	76	G5
Borovo Selo	HR	76	G5
Borşa	RO	78	B3
Borsbeek	B	10	F5
Boryslav	UA	73	F5
Bosa	I	32	E2
Bosanska Dubica	BIH	76	G2
Bosanska Gradiška	BIH	76	G3
Bosanska Krupa	BIH	80	B4
Bosanski Brod	BIH	76	G4
Bosanski Novi	BIH	76	G1
Bosanski Šamac	BIH	76	G5
Boscotrecase	I	30	B5
Bosilegrad	SRB	82	F4
Boskovice	CZ	74	E6
Boston	GB	5	H10
Boteå	S	52	B6
Boteşti	RO	79	C7
Botevgrad	BG	82	E6
Botoroaga	RO	83	C9
Botoşani	RO	79	B7
Botricello	I	31	F9
Boucau	F	16	H2
Bouc-Bel-Air	F	18	D6
Bouchemaine	F	15	G8
Bouguenais	F	14	G6
Bouillargues	F	17	G12
Boulazac	F	16	E6
Boulogne-Billancourt	F	12	D2
Boulogne-sur-Mer	F	9	F12
Bourbon-Lancy	F	17	F11
Bourg-en-Bresse	F	36	E2
Bourges	F	12	G2
Bourgoin-Jallieu	F	36	G2
Bourg-St-Andéol	F	17	F12
Bourg-St-Maurice	F	36	F5
Bourgueil	F	15	G9
Bourne	GB	5	H10
Bournemouth	GB	8	F7
Bourron-Marlotte	F	12	E3
Bovalino	I	31	G8
Boves	I	19	C9
Boville Ernica	I	33	D7
Boxmeer	NL	11	E7
Božava	HR	80	D2
Bra	I	19	B10
Bracciano	I	32	C5
Bräcke	S	52	B3
Brackley	GB	9	D8
Bracknell	GB	9	E8
Brad	RO	77	E12
Bradford	GB	5	F8
Brae	GB	3	B12
Braga	P	22	F2
Bragadiru	RO	83	B10
Bragadiru	RO	83	D9
Bragança	P	22	E5
Brăhăşeşti	RO	79	E8
Brăila	RO	79	G9
Braine-l'Alleud	B	10	G5
Braintree	GB	9	D10
Brakel	B	10	F4
Bramming	DK	44	F2
Bramsche	D	11	C10
Bran	RO	78	F5
Brande	DK	44	E3
Brandenburg	D	43	F9
Brandon	GB	9	C10
Brăneşti	RO	83	B10
Braniewo	PL	68	G1
Braslaw	BY	69	D10
Braşov	RO	78	F5
Brastavăţu	RO	83	C7
Bratca	RO	77	D12
Bratislava	SK	75	H7
Bratovoeşti	RO	82	C6
Bratsigovo	BG	83	G7
Bratunac	BIH	81	D9
Braunau am Inn	A	39	B7
Braunschweig	D	42	F6
Braunton	GB	8	E3
Bray	IRL	4	G3
Brbinj	HR	80	D2
Brčko	BIH	76	H5
Bré	IRL	4	G3
Breaza	RO	78	G5
Brebu	RO	78	G5
Brechin	GB	3	F7
Brecht	B	10	E6
Břeclav	CZ	75	G7
Brecon	GB	8	D4
Breda	NL	10	E6
Bregenz	A	37	C9
Breitenfelde	D	42	C6
Brekken	N	51	C9
Brekstad	N	54	G2
Bremen	D	11	B12
Bremerhaven	D	42	C4
Bremervörde	D	11	A12
Brenes	E	25	J7
Brentwood	GB	9	D10
Bresalc	RKS	82	F2
Brescia	I	34	C6
Bressanone	I	37	D12
Bressuire	F	15	H8
Brest	BY	72	G6
Brest	F	14	E2
Brevik	S	47	C9
Brežice	SLO	39	G11
Breznik	BG	82	F5
Brezno	SK	75	F11
Briançon	F	19	A8
Briare	F	12	F3
Bridgend	GB	2	H3
Bridgend	GB	8	E4
Bridgnorth	GB	8	C6
Bridgwater	GB	8	E5
Bridlington	GB	5	E10
Bridport	GB	8	F5
Brig	CH	34	A2
Brigg	GB	5	F10
Brightlingsea	GB	9	D11
Brighton	GB	9	F9
Brignais	F	36	F2
Brignoles	F	19	D7
Brilon	D	11	E11
Brindisi	I	31	B11
Brioude	F	17	D10
Brisighella	I	35	E8
Bristol	GB	8	E6
Brive-la-Gaillarde	F	17	E7
Briviesca	E	20	D1
Brixham	GB	8	G4
Brixworth	GB	9	C8
Brno	CZ	74	F6
Bro	S	47	C9
Broadstairs	GB	9	E11
Brod	MK	86	B4
Brodick	GB	4	B4
Brodnica	PL	71	D9
Bromarv	FIN	53	H11
Bromma	S	47	C9
Bromölla	S	45	E9
Bromsgrove	GB	8	C6
Bron	F	36	F2
Brønderslev	DK	44	B4
Bronte	I	30	E5
Broşteni	RO	78	C5
Brou	F	15	E10
Broumov	CZ	74	C6
Broxburn	GB	2	G6
Bruchhausen-Vilsen	D	11	B12
Bruchmühlbach	D	13	C10
Bruck an der Mur	A	39	D10
Bruges	B	10	F4
Brugge	B	10	F4
Brumunddal	N	51	G8
Brunflo	S	51	B12
Brunico	I	38	E5

Brunkeberg	N	48	D5	Burton upon Trent	GB	5	H8	Caivano	I	30	B5
Brunsbüttel	D	42	C4	Burwell	GB	9	C10	Cajvana	RO	78	B6
Bruntál	CZ	75	D8	Bury	GB	5	F7	Čakovec	HR	76	E1
Bruravik	N	48	B3	Bury St Edmunds	GB	9	C10	Calafat	RO	82	C5
Brussel	B	10	F5	Busalla	I	19	B11	Calafell	E	21	F9
Brusturi-Drăgănești	RO	78	C6	Busca	I	19	B9	Calafindești	RO	78	B6
Bruxelles	B	10	F5	Bushtyna	UA	78	A1	Calahorra	E	20	D3
Bruz	F	14	E6	Busko-Zdrój	PL	73	C1	Calais	F	9	F12
Brymbo	GB	4	G6	Bussolengo	I	35	C7	Calamonte	E	24	F6
Bryne	N	48	E2	Bușteni	RO	78	G5	Călan	RO	77	F12
Bryukhovychi	UA	73	E6	Busto Arsizio	I	34	C3	Calañas	E	25	J6
Brzeg	PL	75	B8	Büsum	D	42	B4	Călărași	MD	79	C10
Brzeg Dolny	PL	75	B7	Butera	I	30	G4	Călărași	RO	82	D6
Brzesko	PL	73	D1	Butzbach	D	11	G11	Călărași	RO	83	C12
Brzeszcze	PL	75	D10	Bützow	D	43	C8	Calascibetta	I	30	F4
Brzeziny	PL	71	G10	Buxerolles	F	16	B5	Calasetta	I	32	H1
Brzozów	PL	73	E3	Buxtehude	D	42	D5	Calasparra	E	29	B9
Buarcos	P	24	B2	Buxton	GB	5	G8	Calatafimi	I	30	E2
Buca	TR	85	H3	Büyükçekmece	TR	85	B5	Calatayud	E	20	F4
Buccino	I	31	B7	Buzău	RO	79	G7	Calbe (Saale)	D	43	G8
Bucecea	RO	78	B6	Buziaș	RO	77	F10	Caldas da Rainha	P	24	D2
Bucharest	RO	83	B10	Buzoești	RO	83	B8	Caldas de Reis	E	22	C2
Buchs	CH	37	C8	Byahoml'	BY	69	F12	Caldes de Montbui	E	21	E10
Bucine	I	35	G8	Byala	BG	83	D9	Caldicot	GB	8	E5
Buciumeni	RO	78	G5	Byala Slatina	BG	82	D6	Calenzano	I	35	F7
Bückeburg	D	11	D12	Byarozawka	BY	69	H8	Călimănești	RO	78	G3
Buckhaven	GB	3	G7	Bychawa	PL	73	B4	Calimera	I	31	C11
Buckie	GB	3	D7	Bydgoszcz	PL	71	D7	Călinești	RO	78	H4
Buckingham	GB	9	D8	Bygland	N	48	E5	Calitri	I	31	B7
Buckley	GB	4	G6	Byrum	DK	44	B5	Callosa d'En Sarrià	E	27	G10
Bucov	RO	78	H6	Bystřice nad Pernštejnem	CZ	74	E6	Calne	GB	8	E6
Bučovice	CZ	75	F7	Bytča	SK	75	F9	Calpe	E	27	G11
București	RO	83	B10	Bytom	PL	75	C10	Caltabellotta	I	30	F3
Bud	N	50	B4	Bytów	PL	71	B7	Caltagirone	I	30	F5
Budaörs	H	76	C5	Byxelkrok	S	45	B12	Caltanissetta	I	30	F4
Budapest	H	76	C6					Caltavuturo	I	30	E4
Buddusò	I	32	E3					Călugăreni	RO	83	C10
Budești	RO	83	C10	**C**				Calvi	F	19	E10
Bueu	E	22	D2					Calzada de Calatrava	E	26	G4
Buftea	RO	83	B10	Cabañaquinta	E	23	B7	Camariñas	E	22	B1
Bugojno	BIH	80	D6	Čabar	HR	39	H9	Camas	E	25	J7
Bugyi	H	76	C6	Cabeza del Buey	E	26	G2	Cambados	E	22	D2
Buhuși	RO	79	D7	Cabezón de la Sal	E	23	B9	Camborne	GB	8	G2
Builth Wells	GB	8	C4	Cabra	E	28	D5	Cambrai	F	10	H4
Bujalance	E	28	C5	Cabras	I	32	F2	Cambridge	GB	9	C9
Bujanovac	SRB	82	F3	Čačak	SRB	81	D11	Cambrils	E	21	G8
Buk	PL	70	F6	Caccamo	I	30	E3	Camenca	MD	79	A10
Bullas	E	29	C9	Cacém	P	24	F2	Camerano	I	35	G11
Bulle	CH	36	D5	Cáceres	E	24	D6	Camerino	I	35	H10
Bulqizë	AL	86	B3	Čadca	SK	75	E9	Camerota	I	31	C7
Bumbești-Jiu	RO	78	G1	Cadeo	I	34	D5	Cammarata	I	30	F3
Buñol	E	27	F9	Cádiz	E	25	L7	Campagnano di Roma	I	32	C5
Buntești	RO	77	D11	Caen	F	15	C8	Campanario	E	24	F8
Burbach	D	11	G10	Caerdydd	GB	8	E5	Campbeltown	GB	4	C3
Burgas	BG	83	F12	Caerfyrddin	GB	8	D3	Câmpeni	RO	77	E12
Burg bei Magdeburg	D	43	F8	Caergybi	GB	4	G4	Câmpia Turzii	RO	78	D2
Burgdorf	CH	13	G10	Caernarfon	GB	4	G5	Campi Bisenzio	I	35	F7
Burghausen	D	39	C7	Caerphilly	GB	8	E5	Campiglia Marittima	I	32	A2
Burglengenfeld	D	41	F8	Cagli	I	35	G10	Campillos	E	28	E4
Burgos	E	23	D10	Cagliari	I	32	G3	Câmpina	RO	78	G5
Burgstädt	D	41	B9	Cagnano Varano	I	33	D11	Campi Salentina	I	31	C11
Burgsvik	S	41	H9	Cagnes-sur-Mer	F	19	D8	Campli	I	33	B7
Burgum	NL	11	B8	Cahors	F	17	F7	Campobasso	I	33	D9
Burhaniye	TR	85	F3	Cahul	MD	79	F9	Campobello di Licata	I	30	F4
Burlada	E	20	C4	Căianu Mic	RO	78	C3	Campobello di Mazara	I	30	F2
Burnley	GB	5	F7	Caiazzo	I	30	A5	Campo de Criptana	E	26	F5
Burntisland	GB	2	G6	Cairo Montenotte	I	19	B10	Campofelice di Roccella	I	30	E4
Burrel	AL	86	B2	Caisleán an Bharraigh	IRL	7	H3	Campo Maior	P	24	E5
Burriana	E	27	E10	Caister-on-Sea	GB	9	B12	Campomarino	I	33	C9
Burton Latimer	GB	9	C8	Căiuți	RO	79	E7	Campomorone	I	19	B11

Campos	E	29	F10
Câmpulung	RO	78	G4
Câmpulung la Tisa	RO	78	B2
Câmpulung Moldovenesc	RO	78	B5
Çan	TR	85	D1
Çanakkale	TR	85	D2
Canals	E	27	G10
Cancale	F	14	D6
Candeleda	E	24	B8
Canelli	I	19	B10
Canet-en-Roussillon	F	18	F2
Cangas	E	22	D2
Cangas del Narcea	E	22	B6
Cangas de Onís	E	23	B8
Canicattì	I	30	F4
Canicattini Bagni	I	30	G6
Caniles	E	29	D8
Canino	I	32	B4
Cannes	F	19	D8
Cannobio	I	34	B3
Cannock	GB	8	B6
Canosa di Puglia	I	31	A8
Čantavir	SRB	77	F7
Cantemir	MD	79	E9
Canterbury	GB	9	E11
Cantillana	E	25	J7
Canvey Island	GB	9	E10
Caorle	I	35	C10
Capaccio	I	30	C6
Capaci	I	30	E3
Capannori	I	34	F6
Capbreton	F	16	H2
Capdenac-Gare	F	17	F8
Capdepera	E	29	F10
Cap Ferret	F	16	F2
Capistrello	I	33	C7
Čapljina	BIH	80	F6
Capo d'Orlando	I	30	E5
Capoterra	I	32	G2
Capri	I	30	B5
Capua	I	30	A5
Capurso	I	31	A9
Caracal	RO	83	C7
Caraglio	I	19	B9
Caransebeş	RO	77	G11
Caravaca de la Cruz	E	29	C9
Carballo	E	22	B2
Carboneras	E	29	E9
Carbonia	I	32	G2
Carcaixent	E	27	F10
Carcare	I	19	C10
Carcassonne	F	21	B10
Cardedeu	E	21	E10
Cardiff	GB	8	E5
Cardona	E	21	E9
Carei	RO	77	B11
Carentan	F	15	C7
Carhaix-Plouguer	F	14	E3
Cariati	I	31	E9
Carignano	I	19	A9
Carini	I	30	E3
Carlentini	I	30	F6
Carlet	E	27	F10
Carlisle	GB	5	D7
Carloforte	I	32	G1
Carlow	IRL	4	H2
Carlton	GB	5	H9
Carmagnola	I	19	B9
Carmarthen	GB	8	D3
Carmaux	F	17	G8

Carmiano	I	31	C11
Carmona	E	25	J8
Carnac	F	14	F4
Carnforth	GB	5	E7
Carnoustie	GB	3	F7
Carnoux-en-Provence	F	18	E6
Carosino	I	31	C10
Carovigno	I	31	B10
Carpentras	F	18	C5
Carpi	I	35	D7
Carpineto Romano	I	32	D6
Cărpiniş	RO	77	F9
Carpino	I	33	D11
Carquefou	F	14	G6
Carqueiranne	F	18	E7
Carraig na Siuire	IRL	7	L5
Carrara	I	34	F5
Carrickfergus	GB	4	D3
Carrick-on-Shannon	IRL	6	G4
Carrick-on-Suir	IRL	7	L5
Carros	F	19	D8
Carryduff	GB	4	D3
Carry-le-Rouet	F	18	E5
Cartagena	E	29	D11
Cártama	E	28	E4
Cartaxo	P	24	C2
Carteret	F	14	C6
Carterton	GB	9	D7
Cartoceto	I	35	F10
Casagiove	I	30	A5
Casalbordino	I	33	C9
Casalecchio di Reno	I	35	E7
Casale Monferrato	I	19	A11
Casalmaggiore	I	34	D6
Casalpusterlengo	I	34	D5
Casamassima	I	31	B9
Casarano	I	31	C11
Cascina	I	34	G6
Caserta	I	30	A5
Čáslav	CZ	74	D5
Casnewydd	GB	8	E5
Casoli	I	33	C8
Casoria	I	30	B5
Caspe	E	20	F6
Cassano allo Ionio	I	31	D8
Cassino	I	33	D7
Cassis	F	18	E6
Castagneto Carducci	I	34	H6
Casteggio	I	19	A12
Castèl Bolognese	I	35	E8
Castelbuono	I	30	E4
Castèl di Iudica	I	30	F5
Castèl di Sangro	I	33	D8
Castelfidardo	I	35	G11
Castelfiorentino	I	35	G7
Castellabate	I	30	C6
Castellammare del Golfo	I	30	E2
Castellammare di Stabia	I	30	B5
Castellaneta	I	31	B9
Castelldefels	E	21	F10
Castellón de la Plana	E	27	E10
Castell-y-Nedd	GB	8	D4
Castelnaudary	F	21	B10
Castelnau-le-Lez	F	17	H11
Castelnovo ne'Monti	I	34	E6
Castelnuovo di Garfagnana	I	34	F6
Castelnuovo di Porto	I	32	C5
Castelo Branco	P	24	C5
Castèl San Pietro Terme	I	35	E8
Castelsardo	I	32	D2

Castelsarrasin	F	16	G6
Casteltermini	I	30	F3
Castelu	RO	84	C4
Castelvetrano	I	30	F2
Castèl Volturno	I	30	A4
Castiglione dei Pepoli	I	35	F7
Castiglione del Lago	I	35	H9
Castiglione della Pescaia	I	32	B2
Castiglione Falletto	I	19	B10
Castiglion Fiorentino	I	35	G9
Castilleja de la Cuesta	E	25	J7
Castillon-la-Bataille	F	16	E4
Castlebar	IRL	7	H3
Castlebay	GB	2	E1
Castres	F	17	H8
Castricum	NL	10	C6
Castries	F	17	H11
Castrignano del Capo	I	31	D12
Castrocaro Terme	I	35	F9
Castro del Río	E	28	D5
Castro de Rei	E	22	B4
Castropol	E	22	B5
Castro-Urdiales	E	20	B1
Castrovillari	I	31	D8
Castuera	E	24	F8
Çatalca	TR	85	B5
Catania	I	30	F6
Catanzaro	I	31	F9
Catarroja	E	27	F10
Cattolica	I	35	F10
Cattolica Eraclea	I	30	F3
Caudete	E	27	G9
Caudry	F	10	H4
Caulonia	I	31	G8
Căuşeni	MD	79	D11
Caussade	F	17	G7
Cava de'Tirreni	I	30	B6
Cavaillon	F	18	D5
Cavalaire-sur-Mer	F	19	E7
Cavan	IRL	4	F1
Cavour	I	19	B9
Cavriglia	I	35	G8
Cazalla de la Sierra	E	25	H7
Cazasu	RO	79	G9
Ceanannus	I	35	F10
Ceatharlach	IRL	4	H2
Ceauşu de Câmpie	RO	78	D3
Cébazat	F	17	C10
Ceccano	I	33	D7
Cecina	I	34	G6
Cedeira	E	22	A3
Cee	E	22	C1
Cefa	RO	77	D10
Cefalù	I	30	E4
Cefn-mawr	GB	4	H6
Cegléd	H	77	C7
Ceglie Messapica	I	31	B10
Čegrane	MK	82	G1
Cehegín	E	29	C9
Cehu Silvaniei	RO	77	C12
Čelákovice	CZ	41	D11
Celano	I	33	C7
Celanova	E	22	D3
Celaru	RO	83	C7
Celbridge	IRL	4	G2
Celje	SLO	39	F10
Celldömölk	H	76	C2
Celle	D	42	E5
Centelles	E	21	E10
Cento	I	35	D7
Centuripe	I	30	F5

Cepagatti	I	33	C8	Châteaudun	F	15	E10	Cholet	F	15	G7
Čepin	HR	76	F5	Châteaugiron	F	14	E6	Chomutov	CZ	41	C9
Ceprano	I	33	D7	Château-Gontier	F	15	F7	Chop	UA	73	G3
Cerașu	RO	78	G6	Châteaulin	F	14	E3	Chora	GR	87	G9
Cerda	I	30	E4	Châteaurenard	F	18	D5	Chora Sfakion	GR	89	G8
Cerdanyola del Vallès	E	21	F10	Château-Renault	F	15	F10	Chorley	GB	5	F7
Cerea	I	35	D7	Châteauroux	F	15	H11	Choszczno	PL	70	D4
Céret	F	18	F1	Château-Thierry	F	12	C4	Chotěboř	CZ	74	E5
Cerignola	I	31	A8	Châtelguyon	F	17	C10	Christchurch	GB	9	F7
Çerkezköy	TR	85	B4	Châtellerault	F	15	H9	Chrudim	CZ	74	D5
Cerknica	SLO	39	G9	Chatham	GB	9	E10	Chrysoupoli	GR	87	C10
Cernavodă	RO	84	B4	Châtillon-sur-Seine	F	12	F5	Chrzanów	PL	75	D10
Cernica	RO	83	B10	Chatteris	GB	9	C9	Chur	CH	37	D9
Cërrik	AL	86	C2	Chaumont	F	12	E6	Chynadiyeve	UA	73	G4
Certaldo	I	35	G7	Chauny	F	12	B4	Ciacova	RO	77	F9
Cervera	E	21	E8	Chauvigny	F	16	B6	Ciadîr-Lunga	MD	79	E10
Cerveteri	I	32	C5	Chaves	P	22	E4	Ciampino	I	32	D5
Cervia	I	35	E9	Cheadle	GB	5	H8	Cianciana	I	30	F3
Cervignano del Friuli	I	35	B11	Cheb	CZ	41	D8	Cicciano	I	30	B5
Cervo	E	22	A4	Chechel'nyk	UA	79	A11	Ćićevac	SRB	82	D2
Cesena	I	35	F9	Chełm	PL	73	B5	Ciechanów	PL	71	E11
Cesenatico	I	35	E9	Chełmno	PL	71	D8	Ciechocinek	PL	71	E8
Cēsis	LV	66	F6	Chelmsford	GB	9	D10	Ciempozuelos	E	26	D4
Česká Lípa	CZ	41	C11	Chełmża	PL	71	D8	Čierny Balog	SK	75	G11
České Budějovice	CZ	41	F11	Cheltenham	GB	8	D6	Cieszyn	PL	75	E9
Český Krumlov	CZ	39	A9	Chemillé	F	15	G7	Cieza	E	29	B10
Çeşme	TR	89	B11	Chemnitz	D	41	B9	Cill Airne	IRL	7	M3
Cesson-Sévigné	F	14	E6	Chenôve	F	12	G6	Cill Chainnigh	IRL	7	L5
Cestas	F	16	E3	Chepelare	BG	83	H7	Cill Mhantáin	IRL	4	H3
Cetate	RO	78	C3	Chepstow	GB	8	D5	Cimişlia	MD	79	D10
Cetate	RO	82	C5	Cherasco	I	19	B10	Ciney	B	10	H6
Cetinje	MNE	81	G8	Cherbourg-Octeville	F	14	B6	Cingoli	I	35	G11
Cetraro	I	31	D8	Chernyakhovsk	RUS	68	F4	Cinisello Balsamo	I	34	C4
Ceuta		28	G3	Cherven Bryag	BG	82	E6	Cinquefrondi	I	31	G8
Ceva	I	19	C10	Cheshunt	GB	9	D9	Cintruénigo	E	20	E3
Chabeuil	F	18	A5	Chester	GB	5	G7	Ciocăneşti	RO	83	B9
Chagny	F	12	H6	Chesterfield	GB	5	G8	Ciocăneşti	RO	83	C11
Chalandri	GR	89	B7	Chiajna	RO	83	B10	Ciorani	RO	78	H6
Chalastra	GR	87	D7	Chianciano Terme	I	32	A4	Cirencester	GB	8	D6
Chalford	GB	8	D6	Chiaramonte Gulfi	I	30	G5	Cirò	I	31	E9
Chalki	GR	88	G3	Chiaravalle	I	35	G11	Cirò Marina	I	31	E10
Chalkida	GR	89	B7	Chiaravalle Centrale	I	31	F8	Cisláu	RO	78	G6
Challans	F	14	H6	Chiari	I	34	C5	Cisnădie	RO	78	F3
Chalonnes-sur-Loire	F	15	G7	Chiavenno	I	34	A4	Cisterna di Latina	I	32	D6
Châlons-en-Champagne	F	12	D5	Chichester	GB	9	F8	Cisternino	I	31	B10
Chalon-sur-Saône	F	12	H6	Chiclana de la Frontera	E	25	M7	Cistierna	E	23	C8
Cham	D	41	F8	Chieti	I	33	C8	Città della Pieve	I	32	A4
Chamalières	F	17	C10	Chingford	GB	9	D9	Città di Castello	I	35	G9
Chambéry	F	36	G3	Chinon	F	15	G9	Cittanova	I	31	G8
Chambourcy	F	15	D11	Chioggia	I	35	C9	Città Sant'Angelo	I	33	B8
Chamonix-Mont-Blanc	F	36	F5	Chiojdu	RO	78	G6	Ciudad Real	E	26	G4
Champagnole	F	13	H7	Chios	GR	85	H1	Ciudad Rodrigo	E	22	G6
Champ-sur-Drac	F	18	A6	Chipiona	E	25	L6	Ciupercenii Noi	RO	82	C5
Changé	F	15	F9	Chippenham	GB	8	E6	Ciutadella	E	29	E11
Chania	GR	89	F8	Chipping Norton	GB	9	D7	Cividale del Friuli	I	35	B11
Chantada	E	22	G4	Chipping Sodbury	GB	8	E6	Civita Castellana	I	32	C5
Chantilly	F	12	C2	Chirnogi	RO	83	C11	Civitanova Marche	I	35	G12
Chantonnay	F	16	B3	Chirpan	BG	83	G9	Civitavecchia	I	32	C4
Chapeltown	GB	5	G8	Chiscani	RO	79	G9	Civitella del Tronto	I	33	B7
Chard	GB	8	F5	Chişinău	MD	79	C10	Civitella in Val di Chiana	I	35	G8
Charleroi	B	10	G5	Chişineu-Criş	RO	77	D10	Clacton-on-Sea	GB	9	D11
Charleville-Mézières	F	12	B6	Chitila	RO	83	B10	Clamecy	F	12	G4
Charlieu	F	17	C11	Chiusi	I	32	A4	Cleator Moor	GB	4	D6
Charly	F	12	D4	Chiva	E	27	F9	Cleethorpes	GB	5	F10
Charmes	F	13	E8	Chivasso	I	19	A10	Cleja	RO	79	E7
Chartres	F	12	E1	Chocianów	PL	70	H5	Cléon	F	15	C10
Château-Arnoux	F	18	C6	Chodzież	PL	70	E6	Clermont	F	12	C2
Châteaubriant	F	15	F7	Chojna	PL	43	E11	Clermont-Ferrand	F	17	C10
Château-d'Olonne	F	16	B2	Chojnice	PL	71	C7	Clermont-l'Hérault	F	17	H10
Château-du-Loir	F	15	F9	Chojnów	PL	74	B5	Cles	I	37	E11

C

C

Cuenca	E	27	E7	Dărmănești	RO	78	B6	Detva	SK	75	G10
Cuers	F	19	E7	Dărmănești	RO	78	E6	Deutschlandsberg	A	39	E10
Cuevas de Almanzora	E	29	D9	Dărmănești	RO	78	H5	Deva	RO	77	F12
Cugir	RO	78	F1	Darmstadt	D	13	B11	Dévaványa	H	77	C9
Cugnaux	F	17	H7	Darque	P	22	E2	Devecser	H	76	C3
Cuijk	NL	11	E7	Dartford	GB	9	E10	Deventer	NL	11	D8
Cúllar-Baza	E	29	D8	Dartmouth	GB	8	G4	Devin	BG	83	H7
Cullera	E	27	F10	Daruvar	HR	76	F3	Devizes	GB	8	E6
Cullompton	GB	8	F4	Dassel	D	42	G5	Devnya	BG	83	E12
Cumbernauld	GB	2	G5	Datça	TR	88	F3	Dewsbury	GB	5	F8
Cumnock	GB	4	C5	Daugavpils	LV	69	D10	Diamante	I	31	D7
Cumpăna	RO	84	C4	Daventry	GB	9	C8	Diano Marina	I	19	C10
Cuneo	I	19	C9	Davoli	I	31	F8	Didcot	GB	9	D7
Cuorgnè	I	34	C1	Davos	CH	37	D9	Didymoteicho	GR	85	B2
Cupar	GB	3	G7	Davutlar	TR	88	D2	Diekirch	L	13	B8
Cupcina	MD	79	A8	Dawlish	GB	8	G4	Diepholz	D	11	C11
Ćuprija	SRB	82	C2	Dax	F	16	G3	Dieppe	F	9	H11
Curcani	RO	83	C11	Deal	GB	9	E11	Dietikon	CH	13	G11
Curinga	I	31	F8	Debar	MK	86	B3	Digne-les-Bains	F	19	C7
Curtea de Argeș	RO	78	G3	Debeljača	SRB	77	G8	Digoin	F	17	B11
Curtici	RO	77	E9	Dębica	PL	73	D2	Dijon	F	12	G6
Čurug	SRB	77	G7	Dęblin	PL	72	H4	Dikili	TR	85	F2
Cusset	F	17	C10	Dębno	PL	43	E11	Dilbeek	B	10	F5
Cutro	I	31	E9	Debrecen	H	77	B10	Dimitrovgrad	BG	83	G9
Cutrofiano	I	31	C11	Debrzno	PL	70	D6	Dimitrovgrad	SRB	82	E4
Cuxhaven	D	42	C4	Decazeville	F	17	F8	Dinan	F	14	E6
Cwmbrân	GB	8	D5	Děčín	CZ	41	C11	Dinard	F	14	D6
Czaplinek	PL	70	D5	Decize	F	12	H4	Dingolfing	D	38	B6
Czarna Białostocka	PL	72	D5	Dedemsvaart	NL	11	C8	Dingwall	GB	2	D5
Czarne	PL	70	C6	Dedovichi	RUS	67	F12	Dinkelsbühl	D	40	F5
Czarnków	PL	70	E6	Degerfors	S	46	C5	Dinklage	D	11	C11
Czersk	PL	71	C7	Deggendorf	D	39	A7	Diosig	RO	77	C11
Czerwionka-Leszczyny	PL	75	D9	De Haan	B	10	F3	Dippoldiswalde	D	41	B10
Częstochowa	PL	75	B10	Deinze	B	10	F4	Diss	GB	9	C11
Człuchów	PL	71	C7	Dej	RO	78	C2	Ditrău	RO	78	D5
				Delčevo	MK	82	G4	Dives-sur-Mer	F	15	C8
				Delémont	CH	13	G9	Djurås	S	52	G3

D

				Deleni	RO	79	C7	Dnestrovsc	MD	79	D12
				Delft	NL	10	D5	Dno	RUS	67	E12
Dabas	H	76	C6	Delfzijl	NL	11	A9	Dobanovci	SRB	81	B11
Dąbrowa Białostocka	PL	68	H6	Delia	I	30	F4	Dobczyce	PL	75	D11
Dąbrowa Górnicza	PL	75	C10	Delle	F	13	F9	Dobele	LV	66	H4
Dąbrowa Tarnowska	PL	73	D2	Delmenhorst	D	11	B11	Döbeln	D	41	B9
Dăbuleni	RO	82	D6	Delsbo	S	52	D4	Doberlug-Kirchhain	D	43	G10
Dachau	D	37	A11	Deltebre	E	21	G8	Doboj	BIH	81	B7
Dačice	CZ	74	F5	Delvinë	AL	86	E3	Dobre Miasto	PL	68	G2
Dafni	GR	89	B7	Demirci	TR	85	F5	Dobreşti	RO	77	D11
Daimiel	E	26	G5	Demir Hisar	MK	86	C4	Dobrich	BG	84	D3
Đakovo	HR	76	G5	Demirköy	TR	84	G3	Dobříš	CZ	41	E11
Dalarö	S	47	C10	Demmin	D	43	C9	Dobrotești	RO	83	C8
Dalby	S	45	E8	Denbigh	GB	4	G6	Dobruška	CZ	74	D6
Dalj	HR	76	G5	Den Burg	NL	10	B6	Doetinchem	NL	11	D8
Dalkeith	GB	3	H7	Dendermonde	B	10	F5	Dofteana	RO	78	E7
Dalmine	I	34	C5	Den Haag	NL	10	D5	Dokkum	NL	11	A7
Dalsbruk	FIN	53	H11	Den Helder	NL	10	B6	Dokshytsy	BY	69	F11
Dalton-in-Furness	GB	4	E6	Denia	E	27	G11	Doksy	CZ	41	C11
Damme	B	10	F4	Denny	GB	2	G5	Dole	F	13	G7
Damme	D	11	C11	Densburen	CH	13	G10	Dolhasca	RO	79	C7
Damwoude	NL	11	B8	Déols	F	15	H11	Dolianova	I	32	G3
Daneţi	RO	82	C6	Derby	GB	5	H8	Dolni Chiflik	BG	84	E3
Dannenberg (Elbe)	D	43	D7	Derecske	H	77	C10	Dolni Dŭbnik	BG	83	D7
Darabani	RO	79	A7	Dereham	GB	9	B11	Dolný Kubín	SK	75	F10
Dărăşti Ilfov	RO	83	C10	Derry	GB	4	D1	Dolyna	UA	73	F6
Dar Ben Karricha el Behri	MA	28	H3	Dersca	RO	78	B6	Domat Ems	CH	37	D8
Dar Chaoui	MA	28	H3	Derventa	BIH	76	H4	Domažlice	CZ	41	E9
Darda	HR	76	F5	Descartes	F	15	H10	Dombås	N	50	D6
Dardilly	F	36	F2	Dessau	D	43	G8	Dombóvár	H	76	E4
Darfo Boario Terme	I	34	B6	Deta	RO	77	G9	Domérat	F	17	B9
Darlington	GB	5	D8	Detmold	D	11	D12	Domnești	RO	83	B10
Darłowo	PL	45	H12	Dettelbach	D	40	D5	Domodossola	I	34	B3

D

Dömsöd	H	76	C6	Dubrovnik	HR	81	G7	Eberndorf	A	39	F9
Domusnovas	I	32	G6	Dudestii Vechi	RO	77	E8	Ebersbach	D	41	B11
Domžale	SLO	39	G9	Dudley	GB	8	C6	Eberswalde-Finow	D	43	E10
Donaghadee	GB	4	D3	Dueville	I	35	C8	Eboli	I	30	B6
Don Benito	E	24	E7	Duga Resa	HR	39	H11	Écija	E	28	D4
Doncaster	GB	5	F9	Dugo Selo	HR	39	G12	Ečka	SRB	77	G8
Donduşeni	MD	79	A8	Dülgopol	BG	83	E12	Eckernförde	D	42	B5
Donji Miholjac	HR	76	F4	Dulovo	BG	83	C12	Eckington	GB	5	G9
Donji Vakuf	BIH	80	D6	Dumbarton	GB	2	G5	Edelény	H	73	H1
Donostia-San Sebastián	E	20	B3	Dumbrava Roşie	RO	78	D6	Edemissen	D	42	F6
Đorče Petrov	MK	82	G2	Dumbrăveni	RO	78	B6	Edessa	GR	86	C6
Dorchester	GB	8	F6	Dumbrăveni	RO	78	E3	Edinburgh	GB	2	G6
Dordrecht	NL	10	E6	Dumfries	GB	4	C6	Edincik	TR	85	D4
Dorgali	I	32	E3	Dumitreşti	RO	79	F7	Edineţ	MD	79	A8
Dorking	GB	9	E9	Dumnicë e Poshtme	RKS	82	E2	Edirne	TR	83	H11
Dormagen	D	11	F9	Dunaföldvár	H	76	D5	Edland	N	48	C4
Dor Mărunt	RO	83	B11	Dunaharaszti	H	76	C6	Edremit	TR	85	E3
Dornbirn	A	37	C9	Dunajská Streda	SK	76	B3	Eforie	RO	84	C5
Dorog	H	76	B5	Dunakeszi	H	76	B6	Eger	H	77	B8
Dorohoi	RO	78	B6	Dunaújváros	H	76	D5	Egersund	N	48	F3
Dorsten	D	11	E9	Dunavarsány	H	76	C6	Eggesin	D	43	C10
Dortmund	D	11	E10	Dunbar	GB	3	G7	Eghezée	B	10	G6
Dörverden	D	11	B12	Dunblane	GB	2	G5	Egremont	GB	4	E6
Dos Hermanas	E	25	K7	Dundalk	IRL	4	E2	Éguilles	F	18	D5
Douarnenez	F	14	E2	Dun Dealgan	IRL	4	E2	Egyek	H	77	B9
Doué-la-Fontaine	F	15	G8	Dundee	GB	3	F7	Ehingen (Donau)	D	37	A9
Douglas	GBM	4	E5	Dunfermline	GB	2	G6	Eibar	E	20	B2
Douvaine	F	36	E4	Dungannon	GB	4	D2	Eibenstock	D	41	C8
Dover	GB	9	E11	Dún Garbhán	IRL	7	M5	Eibergen	NL	11	D8
Dovhe	UA	73	H5	Dungarvan	IRL	7	M5	Eichstätt	D	38	A4
Downham Market	GB	9	B10	Dunkerque	F	10	F2	Eidet	N	54	F6
Downpatrick	GB	4	E3	Dún Laoghaire	IRL	4	G3	Eidsbugarden	N	50	F5
Drachten	NL	11	B8	Dunmurry	GB	4	D3	Eilenburg	D	41	A8
Dragalina	RO	83	B12	Dunoon	GB	2	G4	Einbeck	D	42	G5
Drăgăneşti	RO	78	H6	Dunstable	GB	9	D8	Eindhoven	NL	11	E7
Drăgăneşti	RO	79	F8	Dupnitsa	BG	82	G5	Einsiedeln	CH	13	G11
Drăgăneşti-Olt	RO	83	C7	Durango	E	20	B2	Eisenach	D	40	B5
Drăgăneşti-Vlaşca	RO	83	C9	Durban-Corbières	F	18	E1	Eisenberg	D	41	B7
Drăgăşani	RO	83	B7	Dúrcal	E	28	E6	Eisenerz	A	39	D10
Dragør	DK	45	F7	Đurđevac	HR	76	E2	Eisenhüttenstadt	D	43	F11
Draguignan	F	19	D7	Düren	D	11	G8	Eisenstadt	A	76	B1
Drajna	RO	78	G6	Durham	GB	5	D8	Eivissa	E	29	G7
Drama	GR	87	C9	Durlas	IRL	7	L5	Ejea de los Caballeros	E	20	D4
Drammen	N	49	C7	Durleşti	MD	79	C10	Ekenäs	FIN	64	G4
Dravograd	SLO	39	F10	Durrës	AL	86	B1	Ekerö	S	47	C9
Drawsko Pomorskie	PL	70	D5	Dursley	GB	8	D6	Eksjö	S	45	A10
Dresden	D	41	B10	Dursunbey	TR	85	E5	Elassona	GR	86	E6
Dreux	F	12	D1	Düsseldorf	D	11	F9	El Astillero	E	23	B10
Drevsjø	N	51	E9	Dve Mogili	BG	83	D9	Elbasan	AL	86	C2
Drezdenko	PL	70	E5	Dvůr Králové	CZ	74	C5	Elbeuf	F	15	C10
Dridu	RO	83	B10	Dyce	GB	3	E8	Elbląg	PL	71	B9
Driffield	GB	5	E10	Dynów	PL	73	E3	El Burgo de Osma	E	20	F1
Drniš	HR	80	D4	Dzhebel	BG	87	B11	Elche-Elx	E	29	B11
Drobeta-Turnu Severin	RO	82	B4	Działdowo	PL	71	D10	Elda	E	27	H9
Drochia	MD	79	A9	Dzierzgoń	PL	71	C9	Elefsina	GR	89	B7
Drogheda	IRL	4	F2	Dzyarzhynsk	BY	69	H10	El Ejido	E	29	E7
Drohobych	UA	73	F5					Elek	H	77	D9
Droichead Átha	IRL	4	F2					Elektrėnai	LT	69	F7
Droichead Nua	IRL	4	G2					Elena	BG	83	E9
Droitwich Spa	GB	8	C6	**E**				El Escorial	E	23	H10
Dronero	I	19	B9					El Espinar	E	23	G9
Dronfield	GB	5	G8	Eastbourne	GB	9	F10	El Fendek	MA	28	H3
Dronten	NL	11	C7	Eastfield	GB	5	E10	Elgin	GB	2	D6
Druskininkai	LT	69	G7	East Grinstead	GB	9	E9	Elin Pelin	BG	82	F6
Dryanovo	BG	83	E9	East Kilbride	GB	2	H5	Elizondo	E	20	B4
Dryna	N	50	C3	Eastleigh	GB	9	F7	Ełk	PL	68	H4
Dubăsari	MD	79	C11	East Wittering	GB	9	F8	Elkhovo	BG	83	G11
Dublin	IRL	4	G2	Ebbw Vale	GB	8	D5	Elland	GB	5	F8
Dublyany	UA	73	E6	Ebensee	A	39	C8	Ellesmere Port	GB	5	G7
Dubove	UA	78	A2	Ebensfeld	D	40	D6	Ellon	GB	3	E8
				Ebenthal	A	39	F9				

Ellös	S	46	E2
Ellwangen (Jagst)	D	40	F5
Elmshorn	D	42	C5
Elne	F	18	F1
Elos	GR	89	G7
El Prat de Llobregat	E	21	F10
El Puerto de Santa María	E	25	L7
Elsdorf	D	11	F8
El Serrat	AND	21	C9
Elsterwerda	D	41	A10
Eltmann	D	40	D6
Elva	EST	67	E8
Elvas	P	24	F5
El Vendrell	E	21	F9
Elverum	N	51	G9
Ely	GB	9	C10
Embrun	F	19	B7
Emden	D	11	A9
Emmaboda	S	45	C11
Emmen	NL	11	C9
Emőd	H	77	B9
Empoli	I	35	F7
Emsbüren	D	11	C9
Encamp	AND	21	C9
Encs	H	73	H2
Engan	N	54	B5
Enköping	S	47	B8
Enna	I	30	F4
Ennigerloh	D	11	D10
Ennis	IRL	7	K3
Enniscorthy	IRL	7	L6
Enniskillen	GB	6	F5
Enns	A	39	B9
Enschede	NL	11	D9
Entroncamento	P	24	D3
Enying	H	76	D4
Eochaill	IRL	7	M5
Epe	NL	11	C7
Épernay	F	12	C5
Épinal	F	13	E8
Epsom	GB	9	E9
Eraclea	I	35	C10
Erbach	D	38	B2
Erbach	D	38	B3
Erbiceni	RO	79	C8
Erchie	I	31	C11
Ercsi	H	76	C5
Érd	H	76	C5
Erdek	TR	85	D4
Erfurt	D	40	B6
Ergué-Gabéric	F	14	F3
Erice	I	30	E2
Erkelenz	D	11	F8
Erkner	D	43	F10
Erlangen	D	40	E6
Ermesinde	P	22	F2
Ermioni	GR	88	D6
Ermoupoli	GR	89	D9
Ermua	E	20	B2
Ernée	F	15	E7
Ernei	RO	78	D3
Errenteria	E	20	B3
Erritsø	DK	44	F3
Ersekë	AL	86	D3
Esbjerg	DK	44	F2
Esbo	FIN	64	G5
Eschwege	D	40	B5
Escombreras	E	29	D11
Esens	D	42	C2
Eskilstuna	S	47	C8
Eslohe (Sauerland)	D	11	F11
Eslöv	S	45	E8
Esneux	B	11	G7
Espalion	F	17	F9
Esparreguera	E	21	F9
Espergærde	DK	45	E7
Espezel	F	21	C10
Espinho	P	22	G2
Espoo	FIN	64	G5
Essen	B	10	E5
Essen	D	11	E9
Essenbach	D	38	B6
Esslingen am Neckar	D	38	A2
Este	I	35	C8
Estella	E	20	C3
Estepa	E	28	D4
Estepona	E	28	F4
Estoril	P	24	F1
Estremoz	P	24	F4
Esztergom	H	76	B5
Étampes	F	12	E2
Étaples	F	9	G12
Etropole	BG	82	E6
Eu	F	9	H11
Eupen	B	11	G8
Eura	FIN	53	F10
Euskirchen	D	11	G9
Eutin	D	42	B6
Evdilos	GR	89	C11
Evesham	GB	8	D6
Évian-les-Bains	F	36	E4
Evje	N	48	F5
Évora	P	24	F4
Evosmos	GR	87	D7
Évreux	F	15	C10
Évron	F	15	E8
Évry	F	12	D2
Exeter	GB	8	F4
Exmouth	GB	8	F4
Exochi	GR	87	B9
Eyguières	F	18	D5
Ezine	TR	85	E2
Ézy-sur-Eure	F	12	D1

F

Faaborg	DK	44	G4
Fabero	E	22	C5
Fabrègues	F	17	H11
Fabriano	I	35	G10
Fabrica di Roma	I	32	C5
Făcăeni	RO	84	B3
Faenza	I	35	E8
Fafe	P	22	F3
Făgăraş	RO	78	F4
Fagernes	N	50	F6
Fagersta	S	47	B7
Făget	RO	77	F11
Fagnano Castello	I	31	D8
Fagnières	F	12	D5
Fakenham	GB	9	B10
Falaise	F	15	D8
Fălciu	RO	79	E9
Falconara Marittima	I	35	F11
Făleşti	MD	79	B9
Falkenberg	D	43	G9
Falkenberg	S	44	C7
Falkirk	GB	2	G6
Falköping	S	46	E4
Fallingbostel	D	42	E5
Falmouth	GB	8	G2
Fălticeni	RO	78	C6
Falun	S	52	G3
Fano	I	35	F10
Fântânele	RO	78	E4
Fara in Sabina	I	32	C6
Faringdon	GB	9	D7
Farnham	GB	9	E8
Faro	P	25	K4
Fårösund	S	47	F10
Farsala	GR	86	F6
Farsund	N	48	G3
Fărţăneşti	RO	79	F9
Fasano	I	31	B10
Fátima	P	24	D3
Fauske	N	57	F3
Fåvang	N	51	E7
Favara	I	30	F3
Faverges	F	36	F4
Faversham	GB	9	E10
Fawley	GB	9	F7
Fayence	F	19	D8
Fazeley	GB	9	B7
Fécamp	F	15	B9
Fegersheim	F	13	E10
Fegyvernek	H	77	C8
Fehérgyarmat	H	77	B11
Felanitx	E	29	F10
Feldioara	RO	78	F5
Feldkirch	A	37	C9
Feldkirchen in Kärnten	A	39	E8
Feldru	RO	78	C3
Felixstowe	GB	9	D11
Felsőzsolca	H	73	H1
Feltre	I	35	B9
Fene	E	22	B3
Feolin Ferry	GB	2	H3
Ferentino	I	32	D6
Ferizaj	RKS	81	G12
Ferlach	A	39	F9
Fermignano	I	35	G10
Fermo	I	35	H12
Fernán Núñez	E	28	D4
Ferney-Voltaire	F	36	E4
Ferrandina	I	31	C8
Ferrara	I	35	D8
Ferrol	E	22	B3
Ferryhill	GB	5	D8
Feteşti	RO	84	B3
Feteşti-Gară	RO	84	B3
Fetsund	N	46	B2
Feuchtwangen	D	40	F5
Feytiat	F	17	C7
Ffestiniog	GB	4	H5
Fiano Romano	I	32	C5
Ficarazzi	I	30	E3
Fidenza	I	34	D5
Fieni	RO	78	G5
Fier	AL	86	D2
Fiesole	I	35	F7
Figeac	F	17	F8
Figline Valdarno	I	35	G8
Figueira da Foz	P	24	B2
Figueres	E	18	G1
Filadelfia	I	31	F8
Fiľakovo	SK	75	H11
Filey	GB	5	E10
Filiaşi	RO	82	B6
Filipeştii de Pădure	RO	78	H5

Filipstad	S	46	B5
Filottrano	I	35	G11
Finale Emilia	I	35	D8
Finale Ligure	I	19	C10
Finkenstein	A	39	F8
Finspång	S	47	D7
Finsterwalde	D	43	G10
Fionnphort	GB	2	G2
Fiorenzuola d'Arda	I	34	D5
Firenze	I	35	F7
Fishguard	GB	8	D2
Fisksätra	S	47	C9
Fismes	F	12	C4
Fisterra	E	22	C1
Fiuggi	I	32	D6
Fiumefreddo di Sicilia	I	30	E6
Fivizzano	I	34	E6
Flåmânzi	RO	79	B7
Fleet	GB	9	E8
Fleetwood	GB	4	F6
Flekkefjord	N	48	F3
Flen	S	47	D8
Flensburg	D	44	G3
Flers	F	15	D8
Fleurance	F	16	G6
Flint	GB	4	G6
Flix	E	21	F7
Floda	S	44	A7
Flöha	D	41	B9
Floirac	F	16	E4
Florence	I	35	F7
Florenville	B	13	B7
Floreşti	MD	79	B10
Floreşti	RO	78	D2
Floreşti-Stoeneşti	RO	83	B9
Floridia	I	30	G6
Florina	GR	86	D5
Florø	N	50	E1
Flötningen	S	51	E9
Foča	BIH	81	E8
Foça	TR	85	G2
Focşani	RO	79	F8
Focuri	RO	79	C8
Foggia	I	33	D10
Fohnsdorf	A	39	D9
Foix	F	21	C9
Folignano	I	33	B7
Foligno	I	32	A6
Folkestone	GB	9	F11
Folldal	N	51	D7
Follonica	I	32	A2
Fondevila	E	22	E3
Fondi	I	33	E7
Fonsorbes	F	17	H7
Fontaine	F	18	A6
Fontainebleau	F	12	E3
Fontaine le Comte	F	16	B5
Fontanellato	I	34	D6
Fontenay-le-Comte	F	16	B3
Fonyód	H	76	D3
Forăşti	RO	78	C6
Forcalquier	F	18	C6
Forchheim	D	40	E6
Førde	N	50	E2
Fordingbridge	GB	9	F7
Forfar	GB	3	F7
Forio	I	30	B4
Forlì	I	35	E9
Forlimpopoli	I	35	F9
Formby	GB	4	F6

Formello	I	32	C5
Formia	I	30	A4
Formofoss	N	54	F5
Forres	GB	2	D6
Fors	S	52	B4
Forsand	N	48	E3
Forshaga	S	46	C4
Forsmark	S	52	G6
Forsnes	N	50	A5
Forssa	FIN	53	F12
Forst	D	43	G11
Fortuna	E	29	C10
Fort William	GB	2	F4
Fosnavåg	N	50	D2
Fossano	I	19	B9
Fossombrone	I	35	G10
Fót	H	76	B6
Fougères	F	15	E7
Fourmies	F	12	A5
Fourna	GR	86	G5
Fournoi	GR	89	C12
Foz	E	22	B4
Fraga	E	21	F7
Fragagnano	I	31	C10
Francavilla al Mare	I	33	B8
Francavilla di Sicilia	I	30	E6
Francavilla Fontana	I	31	B10
Frânceşti	RO	78	G3
Francofonte	I	30	F5
Frankenberg (Eder)	D	11	F11
Frankfurt am Main	D	11	H11
Frankfurt an der Oder	D	43	F11
Frascati	I	32	D5
Fraserburgh	GB	3	D8
Frasin	RO	78	B5
Frastanz	A	37	C9
Frăteşti	RO	83	C10
Frauenfeld	CH	13	F12
Fredensborg	DK	44	E7
Fredericia	DK	44	F3
Frederiksberg	DK	44	E7
Frederikshavn	DK	44	B4
Frederikssund	DK	44	E6
Frederiksværk	DK	44	E6
Fredrika	S	55	F11
Fredrikstad	N	46	C1
Fregenal de la Sierra	E	24	G6
Freiberg	D	41	B9
Freiburg im Breisgau	D	13	E10
Freilassing	D	39	C7
Freising	D	38	B5
Freistadt	A	39	B9
Freital	D	41	B10
Fréjus	F	19	D8
Freudenstadt	D	13	E11
Freyung	D	39	A8
Fribourg	CH	13	H9
Friedberg	D	38	B4
Friedland	D	43	C10
Friesach	A	39	E9
Friesoythe	D	11	B10
Friitala	FIN	53	E10
Frinton-on-Sea	GB	9	D11
Friol	E	22	C4
Friville-Escarbotin	F	9	H11
Frohnleiten	A	39	D10
Frome	GB	8	E6
Frontignan	F	18	D3
Frosinone	I	33	D7
Frumuşica	RO	79	B7

Frumuşiţa	RO	79	F9
Frunzivka	UA	79	C12
Frutigen	CH	36	E6
Frýdek-Místek	CZ	75	E9
Fucecchio	I	35	F7
Fuengirola	E	28	F4
Fuenlabrada	E	26	D4
Fuensalida	E	26	E3
Fuente de Cantos	E	24	G6
Fuente del Maestre	E	24	F6
Fuente Obejuna	E	24	G8
Fuentes de Andalucía	E	25	J8
Fuglafjørður	FO	3	B9
Fulda	D	40	C4
Fumay	F	12	B6
Fumel	F	16	F6
Fundão	P	24	B5
Fundeni	RO	83	B10
Fundulea	RO	83	B11
Fürstenau	D	11	C10
Fürstenberg	D	43	D9
Fürstenfeld	A	39	E11
Fürstenfeldbruck	D	37	A11
Fürstenzell	D	39	B7
Fürth	D	40	E6
Furudal	S	52	F3
Furusund	S	47	B10
Fuscaldo	I	31	E8
Fushë Kosovë	RKS	81	G12
Fushë-Krujë	AL	86	B2
Füssen	D	37	C10
Futog	SRB	77	G7
Füzesabony	H	77	B8
Füzesgyarmat	H	77	C9

G

Gabicce Mare	I	35	F10
Gabrovo	BG	83	E9
Gadebusch	D	43	C7
Găeşti	RO	83	B9
Gaeta	I	30	A4
Gafanha da Nazaré	P	22	G2
Gagliano del Capo	I	31	D12
Gagnef	S	52	G3
Gaildorf	D	40	F4
Gaillac	F	17	G8
Gaillimh	IRL	7	J3
Gaillon	F	15	C10
Gainsborough	GB	5	G9
Găiseni	RO	83	B9
Gălăneşti	RO	78	B5
Galanta	SK	75	H8
Galashiels	GB	5	B7
Galata	BG	84	E3
Galaţi	RO	79	G9
Galatina	I	31	C11
Galatone	I	31	C11
Gălăău	RO	83	B12
Galicea Mare	RO	82	C5
Gallardon	F	12	D1
Gallipoli	I	31	C11
Gällivare	S	60	D3
Galston	GB	4	B5
Galway	IRL	7	J3
Gamleby	S	47	F7
Gammelstaden	S	56	C4
Gand	B	10	F4
Gandía	E	27	G10

G

Ganges	F	17	G11
Gangi	I	30	E4
Gannat	F	17	C10
Gap	F	19	B7
Garbsen	D	42	F5
Garching an der Alz	D	38	C6
Gardanne	F	18	D6
Gardelegen	D	43	E7
Gardone Val Trompia	I	34	C6
Gárdony	H	76	C5
Gåre	N	51	B8
Garforth	GB	5	F9
Gargalianoi	GR	88	D4
Gargždai	LT	68	D3
Gârla Mare	RO	82	C4
Gârleni	RO	79	D7
Garliava	LT	68	F6
Garmisch-Partenkirchen	D	37	C11
Garrel	D	11	B10
Garstang	GB	5	F7
Garwolin	PL	72	G3
Gata de Gorgos	E	27	G11
Gătaia	RO	77	G10
Gatchina	RUS	67	B12
Gateshead	GB	5	D8
Gattinara	I	34	C3
Gauchy	F	12	B4
Gaupne	N	50	E4
Gävle	S	52	G5
Gavrio	GR	89	C9
Gdańsk	PL	71	B8
Gdov	RUS	67	D9
Gdynia	PL	71	B8
Gedser	DK	43	A8
Geel	B	10	F6
Geeste	D	11	C9
Geesthacht	D	42	D6
Geilo	N	48	B5
Geisnes	N	54	E4
Gela	I	30	G4
Geldern	D	11	E8
Geleen	NL	11	F7
Gelibolu	TR	85	D2
Gelnica	SK	73	G2
Gelting	D	37	B11
Gémenos	F	18	E6
Gemert	NL	11	E7
Gemona del Friuli	I	35	A11
General Toshevo	BG	84	D4
Genève	CH	36	E4
Genk	B	11	F7
Genova	I	19	B11
Gent	B	10	F4
Genthin	D	43	F8
Genzano di Lucania	I	31	B8
Genzano di Roma	I	32	D5
Geoagiu	RO	77	F12
Gera	D	41	B8
Germersheim	D	13	C11
Gernika-Lumo	E	20	B2
Gerona	E	18	G1
Gerwisch	D	43	F8
Gerzat	F	17	C10
Gescher	D	11	D9
Geta	FIN	53	G8
Getafe	E	26	D4
Gevgelija	MK	87	C6
Gex	F	36	E4
Gheorgheni	RO	78	D5
Gherla	RO	78	C2
Ghidigeni	RO	79	E8
Ghimeş-Făget	RO	78	D6
Ghimpaţi	RO	83	C9
Ghindari	RO	78	E4
Giannitsa	GR	86	D6
Giardini-Naxos	I	30	E6
Giarmata	RO	77	F9
Giarre	I	30	E6
Gibellina Nuova	I	30	E2
Gibraleón	E	25	J5
Gibraltar	GBZ	28	G3
Gien	F	12	F3
Gießen	D	11	G11
Gifhorn	D	42	F6
Gijón-Xixón	E	23	B7
Gilău	RO	78	D1
Gillingham	GB	8	F6
Gillingham	GB	9	E10
Ginosa	I	31	B9
Gioia del Colle	I	31	B9
Gioia Tauro	I	31	G8
Gioiosa Ionica	I	31	G8
Gioiosa Marea	I	30	E5
Giovinazzo	I	31	A9
Girifalco	I	31	F8
Girişu de Criş	RO	77	C10
Giromagny	F	13	F9
Girona	E	18	G1
Gironella	E	21	E9
Girov	RO	78	D7
Girvan	GB	4	C4
Gislaved	S	45	B8
Gisors	F	12	C1
Gistel	B	10	F3
Giubiasco	CH	34	B4
Giugliano in Campania	I	30	B5
Giulianova	I	33	B8
Giurgiu	RO	83	C10
Givors	F	17	D12
Giżycko	PL	68	G4
Gjakovë	RKS	81	G11
Gjerstad	N	48	E6
Gjilan	RKS	82	F2
Gjirokastër	AL	86	E3
Gjøvik	N	49	A8
Gladsaxe	DK	44	E7
Glandorf	D	11	D9
Glarus	CH	37	D8
Glasgow	GB	2	H5
Glastonbury	GB	8	E5
Glein	N	54	B5
Gleisdorf	A	39	E11
Glenrothes	GB	2	G6
Glina	HR	76	G1
Glina	RO	83	B10
Gliwice	PL	75	D9
Gllamnik	RKS	81	F12
Glodeni	MD	79	B8
Gloggnitz	A	39	D11
Głogów	PL	70	G5
Glossa	GR	87	G8
Glossop	GB	5	G8
Gloucester	GB	8	D6
Głowno	PL	71	G10
Głubczyce	PL	75	D8
Głuchołazy	PL	75	C7
Glückstadt	D	42	C5
Glyfada	GR	89	C7
Gmünd	A	39	A10
Gnarrenburg	D	11	A12
Gniew	PL	71	C8
Gniewkowo	PL	71	E8
Gniezno	PL	71	F7
Goch	D	11	E8
Göd	H	76	B6
Godalming	GB	9	E8
Godech	BG	82	E5
Godmanchester	GB	9	C9
Gödöllő	H	76	B6
Goes	NL	10	E4
Gogoşu	RO	82	B4
Göhren, Ostseebad	D	43	B10
Goicea	RO	82	C6
Gökçeören	TR	85	G5
Gol	N	48	A6
Gołdap	PL	68	G4
Goleniów	PL	43	C11
Golfo Aranci	I	32	D3
Gölmarmara	TR	85	G4
Golub-Dobrzyń	PL	71	D9
Gondomar	P	22	F2
Gönen	TR	85	D4
Gonfreville-l'Orcher	F	15	B9
Gonnesa	I	32	G1
Goole	GB	5	F9
Goor	NL	11	D8
Göppingen	D	38	A2
Góra	PL	70	G6
Góra Kalwaria	PL	71	G11
Goražde	BIH	81	E8
Gördes	TR	85	G5
Gorebridge	GB	3	H7
Gorgota	RO	83	B10
Gorizia	I	35	B11
Gorlice	PL	73	E2
Görlitz	D	41	B12
Gorna Oryakhovitsa	BG	83	E9
Gorneşti	RO	78	D3
Gornja Radgona	SLO	39	F11
Gornji Milanovac	SRB	81	D11
Gorredijk	NL	11	B8
Gorseinon	GB	8	D3
Gorssel	NL	11	D8
Görükle	TR	85	D6
Gorzów Wielkopolski	PL	70	E4
Gosforth	GB	5	C8
Goslar	D	42	G6
Gospić	HR	80	C2
Gosport	GB	9	F8
Gostivar	MK	82	H1
Gostyń	PL	70	G6
Gostynin	PL	71	F9
Göteborg	S	44	A6
Götene	S	46	E4
Gotha	D	40	B6
Gothenburg	S	44	A6
Gotse Delchev	BG	87	B8
Göttingen	D	40	A5
Götzis	A	37	C9
Gouda	NL	10	D6
Gouesnou	F	14	E2
Grabow	D	43	D7
Grabs	CH	37	C8
Gračanica	BIH	81	B7
Gradačac	BIH	76	H5
Grădiştea	RO	83	C12
Grado	I	35	C11
Grado	E	22	B6
Grafenwöhr	D	41	E7
Gragnano	I	30	B5

G

Grajewo	PL	68	H5
Grammichele	I	30	F5
Gramsh	AL	86	C3
Granada	E	28	E6
Grândola	P	24	G3
Grangemouth	GB	2	G6
Granollers	E	21	E10
Gransee	D	43	D9
Grantham	GB	5	H9
Granville	F	14	D6
Grao	E	27	E11
Grassano	I	31	B8
Grasse	F	19	D8
Gratkorn	A	39	E10
Graulhet	F	17	G8
Gravelines	F	9	F12
Gravesend	GB	9	E10
Gravina di Catania	I	30	F6
Gravina in Puglia	I	31	B8
Gray	F	13	G7
Graz	A	39	E10
Grazzanise	I	30	A5
Great Dunmow	GB	9	D10
Great Gonerby	GB	5	H9
Great Malvern	GB	8	C6
Great Shelford	GB	9	C9
Great Torrington	GB	8	F3
Great Yarmouth	GB	9	C12
Grebănu	RO	79	G7
Greenisland	GB	4	D3
Greenock	GB	2	G4
Greifswald	D	43	B10
Grenaa	DK	44	D5
Grenade	F	17	G7
Grenchen	CH	13	G10
Grenoble	F	18	A6
Greve in Chianti	I	35	G8
Greven	D	11	D10
Grevena	GR	86	E5
Grevenmacher	L	13	B8
Greystones	IRL	4	G3
Grez-Doiceau	B	10	G6
Grigiškės	LT	69	F8
Grigoriopol	MD	79	C11
Grimma	D	41	B9
Grimmen	D	43	B9
Grimsby	GB	5	F10
Grimstad	N	48	F5
Grindsted	DK	44	E2
Grisslehamn	S	47	A10
Grivița	RO	83	B12
Grocka	SRB	81	C11
Grodków	PL	75	C7
Grodzisk Mazowiecki	PL	71	F11
Grodzisk Wielkopolski	PL	70	F5
Grójec	PL	71	G11
Grömitz	D	43	B7
Groningen	NL	11	B8
Großenhain	D	41	B10
Grosseto	I	32	B3
Grosuplje	SLO	39	G9
Grotli	N	50	D4
Grottaferrata	I	32	D5
Grottaglie	I	31	B10
Grottammare	I	33	A7
Grotte	I	30	F4
Grove	GB	9	D7
Grudziądz	PL	71	D8
Grumo Appula	I	31	A9
Grums	S	46	C4
Grünberg	D	11	G12
Grybów	PL	73	E2
Gryfice	PL	43	C12
Gryfino	PL	43	D11
Gryt	S	47	E8
Guadalajara	E	20	G1
Guadix	E	29	D7
Gualdo Cattaneo	I	32	B5
Gualdo Tadino	I	35	G10
Guarda	P	22	H4
Guardamar del Segura	E	29	C11
Guardavalle	I	31	F8
Guardiagrele	I	33	C8
Guardia Sanframondi	I	30	A5
Guardo	E	23	C8
Guareña	E	24	F7
Guastalla	I	34	D6
Gubbio	I	35	G10
Guben	D	43	G11
Gubin	PL	43	G11
Guénange	F	13	C8
Guer	F	14	F5
Guérande	F	14	G5
Guéret	F	17	C8
Gueugnon	F	17	B11
Gugești	RO	79	F8
Guglionesi	I	33	C9
Guichen	F	14	F6
Guidel	F	14	F4
Guidonia-Montecelio	I	32	C6
Guildford	GB	9	E8
Guillena	E	25	J7
Guimarães	P	22	F3
Guînes	F	9	F12
Guingamp	F	14	D4
Guipavas	F	14	E2
Guisborough	GB	5	D9
Guitiriz	E	22	B3
Gujan-Mestras	F	16	F3
Gulbene	LV	67	G8
Gullegem	B	10	F4
Gülübovo	BG	83	G9
Gunja	HR	76	H5
Günzburg	D	38	B3
Gunzenhausen	D	40	F6
Gura Humorului	RO	78	B5
Gurghiu	RO	78	D4
Gur'yevsk	RUS	68	F2
Gusev	RUS	68	F4
Guspini	I	32	G2
Gussago	I	34	C6
Gustavsberg	S	47	C10
Güstrow	D	43	C8
Gütersloh	D	11	D11
Gvardeysk	RUS	68	F3
Gvarv	N	48	D6
Gyál	H	76	C6
Gyomaendrőd	H	77	D8
Gyöngyös	H	77	B7
Győr	H	76	B3
Gytheio	GR	88	E5
Gyula	H	77	D9

H

Haaksbergen	NL	11	D9
Haapsalu	EST	66	C4
Haarlem	NL	10	C6
Habo	S	46	F5
Haddington	GB	3	G7
Haderslev	DK	44	F3
Hadımköy	TR	85	B5
Hadleigh	GB	9	D11
Hadsten	DK	44	D4
Hagen	D	11	E10
Hagenow	D	43	D7
Hagfors	S	46	B4
Hagsta	S	52	F5
Haguenau	F	13	D10
Hailsham	GB	9	F10
Hainburg an der Donau	A	75	H7
Hainichen	D	41	B9
Hajdúböszörmény	H	77	B10
Hajdúdorog	H	77	B10
Hajdúhadház	H	77	B10
Hajdúnánás	H	77	B10
Hajdúsámson	H	77	B10
Hajdúszoboszló	H	77	C9
Hajnówka	PL	72	E6
Hakkenpää	FIN	53	G10
Hălăucești	RO	79	C7
Halberstadt	D	43	G7
Hălchiu	RO	78	F5
Halden	N	46	C2
Haldensleben	D	43	F7
Halesowen	GB	8	C6
Halesworth	GB	9	C11
Halhjem	N	48	B2
Halifax	GB	5	F8
Hälla	S	55	G10
Halle	B	10	G5
Halle (Saale)	D	41	A7
Hällefors	S	46	B5
Hallein	A	39	D7
Hall in Tirol	A	37	C11
Hallsberg	S	46	D6
Hallstahammar	S	47	B7
Halmeu	RO	77	B12
Halmstad	S	45	C7
Halstead	GB	9	D10
Halstenbek	D	42	C5
Haltingen	D	13	F10
Ham	F	12	B3
Hamar	N	49	A8
Hamburg	D	42	C5
Hämeenlinna	FIN	64	E5
Hameln	D	11	D12
Hamilton	GB	2	H5
Hamina	FIN	65	F8
Hamm	D	11	E10
Hammel	DK	44	D3
Hammelburg	D	40	D4
Hammerdal	S	55	G8
Hammerfest	N	58	B6
Hamminkeln	D	11	E8
Hanau	D	13	A12
Hanko	FIN	64	H4
Hannover	D	42	F5
Hannut	B	10	G6
Hansnes	N	58	D3
Haparanda	S	56	B6
Harburg (Schwaben)	D	38	A4
Hard	A	37	C9
Hardenberg	NL	11	C8
Haren (Ems)	D	11	C9
Hargshamn	S	47	A10
Harjavalta	FIN	53	E10
Hârlău	RO	79	C7
Harlingen	NL	11	B7

Harlow	GB	9	D9	Helsingør	DK	45	E7	Holbæk	DK	44	E6				
Härnösand	S	52	C6	Helsinki	FIN	64	G6	Holbeach	GB	5	H10				
Haro	E	20	D2	Helston	GB	8	G2	Holboca	RO	79	C8				
Harpenden	GB	9	D9	Hemel Hempstead	GB	9	D9	Holešov	CZ	75	E8				
Harrislee	D	44	G3	Hemnesberget	N	54	B6	Holíč	SK	75	F7				
Harrogate	GB	5	F8	Hemsby	GB	9	B12	Holice	CZ	74	D5				
Hârşova	RO	84	B3	Hendaye	F	20	B3	Hollabrunn	A	39	B11				
Harstad	N	57	C4	Hengelo	NL	11	D9	Hollfeld	D	41	D7				
Harsum	D	42	F5	Henley-on-Thames	GB	9	E8	Hollola	FIN	64	E6				
Harsvik	N	54	F2	Hennebont	F	14	F4	Holmestrand	N	49	D7				
Hartberg	A	39	D11	Herborn	D	11	G11	Holmfirth	GB	5	F8				
Hartlepool	GB	5	D9	Herceg-Novi	MNE	81	G8	Holmsund	S	56	G2				
Harwich	GB	9	D11	Hereford	GB	8	D5	Holstebro	DK	44	D2				
Haselünne	D	11	C10	Herford	D	11	D11	Holyhead	GB	4	G4				
Haslemere	GB	9	F8	Herlev	DK	44	E7	Holywood	GB	4	D3				
Haslev	DK	44	F6	Hermagor	A	39	F7	Holzminden	D	11	D12				
Hasparren	F	20	B4	Hermsdorf	D	41	B7	Homocea	RO	79	E8				
Haspe	D	11	E10	Herne	B	10	G5	Hønefoss	N	49	B7				
Hassela	S	52	D4	Herning	DK	44	D2	Honfleur	F	15	C9				
Hasselt	B	11	F7	Hérouville-St-Clair	F	15	C8	Honiton	GB	8	F5				
Haßfurt	D	40	D5	Herrera	E	28	D4	Honley	GB	5	F8				
Hässleholm	S	45	D8	Hersbruck	D	41	E7	Hoofddorp	NL	10	C6				
Hastings	GB	9	F10	Hertford	GB	9	D9	Hook	GB	9	E8				
Hasvik	N	58	C5	Herzberg	D	43	G9	Höör	S	45	E8				
Haţeg	RO	77	F12	Hesdin	F	9	G12	Hoorn	NL	10	C6				
Hatfield	GB	5	F9	Hessigkofen	CH	13	G10	Hope	N	50	F2				
Hattem	NL	11	C8	Hessisch Lichtenau	D	40	B4	Hopsten	D	11	C10				
Hatvan	H	77	B7	Hettstadt	D	40	E4	Horaždovice	CZ	41	E10				
Haugesund	N	48	D2	Hettstedt	D	43	G7	Hörby	S	45	E8				
Hauske	N	48	D2	Heves	H	77	B8	Horda	N	48	C3				
Havant	GB	9	F8	Hexham	GB	5	D8	Horezu	RO	78	G2				
Havârna	RO	79	A7	Heysham	GB	5	E7	Horgoš	SRB	77	E7				
Havelberg	D	43	E8	Highbridge	GB	8	E5	Horia	RO	79	D7				
Haverfordwest	GB	8	D2	Highworth	GB	9	D7	Hořice	CZ	74	C5				
Haverhill	GB	9	D10	High Wycombe	GB	9	D8	Horn	A	39	B11				
Havířov	CZ	75	E9	Hildburghausen	D	40	C6	Horn	N	54	C5				
Havlíčkův Brod	CZ	74	E5	Hildesheim	D	42	F5	Horncastle	GB	5	G10				
Havneby	DK	44	G2	Hillerød	DK	44	E6	Hørning	DK	44	E4				
Havøysund	N	59	B7	Hillswick	GB	3	B11	Hornsea	GB	5	F10				
Havran	TR	85	E3	Hilpoltstein	D	40	F6	Horodok	UA	73	E5				
Havsa	TR	84	H2	Hilversum	NL	10	D6	Horsens	DK	44	E3				
Hawick	GB	5	C7	Hînceşti	MD	79	D10	Horsham	GB	9	F9				
Haxby	GB	5	E9	Hinckley	GB	9	C7	Hørsholm	DK	44	E7				
Hayrabolu	TR	85	B3	Hinnerup	DK	44	D4	Horten	N	49	D7				
Haywards Heath	GB	9	F9	Hinojosa del Duque	E	26	H2	Horwich	GB	5	F7				
Heanor	GB	5	G9	Hinte	D	11	A9	Hosszúpályi	H	77	C10				
Hedemora	S	47	A7	Hirschaid	D	40	D6	Hotarele	RO	83	C10				
Hedeviken	S	51	C11	Hirson	F	12	B5	Hoting	S	55	F9				
Heemskerk	NL	10	C6	Hirtshals	DK	44	B4	Hove	GB	9	F9				
Heemstede	NL	10	C6	Histon	GB	9	C9	Höxter	D	11	E12				
Heeren	D	11	E10	Hitchin	GB	9	D9	Hoyerswerda	D	41	A11				
Heerlen	NL	11	F7	Hitzacker	D	43	D7	Hoylake	GB	4	G6				
Heide	D	42	B4	Hjerkinn	N	50	D6	Hradec Králové	CZ	74	D5				
Heidelberg	D	13	C11	Hjo	S	46	E5	Hranice	CZ	75	E8				
Heidenheim an der Brenz	D	38	B3	Hjørring	DK	44	B4	Hrasnica	BIH	81	D7				
Heikendorf	D	42	B6	Hlinsko	CZ	74	E5	Hrastnik	SLO	39	G10				
Heilbronn	D	40	F4	Hlohovec	SK	75	G8	Hriňová	SK	75	G11				
Heiligenhafen	D	43	B7	Hlyboka	UA	78	A6	Hrodna	BY	68	H6				
Heiloo	NL	10	C6	Hlybokaye	BY	69	E11	Hrubieszów	PL	73	C6				
Heimdal	N	51	B7	Hnúšťa	SK	75	G11	Hucknall	GB	5	G9				
Heinola	FIN	65	E7	Hobro	DK	44	C3	Huddersfield	GB	5	F8				
Helbra	D	43	G7	Hochdorf	D	40	G4	Hudeşti	RO	78	A7				
Helegiu	RO	79	E7	Hoddesdon	GB	9	D9	Hudiksvall	S	52	D5				
Helensburgh	GB	2	G4	Hódmezővásárhely	H	77	E8	Huedin	RO	77	D12				
Helgeroa	N	49	E7	Hof	D	41	C7	Huelma	E	28	D6				
Hellín	E	27	H8	Hofheim in Unterfranken	D	40	D5	Huelva	E	25	K5				
Helmond	NL	11	E7	Hofors	S	52	G4	Huenenberg	CH	37	C7				
Helsingborg	S	45	E7	Höganäs	S	45	D7	Huércal-Overa	E	29	D9				
Helsinge	DK	44	E6	Hoghiz	RO	78	F5	Huesca	E	20	D6				
Helsingfors	FIN	64	G6	Hokksund	N	49	C7	Huéscar	E	29	C8				

I

J

Jesolo	I	35	C10	Kallinge	S	45	D10	Kattavia	GR	88	H3
Jessen	D	43	G9	Kallithea	GR	89	C7	Kattbo	S	51	G12
Jessheim	N	46	A2	Kalmar	S	45	C12	Katwijk aan Zee	NL	10	D5
Jever	D	42	C3	Kalocsa	H	76	D5	Kaufbeuren	D	37	B10
Jiana	RO	82	B4	Kaluđerica	SRB	81	B11	Kaufungen	D	40	B4
Jibou	RO	77	C12	Kalundborg	DK	44	E5	Kauhajoki	FIN	53	C10
Jičín	CZ	74	C5	Kalvåg	N	50	E1	Kauhava	FIN	53	B11
Jidvei	RO	78	E2	Kalvarija	LT	68	F6	Kaunas	LT	68	F6
Jihlava	CZ	74	E5	Kalymnos	GR	88	F2	Kauniainen	FIN	64	G5
Jijila	RO	79	G9	Kamares	GR	89	E9	Kavadarci	MK	86	B6
Jijona-Xixona	E	27	H10	Kamariotissa	GR	87	D11	Kavajë	AL	86	C2
Jilava	RO	83	B10	Kamennogorsk	RUS	65	E10	Kavaklıdere	TR	85	H5
Jimbolia	RO	77	F8	Kameno	BG	83	F12	Kavala	GR	87	C10
Jindřichův Hradec	CZ	41	F12	Kamenz	D	41	B11	Kavarna	BG	84	D4
Jirkov	CZ	41	C10	Kamëz	AL	86	B2	Kävlinge	S	45	E8
Jódar	E	29	C7	Kamienna Gora	PL	74	C6	Kaysersberg	F	13	E9
Joensuu	FIN	65	B10	Kamień Pomorski	PL	43	C11	Kazanlük	BG	83	F9
Jõgeva	EST	67	D8	Kamnik	SLO	39	F9	Kazimierza Wielka	PL	73	D1
Jõhvi	EST	67	B9	Kampen	NL	11	C7	Kazlų Rūda	LT	68	F6
Joigny	F	12	F4	Kamyanyets	BY	72	F6	Kecel	H	76	D6
Joinville	F	12	E6	Kangasala	FIN	64	D5	Kecskemét	H	77	D7
Joiţa	RO	83	B9	Kanjiža	SRB	77	E7	Kėdainiai	LT	68	E6
Jonava	LT	69	E7	Kankaanpää	FIN	53	D11	Kędzierzyn-Koźle	PL	75	C9
Jondal	N	48	B3	Kapaklı	TR	85	B4	Kefalos	GR	88	F2
Joniškis	LT	68	C6	Kapellskär	S	47	B10	Keighley	GB	5	F8
Jönköping	S	45	A9	Kapfenberg	A	39	D10	Keila	EST	66	B5
Jonzac	F	16	D4	Kaplice	CZ	39	A9	Ķekava	LV	66	G5
Jordbro	S	47	C9	Kaposvár	H	76	E3	Kelheim	D	41	F7
Joué-lès-Tours	F	15	G9	Kappeln	D	42	A5	Kelmė	LT	68	D5
Joure	NL	11	B7	Kapuvár	H	76	B2	Kelso	GB	5	B7
Joutseno	FIN	65	E9	Karacabey	TR	85	D5	Kemalpaşa	TR	85	H3
Józefów	PL	71	F11	Karavukovo	SRB	76	G6	Kemi	FIN	56	C6
Juan-les-Pins	F	19	D8	Kårböle	S	52	D3	Kemijärvi	FIN	61	D9
Judenburg	A	39	E9	Karcag	H	77	C9	Kemnath	D	41	D7
Jülich	D	11	F8	Karczew	PL	71	G11	Kempele	FIN	62	D6
Jumilla	E	27	H8	Karditsa	GR	86	F6	Kempston	GB	9	C9
Junsele	S	55	G9	Kärdla	EST	66	C3	Kempten (Allgäu)	D	37	B10
Jurançon	F	20	B6	Karis	FIN	64	G4	Kendal	GB	5	E7
Jurbarkas	LT	68	E5	Karkkila	FIN	64	F5	Kenderes	H	77	C8
Jurilovca	RO	84	B5	Karleby	FIN	56	F5	Kenilworth	GB	9	C7
Jūrmala	LV	66	G4	Karlino	PL	70	C5	Kępno	PL	75	B8
Jüterbog	D	43	G9	Karlovac	HR	39	H11	Kepsut	TR	85	E5
Jyllinge	DK	44	E6	Karlovasi	GR	88	D2	Keramoti	GR	87	C10
Jyväskylä	FIN	64	C6	Karlovo	BG	83	F8	Keratea	GR	89	C7
				Karlovy Vary	CZ	41	D9	Kerava	FIN	64	G6
				Karlshamn	S	45	D10	Kerepestarcsa	H	76	B6

				Karlskoga	S	46	C5	Kerkrade	NL	11	F8
				Karlskrona	S	45	D11	Kerkyra	GR	86	F2
Kaarina	FIN	53	G11	Karlsruhe	D	13	C11	Kerstinbo	S	47	A8
Kaba	H	77	C9	Karlstad	S	46	C4	Kerteminde	DK	44	F4
Kać	SRB	77	G7	Karlstadt	D	40	D4	Keşan	TR	85	C2
Kaçanik	RKS	82	G2	Karnobat	BG	83	F11	Keszthely	H	76	D3
Kadaň	CZ	41	C9	Karpenisi	GR	86	G5	Kętrzyn	PL	68	G3
Kağıthane	TR	85	B6	Karşıyaka	TR	85	H3	Kettering	GB	9	C8
Kahla	D	41	C7	Kartal	H	76	B6	Kęty	PL	75	D10
Kaiserslautern	D	13	C10	Kartuzy	PL	71	B8	Keuruu	FIN	64	C5
Kajaani	FIN	63	E8	Karvala	FIN	53	B12	Keynsham	GB	8	E6
Kakanj	BIH	81	D7	Karviná	CZ	75	D9	Kežmarok	SK	73	F1
Kalajoki	FIN	56	F6	Karystos	GR	89	B8	Kharmanli	BG	83	G9
Kalamaki	GR	89	C7	Kassel	D	40	A4	Khaskovo	BG	83	G9
Kalamaria	GR	87	D7	Kastania	GR	86	G5	Khisarya	BG	83	F8
Kalamata	GR	88	D4	Kaštel Stari	HR	80	E4	Khust	UA	73	H5
Kalampaka	GR	86	F5	Kaštel Sućurac	HR	80	E4	Kiato	GR	88	B5
Kälarne	S	52	B4	Kasterlee	B	10	F6	Kičevo	MK	86	B4
Kalety	PL	75	C10	Kastoria	GR	86	D4	Kidderminster	GB	8	C6
Kalevala	RUS	63	C12	Ka-Stutensee	D	13	C11	Kidlington	GB	9	D7
Kaliningrad	RUS	68	F2	Katapola	GR	89	E11	Kidsgrove	GB	5	G7
Kalisz	PL	71	G7	Katerini	GR	87	E7	Kiel	D	42	B6
Kalix	S	56	B5	Katowice	PL	75	D10	Kielce	PL	73	C1
Kållered	S	44	A6	Katrineholm	S	47	D7	Kietrz	PL	75	D8

L

Name				Name				Name			
Larvik	N	49	E7	Leeuwarden	NL	11	B7	Lereşti	RO	78	G4
Las Cabezas de San Juan	E	25	K7	Lefkada	GR	86	G4	Lerici	I	34	F5
La Seyne-sur-Mer	F	18	E6	Leganés	E	26	D4	Lerida	E	21	E7
Laško	SLO	39	G10	Legazpi	E	20	C2	Lerum	S	44	A6
La Solana	E	26	G5	Lège-Cap-Ferret	F	16	E3	Lerwick	GB	3	C12
La Souterraine	F	17	B7	Legionowo	PL	71	F11	Les Arcs	F	19	D7
La Spezia	I	34	F5	Legnano	I	34	C4	Les Borges Blanques	E	21	F8
Las Rozas de Madrid	E	23	H10	Legnica	PL	74	B6	Lescar	F	20	B6
Lastra a Signa	I	35	F7	Le Gond-Pontouvre	F	16	D5	Les Escaldes	AND	21	D9
La Suze-sur-Sarthe	F	15	F9	Le Grand-Lemps	F	36	G3	Le Seu d'Urgell	E	21	D9
Laterza	I	31	B9	Le Grand-Quevilly	F	15	C10	Les Herbiers	F	15	H7
La Teste-de-Buch	F	16	F3	Le Grau-du-Roi	F	17	H11	Lesina	I	33	D10
Latiano	I	31	B11	Le Havre	F	15	B9	Lesko	PL	73	E4
Latina	I	32	D6	Lehliu-Gară	RO	83	B11	Leskovac	SRB	82	E3
Latisana	I	35	B10	Lehre	D	42	F6	Lesparre-Médoc	F	16	D3
La Tremblade	F	16	C3	Lehrte	D	42	F5	Les Pavillons sous Bois	F	12	D2
La Trinité	F	19	D9	Leibnitz	A	39	E11	Les Pennes-Mirabeau	F	18	D5
Latronico	I	31	C8	Leicester	GB	9	B8	Les Ponts-de-Cé	F	15	G8
Lattes	F	17	H11	Leiden	NL	10	D5	Les Sables-d'Olonne	F	16	B2
La Turballe	F	14	G5	Leighton Buzzard	GB	9	D8	Leszno	PL	70	G6
Lauda-Königshofen	D	40	E4	Leikanger	N	50	D2	Létavértes	H	77	C10
Laudun	F	17	G12	Leikanger	N	50	F3	Leţcani	RO	79	C8
Lauenburg (Elbe)	D	42	D6	Leioa	E	20	B1	Le Teil	F	17	F12
Launceston	GB	8	F3	Leipzig	D	41	A8	Le Thillot	F	13	F9
La Unión	E	29	D11	Leiria	P	24	C2	Le Thor	F	18	C5
Laupheim	D	37	A9	Leirvåg	N	50	G1	Le Touquet-Paris-Plage	F	9	G11
Laureana di Borrello	I	31	G8	Leirvik	N	48	C2	Letovice	CZ	74	E6
Lauria	I	31	C7	Leiston	GB	9	C11	Le Tréport	F	9	H11
Lausanne	CH	36	E4	Leixlip	IRL	4	G2	Letterkenny	IRL	6	E5
Lauta	D	41	A11	Leksand	S	52	F3	Leu	RO	82	C6
Lautersbach (Hessen)	D	40	C4	Le Lavandou	F	19	E7	Leuze-en-Hainaut	B	10	G4
Lauvsnes	N	54	F3	Le Lignon	CH	36	E4	Levang	N	54	B5
Lavagna	I	19	C12	Le Locle	CH	13	G9	Levanger	N	54	G4
Lavagna	I	34	E4	Lelystad	NL	11	C7	Levanto	I	34	F5
Laval	F	15	E7	Le Mans	F	15	E9	Leven	GB	3	G7
La Vall d'Uixó	E	27	G10	Lemgo	D	11	D12	Leverano	I	31	C11
Lavaur	F	17	H8	Lemmer	NL	11	B7	Le-Verdon-sur-Mer	F	16	D3
Lavelanet	F	21	C9	Lempäälä	FIN	53	E12	Leverkusen	D	11	F9
Lavello	I	31	A7	Lempdes	F	17	C10	Levice	SK	75	H9
Lavena Ponte Tresa	I	34	B3	Le Muy	F	19	D7	Levico Terme	I	35	B8
Lavis	I	35	B7	Lemvig	DK	44	D2	Le Vigan	F	17	G10
La Voulte-sur-Rhône	F	18	B4	Lenart	SLO	39	F11	Levoča	SK	73	F1
Lavrio	GR	89	C8	Lenauheim	RO	77	F9	Levski	BG	83	D8
Laxou	F	13	D8	Lendava	SLO	76	D1	Lewes	GB	9	F9
Laza	RO	79	D8	Lendinara	I	35	D8	Lewin Brzeski	PL	75	C8
Lazarevac	SRB	81	C11	Lenggries	D	37	B11	Leyland	GB	5	F7
Lazdijai	LT	68	G6	Lenti	H	76	D1	Leżajsk	PL	73	D4
Lazuri	RO	77	B12	Lentini	I	30	F6	Lezhë	AL	86	B2
Leamington Spa, Royal	GB	9	C7	Lentvaris	LT	69	F8	Lézignan-Corbières	F	18	E1
Leatherhead	GB	9	E9	Leoben	A	39	D10	L'Hospitalet de Llobregat	E	21	F10
Lebane	SRB	82	E3	Léognan	F	16	E4	Liberec	CZ	41	C12
Le Blanc	F	16	B6	Leominster	GB	8	C5	Libourne	F	16	E4
Lębork	PL	71	B7	León	E	23	D7	Librazhd	AL	86	C3
Lebrija	E	25	K7	Leonberg	D	13	D12	Licata	I	30	G4
Lebyazh'ye	RUS	65	G10	Leonding	A	39	B9	Lichfield	GB	9	B7
Leça do Bailio	P	22	F2	Leonforte	I	30	F5	Lichtenfels	D	40	D6
Le Cannet	F	19	D8	Leova	MD	79	E9	Lida	BY	69	H8
Lecce	I	31	C11	Le Palais-sur-Vienne	F	17	C7	Lidingö	S	47	C9
Lecco	I	34	B4	Le Passage	F	16	G5	Lidköping	S	46	E4
Lechinţa	RO	78	C3	Le Petit-Quevilly	F	15	C10	Lidzbark	PL	71	D10
Leck	D	44	G2	Le Pian-Médoc	F	16	E3	Lidzbark Warmiński	PL	68	G2
Le Conquet	F	14	E2	Le Poinçonnet	F	15	H11	Liège	B	11	G7
Le Coteau	F	17	C11	Le Poiré-sur-Vie	F	16	A2	Lieksa	FIN	63	G11
Le Creusot	F	12	H5	Le Pont-de-Beauvoisin	F	36	G3	Lielvārde	LV	66	H6
Łęczna	PL	73	B4	Le Pontet	F	18	C5	Lienz	A	39	E7
Łęczyca	PL	71	G9	Leporano	I	31	C10	Liepāja	LV	68	B3
Ledbury	GB	8	D6	Le Puy-en-Velay	F	17	E11	Lier	B	10	F5
Leeds	GB	5	F8	Lequile	I	31	C11	Liestal	CH	13	G10
Leek	GB	5	G8	Lercara Friddi	I	30	E3	Lieşti	RO	79	F8
Leer (Ostfriesland)	D	11	B10					Liezen	A	39	D9

Name	Country	Page	Grid
Lifford	IRL	6	E5
Liffré	F	14	E6
Lignano Sabbiadoro	I	35	C11
Ligny-en-Barrois	F	13	D7
Lilienthal	D	11	B12
Lilla Edet	S	46	E3
Lille	F	10	G3
Lillehammer	N	51	F7
Lillestrøm	N	46	B1
Lille Værløse	DK	44	E7
Lillhamra	S	51	E12
Lillholmsjö	S	55	G7
Limanowa	PL	73	E1
Limavady	GB	4	C2
Limay	F	12	C1
Limbaži	LV	66	F6
Limerick	IRL	7	L4
Limoges	F	17	C7
Limoux	F	21	C10
Linares	E	28	C6
Linaria	GR	87	G10
Lincoln	GB	5	G10
Lindau (Bodensee)	D	37	C9
Lindesberg	S	46	C6
Lindome	S	44	B6
Lindos	GR	88	G4
Lindsdal	S	45	C12
Lingen (Ems)	D	11	C9
Linguaglossa	I	30	E6
Linköping	S	46	E7
Linnich	D	11	F8
Linz	A	39	B9
Lioboml'	UA	73	B6
Lioni	I	30	B6
Lipany	SK	73	F2
Lipari	I	30	D6
Lipcani	MD	79	A7
Liphook	GB	9	F8
Lipjan	RKS	81	G12
Lipno	PL	71	E9
Lipova	RO	77	E10
Lipsko	PL	73	B3
Liptovský Mikuláš	SK	75	F11
Lisboa	P	24	F2
Lisburn	GB	4	D3
Lisieux	F	15	C9
Liskeard	GB	8	G3
L'Isle-Jourdain	F	16	H6
L'Isle-sur-la-Sorgue	F	18	C5
Liss	GB	9	F8
Liteni	RO	78	B7
Litija	SLO	39	G10
Litochoro	GR	87	E7
Litoměřice	CZ	41	C11
Litomyšl	CZ	74	D6
Litovel	CZ	75	E7
Littlehampton	GB	9	F8
Littleport	GB	9	C10
Littoinen	FIN	53	G11
Litvínov	CZ	41	C10
Livadeia	GR	88	B6
Līvāni	LV	69	C9
Liverpool	GB	5	G7
Livingston	GB	2	G6
Livorno	I	34	G6
Lizard	GB	8	H2
Lizzanello	I	31	C11
Lizzano	I	31	C10
Ljubljana	SLO	39	G9
Ljugarn	S	47	G10
Ljungby	S	45	C9
Ljungsbro	S	46	E6
Ljusdal	S	52	D4
Ljutomer	SLO	39	F11
Llagostera	E	21	E11
Llandrindod Wells	GB	8	C4
Llandudno	GB	4	G5
Llanelli	GB	8	D3
Llanes	E	23	B9
Llannon	GB	8	D3
Llantwit Major	GB	8	E4
Lleida	E	21	E7
Llerena	E	24	G7
Lliria	E	27	E10
Llodio	E	20	B1
Lloret de Mar	E	21	E11
Llucmajor	E	29	F9
Loano	I	19	C10
Löbau	D	41	B11
Łobez	PL	70	C4
Locarno	CH	34	B3
Lochaline	GB	2	F3
Lochboisdale	GB	2	E1
Lochem	NL	11	D8
Loches	F	15	G10
Loch Garman	IRL	7	L6
Lochgilphead	GB	2	G4
Lochmaddy	GB	2	D1
Łochów	PL	72	F3
Locri	I	31	G8
Löddeköpinge	S	45	E7
Lodève	F	17	G10
Łódź	PL	71	G9
Loftahammar	S	47	F8
Logatec	SLO	35	B12
Logroño	E	20	D2
Lohals	DK	44	F5
Lohja	FIN	64	G5
Lohne (Oldenburg)	D	11	C11
Loimaa	FIN	53	F11
Loja	E	28	E5
Lom	BG	82	C5
Lom	N	50	E5
Łomianki	PL	71	F11
Lomma	S	45	E7
Lomonosov	RUS	65	G10
Łomża	PL	72	D4
Lonato	I	34	C6
London	GB	9	E9
Londonderry	GB	4	D1
Long Eaton	GB	5	H9
Longford	IRL	7	H5
Longobucco	I	31	E9
Longueau	F	12	B2
Longué-Jumelles	F	15	G8
Longuenesse	F	10	G2
Longuyon	F	13	C7
Longwy	F	13	B7
Lonigo	I	35	C8
Löningen	D	11	C10
Lons-le-Saunier	F	36	D3
Lopătari	RO	79	G7
Lora del Río	E	25	J8
Lorca	E	29	D9
Loreto	I	35	G11
Lorient	F	14	F4
Łőrinci	H	77	B7
Loriol-sur-Drôme	F	18	B5
Los	S	52	D3
Los Barrios	E	25	M8
Los Corrales de Buelna	E	23	B10
Łosice	PL	72	F5
Los Palacios y Villafranca	E	25	K7
Los Santos de Maimona	E	24	G6
Lossiemouth	GB	2	D6
Lößnitz	D	41	C9
Los Yébenes	E	26	F4
Loudéac	F	14	E5
Loudun	F	15	G9
Loughborough	GB	5	H9
Loughton	GB	9	D9
Louhans	F	36	D2
Loulé	P	25	K4
Louny	CZ	41	C10
Lourdes	F	20	C6
Louth	GB	5	G10
Loutraki	GR	88	C6
Loutra Smokovou	GR	86	G6
Louviers	F	15	C10
Lovech	BG	83	E7
Loviisa	FIN	65	F7
Lovraeid	N	48	D3
Lovrin	RO	77	F8
Lowestoft	GB	9	C12
Łowicz	PL	71	F10
Loxstedt	D	11	A11
Loznica	SRB	81	C9
Lozovik	SRB	81	C12
Luanco	E	23	A7
Luarca	E	22	B6
Lubaczów	PL	73	D5
Lubań	PL	41	B12
Lubartów	PL	72	H5
Lubawa	PL	71	D10
Lübbecke	D	11	C11
Lübben	D	43	G10
Lübeck	D	42	C6
Lubin	PL	70	H5
Lublin	PL	73	B4
Lubliniec	PL	75	C9
Luboń	PL	70	F6
Lubsko	PL	43	G12
Lübz	D	43	D8
Lucan	IRL	4	G2
Lucca	I	34	F6
Lucé	F	12	E1
Lucena	E	28	D5
Lučenec	SK	75	G11
Lucera	I	33	D10
Lüchow	D	43	E7
Lucieni	RO	78	H5
Lucija	SLO	35	C11
Luckau	D	43	G10
Luckenwalde	D	43	F9
Luco dei Marsi	I	33	C7
Luçon	F	16	B3
Luc-sur-Mer	F	15	C8
Ludlow	GB	8	C5
Luduş	RO	78	E2
Ludvika	S	46	A6
Ludwigsburg	D	40	F4
Ludwigslust	D	43	D7
Ludza	LV	69	J8
Luga	RUS	67	D12
Lugano	CH	34	B4
Lugo	I	35	E9
Lugo	E	22	C4
Lugoj	RO	77	F10
Luik	B	11	G7
Luimneach	IRL	7	L4

L

Luino	I	34	B3	Mæl	N	48	C6	Mandal	N	48	G4
Luizi Călugăra	RO	79	D7	Mafra	P	24	E1	Mandelieu-la-Napoule	F	19	D8
Lukavac	BIH	81	C8	Magdeburg	D	43	F7	Mandello del Lario	I	34	B4
Lukovit	BG	83	E7	Magherafelt	GB	4	D2	Mandra	GR	89	B7
Łuków	PL	72	G4	Magione	I	35	G9	Manduria	I	31	C10
Luleå	S	56	C4	Maglaj	BIH	81	C7	Măneciu	RO	78	G6
Lüleburgaz	TR	85	B3	Maglavit	RO	82	C5	Manerbio	I	34	C6
Lumbres	F	9	F12	Maglie	I	31	C11	Mănești	RO	78	H5
Lumezzane	I	34	C6	Maglód	H	76	C6	Manfredonia	I	33	D11
Lumina	RO	84	C4	Magura	SRB	81	G12	Mangalia	RO	84	C4
Lumparland	FIN	47	A12	Măgurele	RO	83	B10	Mangualde	P	22	G4
Lunca	RO	79	B7	Mahmudia	RO	79	G11	Maniago	I	35	B10
Lunca	RO	83	C8	Mahón	E	29	E12	Manisa	TR	85	G3
Lunca de Jos	RO	78	D6	Maia	P	22	F2	Manlleu	E	21	E10
Luncavița	RO	79	G9	Măicănești	RO	79	G8	Mannheim	D	13	C11
Lund	S	45	E8	Maidenhead	GB	9	E8	Manningtree	GB	9	D11
Lüneburg	D	42	D6	Maidstone	GB	9	E10	Manno	CH	34	B4
Lunel	F	17	H11	Maieru	RO	78	C4	Manoppello	I	33	C8
Lunéville	F	13	D8	Mainburg	D	38	B5	Manosque	F	18	D6
Lungulețu	RO	83	B9	Maintenon	F	12	D1	Manresa	E	21	E9
L'Union	F	11	H7	Mainz	D	13	A11	Mansfield	GB	5	G9
Lupeni	RO	77	G12	Maiolati Spontini	I	35	G11	Mantes-la-Ville	F	12	D1
Lure	F	13	F8	Majadahonda	E	23	H10	Mantova	I	35	D7
Lurgan	GB	4	E2	Majdanpek	SRB	82	B3	Mäntsälä	FIN	64	F6
Lu-Ruchheim	D	13	C11	Makarska	HR	80	E5	Mänttä	FIN	64	C5
Lusciano	I	30	B5	Makó	H	77	E8	Mäntyluoto	FIN	53	E10
Lushnjë	AL	86	C2	Maków Mazowiecki	PL	71	E11	Manyas	TR	85	D4
Lustenau	A	37	C9	Maków Podhalański	PL	75	E11	Manzanares	E	26	G5
Lutherstadt Wittenberg	D	43	G9	Mala	IRL	7	M4	Manziana	I	32	C5
Lütjenburg	D	42	B6	Malacky	SK	75	G7	Maracena	E	28	D6
Luton	GB	9	D9	Maladzyechna	BY	69	G10	Mărăcineni	RO	79	G7
Luxembourg	L	13	B8	Málaga	E	28	E5	Maranello	I	35	E7
Luxeuil-les-Bains	F	13	F8	Malagón	E	26	F4	Marano di Napoli	I	30	B5
Luzern	CH	13	G11	Malahide	IRL	4	G3	Mărășești	RO	79	F8
Luzzi	I	31	E8	Malalbergo	I	35	D8	Maratea	I	31	D7
L'viv	UA	73	E6	Malaryta	BY	72	G6	Marbella	E	28	F4
Lwówek Śląski	PL	74	B5	Malbork	PL	71	C9	Marburg an der Lahn	D	11	G11
Lyaskovets	BG	83	E9	Malchin	D	43	C9	Marby	S	51	B12
Lycksele	S	55	E11	Malchow	D	43	D8	Marcali	H	76	D3
Lydney	GB	8	D6	Măldăeni	RO	83	C8	March	GB	9	C9
Lymans'ke	UA	79	D12	Maldon	GB	9	D10	Marche-en-Famenne	B	11	H7
Lymington	GB	9	F7	Malemort-sur-Corrèze	F	17	E7	Marchena	E	25	J8
Lyneham	GB	8	E6	Malente	D	42	B6	Marchtrenk	A	39	C9
Lyon	F	36	F2	Malesherbes	F	12	E2	Marcianise	I	30	A5
Lysekil	S	46	E2	Mali Idoš	SRB	77	F7	Marciano della Chiana	I	35	G8
Lyss	CH	13	G9	Mali Lošinj	HR	80	C1	Marennes	F	16	C3
Lytham St Anne's	GB	4	F6	Malines	B	10	F5	Margate	GB	9	E11
Lyubashivka	UA	79	B12	Malkara	TR	85	C3	Margherita di Savoia	I	33	E11
Lyubimets	BG	83	G10	Mallaig	GB	2	E3	Marghita	RO	77	C11
				Mallorca	E	29	F9	Marginea	RO	78	B5
				Mallow	IRL	7	M4	Mărgineni	RO	79	D7
M				Malmberget	S	60	D3	Mariánské Lázně	CZ	41	D8
				Malmesbury	GB	8	E6	Maribo	DK	44	G5
Maardu	EST	66	B6	Malmö	S	45	F7	Maribor	SLO	39	F11
Maaseik	B	11	F7	Malmslätt	S	46	E6	Mariehamn	FIN	47	A11
Maastricht	NL	11	F7	Malnaș	RO	78	E5	Marienberg	D	41	C9
Mablethorpe	GB	5	G11	Måløy	N	50	D2	Mariestad	S	46	D5
Macclesfield	GB	5	G8	Malpica	E	22	B2	Marigliano	I	30	B5
Macea	RO	77	E9	Malton	GB	5	E9	Marignane	F	18	D5
Macerata	I	35	G11	Malu Mare	RO	82	C6	Marijampolė	LT	68	F6
Machecoul	F	14	H6	Malung	S	49	A11	Marín	E	22	D2
Măcin	RO	79	G9	Mamers	F	15	E9	Marina di Gioiosa Ionica	I	31	G8
Macomer	I	32	E2	Mamonovo	RUS	68	F1	Marineo	I	30	E3
Mâcon	F	17	B12	Mamuras	AL	86	B2	Marinha Grande	P	24	C2
Madan	BG	87	B11	Manacor	E	29	F10	Marino	I	32	D5
Maddaloni	I	30	A5	Mânăstirea	RO	83	C11	Markdorf	D	37	B8
Made	NL	10	E6	Mânăstirea Cașin	RO	79	E7	Market Deeping	GB	9	B9
Madona	LV	67	G7	Mancha Real	E	28	C6	Market Drayton	GB	5	H7
Madrid	E	23	H10	Manchester	GB	5	G7	Market Harborough	GB	9	C8
Madridejos	E	26	F5	Manciano	I	32	B4	Marki	PL	71	F11

Name	Country	No.	Grid
Markkleeberg	D	41	B8
Markopoulo	GR	89	C7
Marktoberdorf	D	37	B10
Marktredwitz	D	41	D8
Marl	D	11	E9
Marlborough	GB	9	E7
Marly	CH	13	H9
Marmande	F	16	F5
Marmaraereğlisi	TR	85	C4
Marmari	GR	89	B8
Marmolejo	E	28	C5
Marne	D	42	C4
Marne-la-Vallée	F	12	D3
Maromme	F	15	C10
Marousi	GR	89	B7
Marquise	F	9	F12
Marsala	I	30	E1
Mârşani	RO	82	C6
Marsberg	D	11	E12
Marsciano	I	32	A5
Marseillan	F	18	E2
Marseille	F	18	E5
Marsillargues	F	17	H11
Märsta	S	47	B9
Marstrand	S	46	F2
Martano	I	31	C12
Martfű	H	77	C8
Martigny	CH	34	B1
Martil	MA	28	H3
Martin	SK	75	F10
Martina Franca	I	31	B10
Martinsicuro	I	33	B8
Martorell	E	21	F10
Martos	E	28	C6
Maruggio	I	31	C10
Marvejols	F	17	F10
Maryport	GB	4	D6
Marzabotto	I	35	E7
Mascali	I	30	E6
Mascalucia	I	30	F6
Massa	I	34	F6
Massafra	I	31	B10
Massa Lombarda	I	35	E8
Massamagrell	E	27	F10
Massa Marittimo	I	32	A2
Massarosa	I	34	F6
Mǎstǎcani	RO	79	F9
Matala	GR	89	G9
Mataró	E	21	F10
Mǎtǎsari	RO	82	A5
Matca	RO	79	F8
Matelica	I	35	G10
Matera	I	31	B9
Mátészalka	H	77	B11
Matino	I	31	C11
Matlock	GB	5	G8
Mattersburg	A	39	C12
Mattinata	I	33	D11
Maubeuge	F	10	H5
Mauguio	F	17	H11
Mauléon	F	15	H7
Mauléon-Licharre	F	20	B5
Maurset	N	48	B4
Mavrodin	RO	83	C8
Mayen	D	11	G9
Mayenne	F	15	E8
Mazamet	F	21	B10
Mazara del Vallo	I	30	F2
Mazarrón	E	29	D10
Mažeikiai	LT	68	C4
Mazzarino	I	30	F4
Meadela	P	22	E2
Meaux	F	12	D3
Mechelen	B	10	F5
Medemblik	NL	10	C6
Medgidia	RO	84	C4
Mediaş	RO	78	E3
Medicina	I	35	E8
Medieşu Aurit	RO	77	B12
Medina del Campo	E	23	F8
Medina de Pomar	E	23	C11
Medina-Sidonia	E	25	M7
Medzilaborce	SK	73	F3
Megara	GR	88	B6
Mehadia	RO	77	H11
Meilen	CH	13	G11
Meinerzhagen	D	11	F10
Meiningen	D	40	C5
Meißen	D	41	B10
Mejorada del Campo	E	23	H11
Meldola	I	35	F9
Meldorf	D	42	B4
Melenci	SRB	77	F8
Melendugno	I	31	C12
Melfi	I	31	B7
Melicucco	I	31	G8
Melide	E	22	C3
Melilli	I	30	G6
Melissano	I	31	D11
Melito di Porto Salvo	I	31	H7
Melk	A	39	B10
Melksham	GB	8	E6
Melle	F	16	B4
Mellrichstadt	D	40	C5
Mělník	CZ	41	C11
Mels	CH	37	D8
Melton Mowbray	GB	5	H9
Melun	F	12	D3
Mélykút	H	76	E6
Memaliaj	AL	86	D2
Memmingen	D	37	B9
Mende	F	17	F10
Menemen	TR	85	G3
Menfi	I	30	F2
Mengeš	SLO	39	G9
Mengíbar	E	28	C6
Mennecy	F	12	D2
Mentana	I	32	C5
Menton	F	19	D9
Meppel	NL	11	C8
Meppen	D	11	C9
Mer	F	12	F1
Merag	HR	80	B1
Merano	I	37	D11
Mercato San Severino	I	30	B6
Mercato Saraceno	I	35	F9
Mercogliano	I	30	B6
Merei	RO	79	G7
Meriç	TR	85	B2
Merichas	GR	89	D8
Mérida	E	24	E6
Merseburg (Saale)	D	41	A7
Merthyr Tydfil	GB	8	D4
Méru	F	12	C2
Merzig	D	13	C8
Mesagne	I	31	B11
Mesimeri	GR	87	D7
Mesola	I	35	D9
Mesolongi	GR	88	B3
Mesoraca	I	31	E9
Messina	I	31	E7
Messini	GR	88	D4
Meta	I	30	B5
Metallostroy	RUS	65	H11
Metković	HR	80	F6
Metlika	SLO	39	H10
Metz	F	13	C8
Meximieux	F	36	F2
Meylan	F	18	A6
Mezdra	BG	82	E6
Mèze	F	18	D3
Mezőberény	H	77	D9
Mezőcsát	H	77	B9
Mezőhegyes	H	77	E9
Mezőkeresztes	H	77	B8
Mezőkovácsháza	H	77	E9
Mezőkövesd	H	77	B8
Mezőtúr	H	77	D8
Mezzolombardo	I	35	A7
Miajadas	E	24	E7
Miastko	PL	70	C6
Michalovce	SK	73	G3
Middelburg	NL	10	E4
Middelfart	DK	44	F3
Middelharnis	NL	10	E5
Middlesbrough	GB	5	D9
Middleton	GB	5	F7
Middlewich	GB	5	G7
Midhurst	GB	9	F8
Midleton	IRL	7	M4
Miðvágur	FO	3	B8
Miechów	PL	75	C11
Międzychód	PL	70	E5
Międzyrzec Podlaski	PL	72	G5
Międzyrzecz	PL	70	F4
Międzyzdroje	PL	43	C11
Mielec	PL	73	D2
Miercurea-Ciuc	RO	78	E5
Mieres	E	23	B7
Miesbach	D	37	B12
Migennes	F	12	F4
Migné-Auxances	F	16	B5
Miguelturra	E	26	G4
Mihăeşti	RO	78	G3
Mihăeşti	RO	78	G4
Mihăileşti	RO	83	B10
Mihail Kogălniceanu	RO	84	B4
Mihai Viteazu	RO	78	D2
Mijas	E	28	F4
Mikkeli	FIN	65	D8
Milan	I	34	C4
Milano	I	34	C4
Milas	TR	88	E3
Milazzo	I	30	D6
Milcovul	RO	79	F8
Mildenhall	GB	9	C10
Mileto	I	31	F8
Mílevsko	CZ	41	E11
Milford Haven	GB	8	D2
Milicz	PL	70	H6
Militello in Val di Catania	I	30	F5
Millau	F	17	G10
Millom	GB	4	E6
Milly-la-Forêt	F	12	E2
Milna	HR	80	E4
Milton Keynes	GB	9	D8
Mimizan	F	16	F2
Mimoň	CZ	41	C11
Minas de Riotinto	E	25	H6
Mindelheim	D	37	B10

M

Minden	D	11	D12	Mollerussa	E	21	E8	Montesano sulla Marcellana	I	31	C7
Mindszent	H	77	D7	Mölln	D	42	C6	Monte San Savino	I	35	G8
Minehead	GB	8	E4	Mölndal	S	46	F3	Monte Sant'Angelo	I	33	D11
Mineo	I	30	F5	Mölnlycke	S	44	A6	Montesarchio	I	30	A5
Minervino Murge	I	31	A8	Molpe	FIN	53	B10	Montescaglioso	I	31	B9
Minsk	BY	69	H11	Momchilgrad	BG	87	B11	Montesilvano	I	33	B8
Minturno	I	30	A4	Monaghan	IRL	4	E2	Montespertoli	I	35	G7
Mira	I	35	C9	Moncada	E	27	F10	Montevarchi	I	35	G8
Mirabella Eclano	I	30	A6	Moncalieri	I	19	A9	Monthey	CH	36	E5
Mirabella Imbaccari	I	30	F5	Monchaltorf	CH	37	C7	Montignoso	I	34	F6
Miramas	F	18	D5	Mondolfo	I	35	F10	Montijo	E	24	E6
Miramont-de-Guyenne	F	16	F5	Mondoñedo	E	22	B4	Montilla	E	28	D4
Miranda de Ebro	E	20	C1	Mondovì	I	19	C10	Montivilliers	F	15	B9
Mirandela	P	22	F5	Mondragone	I	30	A4	Montluçon	F	17	B9
Mirandola	I	35	D7	Monemvasia	GR	88	E6	Montmélian	F	36	G4
Mircea Vodă	RO	84	C4	Monesterio	E	25	H7	Montmorillon	F	16	B6
Mirceşti	RO	79	C7	Monfalcone	I	35	B11	Montorio al Vomano	I	33	B7
Mirecourt	F	13	E8	Monforte de Lemos	E	22	D4	Montoro	E	28	C5
Mireşu Mare	RO	77	C12	Monifieth	GB	3	F7	Montpellier	F	17	H11
Misano Adriatico	I	35	F10	Mońki	PL	72	D5	Montpon-Ménestérol	F	16	E5
Misilmeri	I	30	E3	Monmouth	GB	8	D5	Montreuil-Juigné	F	15	F8
Miskolc	H	73	H1	Monolithos	GR	88	G3	Montreux	CH	36	E5
Mistelbach	A	39	B12	Monopoli	I	31	B10	Montrichard	F	15	G10
Misterbianco	I	30	F6	Monor	H	76	C6	Montrond-les-Bains	F	17	D12
Mistretta	I	30	E5	Monóvar	E	27	H9	Montrose	GB	3	F7
Mitreni	RO	83	C11	Monreale	I	30	E3	Monts	F	15	G9
Mitrovicë	RKS	81	F12	Mons	B	10	G5	Mont-St-Aignan	F	15	C10
Mittersill	A	38	D6	Monselice	I	35	C8	Monza	I	34	C4
Mittweida	D	41	B9	Monster	NL	10	D5	Monzón	E	21	E7
Mizhhir''ya	UA	73	G5	Monsummano Terme	I	35	F7	Moorbad Lobenstein	D	41	C7
Mizil	RO	78	G6	Montalbano Jonico	I	31	C9	Moordorf (Südbrookmerland)	D	11	A9
Miziya	BG	82	D6	Montalcino	I	32	A3	Mór	H	76	C4
Mjölby	S	46	E6	Montale	I	35	F7	Mora	E	26	E4
Mjøndalen	N	49	C7	Montalto di Castro	I	32	C4	Mora	S	51	F12
Mladá Boleslav	CZ	41	C12	Montalto Uffugo	I	31	E8	Morąg	PL	68	G1
Mladenovac	SRB	81	C11	Montana	BG	82	D5	Mórahalom	H	77	E7
Mława	PL	71	D10	Montargis	F	12	F3	Moraleja	E	24	C6
Mnichovo Hradiště	CZ	41	C12	Montataire	F	12	C2	Morano Calabro	I	31	D8
Moaña	E	22	D2	Montauban	F	17	G7	Moratalla	E	29	B9
Moara Vlăsiei	RO	83	B10	Montauroux	F	19	D8	Moravská Třebová	CZ	74	E6
Modena	I	35	E7	Montbard	F	12	F5	Moravské Budějovice	CZ	74	F5
Modica	I	30	G5	Montbéliard	F	13	F9	Morbach	D	13	B9
Modra	SK	75	G7	Montbrison	F	17	D11	Morbegno	I	34	B5
Modriča	BIH	76	H4	Montceau-les-Mines	F	17	B12	Morciano di Romagna	I	35	F10
Modugno	I	31	A9	Montchanin	F	12	H5	Morcone	I	33	E9
Moers	D	11	E8	Mont-de-Marsan	F	16	G4	Morecambe	GB	5	E7
Mogilno	PL	71	E7	Montdidier	F	12	B3	Moreni	RO	78	H5
Moguer	E	25	K6	Montebello Ionico	I	31	H7	Morestel	F	36	F3
Mohács	H	76	F5	Monte-Carlo	MC	19	D9	Morez	F	36	E4
Mohelnice	CZ	75	E7	Montechiarugolo	I	34	E6	Morges	CH	36	E4
Moieciu	RO	78	G5	Montefalco	I	32	B5	Morlaix	F	14	D3
Moineşti	RO	78	E6	Montefiascone	I	32	B4	Moroeni	RO	78	G5
Mo i Rana	N	55	B7	Montefrío	E	28	D5	Morón de la Frontera	E	25	K8
Moirans	F	36	G3	Montegiorgio	I	35	H11	Morpeth	GB	5	C8
Moisei	RO	78	B3	Montegranaro	I	35	G11	Morshyn	UA	73	F6
Moissac	F	16	G6	Montehermoso	E	24	C6	Mortagne-au-Perche	F	15	D9
Mojkovac	MNE	81	F9	Monteiasi	I	31	C10	Mortagne-sur-Sèvre	F	15	G7
Mokrin	SRB	77	F8	Montelepre	I	30	E3	Morteau	F	13	G8
Mol	SRB	77	F7	Montelibretti	I	32	C6	Mosbach	D	13	C12
Mola di Bari	I	31	A9	Montélimar	F	18	B4	Moscavide	P	24	E7
Moldava nad Bodvou	SK	73	G2	Montella	I	30	B6	Mosina	PL	70	F6
Molde	N	50	C4	Montellano	E	25	K8	Mosjøen	N	54	C6
Moldova Nouă	RO	82	B2	Montelupo Fiorentino	I	35	F7	Mosonmagyaróvár	H	76	B3
Moldoviţa	RO	78	B5	Montemor-o-Novo	P	24	F3	Moss	N	49	D8
Molétai	LT	69	E8	Montepulciano	I	32	A4	Most	CZ	41	C10
Molfetta	I	31	A9	Monteriggioni	I	35	G7	Mostar	BIH	81	E7
Molina de Segura	E	29	C10	Monteroni d'Arbia	I	35	G8	Mosterhamn	N	48	C2
Moliterno	I	31	C7	Monteroni di Lecce	I	31	C11	Móstoles	E	26	D4
Mölle	S	44	D7	Monterotondo	I	32	C5	Mostys'ka	UA	73	E5
				Monte San Giovanni Campano	I	33	D7	Mota del Cuervo	E	26	F6

Name	Country	Pg	Grid
Motala	S	46	E6
Moţăţei	RO	82	C5
Motherwell	GB	2	H5
Motril	E	28	E6
Motru	RO	82	A5
Motta San Giovanni	I	31	G7
Mottola	I	31	B9
Mougins	F	19	D8
Moulins	F	17	B10
Moulins-les Metz	F	13	C8
Moura	P	24	G5
Mourenx	F	20	B5
Mouscron	B	10	G4
Moutier	CH	13	G9
Moûtiers	F	36	G4
Moyenmoutier	F	13	E9
Mozirje	SLO	39	F10
Mrągowo	PL	68	H3
Mrkonjić-Grad	BIH	80	C5
Mszana Dolna	PL	75	E11
Mszczonów	PL	71	G11
Much	D	11	F9
Mudanya	TR	85	D6
Mugeni	RO	78	E4
Muggia	I	35	C12
Mühlhausen (Thüringen)	D	40	B5
Muineachán	IRL	4	E2
Mukacheve	UA	73	G4
Mula	E	29	C10
Mulhouse	F	13	F9
Müllheim	D	13	F10
Mullingar	IRL	4	F1
Mullsjö	S	46	F5
Mulsanne	F	15	F9
Münchberg	D	41	D7
München	D	38	C5
Munchingen	D	13	D12
Mundolsheim	F	13	D10
Munich	D	38	C5
Munkebo	DK	44	F4
Münnerstadt	D	40	D5
Münsingen	D	38	B2
Münsingen	CH	13	H10
Munster	F	13	E9
Münster	D	11	D10
Münster	D	42	E5
Munteni	RO	79	F8
Muradiye	TR	85	G3
Muratlı	TR	85	B3
Murcia	E	29	C10
Muret	F	21	B9
Murgeni	RO	79	E9
Muriedas	E	23	B10
Murnau am Staffelsee	D	37	B11
Muro	E	29	F10
Muro Lucano	I	31	B7
Muros	E	22	C1
Murowana Goślina	PL	70	F6
Mûrs-Erigné	F	15	G8
Murska Sobota	SLO	39	F11
Mürzzuschlag	A	39	D11
Musselburgh	GB	3	G7
Musselkanaal	NL	11	B9
Mussidan	F	16	E5
Mussomeli	I	30	F4
Mustafakemalpaşa	TR	85	D5
Muxía	E	22	B1
Myadzyel	BY	69	F10
Mykolayiv	UA	73	E6
Mykonos	GR	89	D10
Myllykoski	FIN	65	F7
Myory	BY	69	D11
Myrina	GR	87	E11
Myślenice	PL	75	D11
Myślibórz	PL	43	E11
Myszków	PL	75	C10
Mytilini	GR	85	F2

N

Name	Country	Pg	Grid
Naantali	FIN	53	G10
Naas	IRL	4	G2
Nabburg	D	41	E8
Náchod	CZ	74	C6
Nădlac	RO	77	E8
Nádudvar	H	77	C9
Næstved	DK	44	F6
Nafpaktos	GR	88	B4
Nafplio	GR	88	C6
Nagold	D	13	D11
Nagyatád	H	76	E3
Nagyecsed	H	77	B11
Nagyhalász	H	73	H3
Nagykálló	H	77	B10
Nagykanizsa	H	76	E2
Nagykáta	H	77	C7
Nagykőrös	H	77	C7
Nagyszénás	H	77	D8
Naintré	F	16	A5
Nairn	GB	2	D6
Nájera	E	20	D2
Nakło nad Notecią	PL	71	D7
Nakskov	DK	44	G5
Náměšť nad Oslavou	CZ	74	F6
Namsos	N	54	F4
Namur	B	10	G6
Namysłów	PL	75	B8
Nancy	F	13	D8
Nantes	F	14	G6
Nantwich	GB	5	G7
Naousa	GR	86	D6
Naples	I	30	B5
Napoli	I	30	B5
Narbonne	F	18	E2
Nardò	I	31	C11
Narni	I	32	B5
Naro	I	30	F4
Närpes	FIN	53	C10
Narva	EST	67	B10
Narvik	N	57	D5
Năsăud	RO	78	C3
Našice	HR	76	G4
Nasielsk	PL	71	F11
Naso	I	30	E5
Nässjö	S	45	A10
Nastola	FIN	65	E7
Naujoji Akmenė	LT	68	C5
Naumburg (Saale)	D	41	B7
Navalcarnero	E	26	D4
Navalmoral de la Mata	E	24	C8
Navalvillar de Pela	E	24	E8
Navan	IRL	4	F2
Navarcles	E	21	E10
Navàs	E	21	E9
Navia	E	22	B5
Năvodari	RO	84	B5
Naxos	GR	89	D10
Nazaré	P	24	D2
Nea Alikarnassos	GR	89	G10
Nea Artaki	GR	89	A7
Nea Filadelfeia	GR	89	B7
Nea Ionia	GR	87	F7
Nea Liosia	GR	89	B7
Nea Makri	GR	89	B7
Neapoli	GR	88	E6
Nea Styra	GR	89	B8
Neath	GB	8	D4
Neckartenzlingen	D	38	B2
Nedelino	BG	87	B11
Nedstrand	N	48	D2
Negotin	SRB	82	C4
Negotino	MK	86	B6
Negreşti	RO	79	D8
Negreşti-Oaş	RO	78	B1
Negru Vodă	RO	84	C4
Nehoiu	RO	78	G6
Neksø	DK	45	G10
Neman	RUS	68	E4
Nemenčinė	LT	69	F8
Nemours	F	12	E3
Nenagh	IRL	7	K4
Nepi	I	32	C5
Nérac	F	16	G5
Neratovice	CZ	41	D11
Nerja	E	28	E6
Nerva	E	25	H6
Nes	N	49	B7
Nesna	N	54	B5
Neston	GB	4	G6
Nettuno	I	32	D5
Neuageri	CH	37	C7
Neubrandenburg	D	43	C9
Neuburg an der Donau	D	38	A4
Neuchâtel	CH	13	H9
Neuenhaus	D	11	C9
Neuenkirchen	D	42	D5
Neufchâteau	B	13	B7
Neufchâteau	F	13	E7
Neufchâtel-en-Bray	F	12	B1
Neufchâtel-Hardelot	F	9	F12
Neuhof	D	40	C4
Neumarkt in der Oberpfalz	D	41	F7
Neumünster	D	42	B5
Neunkirchen	A	39	C11
Neunkirchen	D	13	C9
Neuruppin	D	43	E9
Neustadt an der Aisch	D	40	E6
Neustadt an der Weinstraße	D	13	C11
Neustrelitz	D	43	D9
Neutraubling	D	41	F8
Neuville-lès-Dieppe	F	9	H11
Neuwied	D	11	G10
Neviano	I	31	C11
New Alresford	GB	9	F8
Newark-on-Trent	GB	5	G9
Newbridge	IRL	4	G2
Newbury	GB	9	E7
Newcastle	GB	4	E3
Newcastle-under-Lyme	GB	5	G7
Newcastle upon Tyne	GB	5	D8
Newhaven	GB	9	F9
Newmarket	GB	9	C10
Newport	GB	5	H7
Newport	GB	8	E5
Newport	GB	9	F7
Newport Pagnell	GB	9	D8
Newquay	GB	8	G2
New Romney	GB	9	F11
New Ross	IRL	7	L6

N

Newry	GB	4	E2	Nørresundby	DK	44	C4	Nubledo	E	23	B7
Newton Abbot	GB	8	G4	Nørre Vorupør	DK	44	C2	Nuenen	NL	11	E7
Newton Aycliffe	GB	5	D8	Norrköping	S	47	E7	Nuits-St-Georges	F	12	G6
Newtown	GB	8	C4	Norrtälje	S	47	B10	Nules	E	27	E10
Newtownabbey	GB	4	D3	Northallerton	GB	5	E8	Nummela	FIN	64	G5
Newtownards	GB	4	D3	Northam	GB	8	F3	Nuneaton	GB	9	C7
Nicastro	I	31	F8	Northampton	GB	9	C8	Nunspeet	NL	11	C7
Nice	F	19	D9	North Berwick	GB	3	G7	Nuoro	I	32	E3
Nichelino	I	19	A9	Northeim	D	42	G5	Nurmes	FIN	63	G10
Nicolae Bălcescu	RO	79	E7	North Walsham	GB	9	B11	Nurmo	FIN	53	B11
Nicolae Bălcescu	RO	84	B4	Northwich	GB	5	G7	Nürnberg	D	40	E6
Nicolosi	I	30	F6	Norton	GB	5	E9	Nusco	I	30	B6
Nicorești	RO	79	F8	Nortorf	D	42	B5	Nușfalău	RO	77	C12
Nicosia	I	30	E5	Nort-sur-Erdre	F	14	G6	Nybergsund	N	51	F10
Nicotera	I	31	F8	Norwich	GB	9	B11	Nyborg	DK	44	F5
Niculițel	RO	79	G10	Noto	I	30	G6	Nyborg	N	48	B2
Nidda	D	11	G12	Notodden	N	48	D6	Nybro	S	45	C11
Nidzica	PL	71	D10	Notre-Dame-de-Gravenchon	F	15	C9	Nyby	FIN	53	B10
Niebüll	D	44	G2	Nottingham	GB	5	H9	Nyergesújfalu	H	76	B5
Niederbronn-les-Bains	F	13	D10	Nottuln	D	11	D9	Nyíradony	H	77	B10
Nieder Reisbach	D	41	G8	Nouzonville	F	12	B6	Nyírbátor	H	77	B11
Niemodlin	PL	75	C8	Nová Baňa	SK	75	G9	Nyíregyháza	H	77	B10
Nienburg (Saale)	D	43	G8	Novaci	RO	78	G2	Nyírtelek	H	77	A10
Nienburg (Weser)	D	11	C12	Nová Dubnica	SK	75	F9	Nykøbing	DK	44	G6
Niesky	D	41	B12	Novafeltria	I	35	F9	Nykøbing Mors	DK	44	C2
Nigrita	GR	87	C8	Nova Gorica	SLO	35	B11	Nykøbing Sjælland	DK	44	E6
Nijar	E	29	E8	Nova Gradiška	HR	76	G3	Nyköping	S	47	D8
Nijmegen	NL	11	D7	Nova Pazova	SRB	77	H8	Nykvarn	S	47	C9
Nijverdal	NL	11	C8	Novara	I	34	C3	Nymburk	CZ	41	D12
Nikel'	RUS	59	E11	Nova Siri	I	31	C9	Nynäshamn	S	47	D9
Nikopol	BG	83	D8	Nova Varoš	SRB	81	E10	Nyon	CH	36	E4
Nikšić	MNE	81	F8	Nova Zagora	BG	83	F10	Nyons	F	18	C5
Nîmes	F	17	G12	Novelda	E	27	H9	Nýřany	CZ	41	E9
Nimigea	RO	78	C3	Novellara	I	35	D7	Nýrsko	CZ	41	F9
Niort	F	16	B4	Nové Mesto nad Váhom	SK	75	G8	Nysa	PL	75	C7
Niš	SRB	82	D3	Nové Město na Moravě	CZ	74	E6				
Niscemi	I	30	G5	Nové Zámky	SK	76	B4				
Nisko	PL	73	C3	Novi Bečej	SRB	77	F7	O			
Nisporeni	MD	79	C9	Novi Iskŭr	BG	82	F5				
Nitra	SK	75	G8	Novi Kneževac	SRB	77	E7	Oadby	GB	9	B8
Nittenau	D	41	F8	Novi Ligure	I	19	B11	Oakham	GB	9	B8
Nittendorf	D	41	F7	Novi Pazar	BG	83	D12	Oban	GB	2	F4
Nivala	FIN	62	F5	Novi Pazar	SRB	81	F11	O Barco	E	22	D5
Nizza Monferrato	I	19	B10	Novi Sad	SRB	77	G7	Oberammergau	D	37	B11
Nocera Terinese	I	31	E8	Novi Travnik	BIH	80	D6	Obernai	F	13	E10
Nocera Umbra	I	32	A6	Novo Beograd	SRB	81	B11	Oberriet	CH	37	C9
Noci	I	31	B10	Novo Mesto	SLO	39	G10	Oberstdorf	D	37	C10
Nogent-le-Roi	F	12	D1	Novo Miloševo	SRB	77	F8	Obiliq	RKS	81	G12
Nogent-le-Rotrou	F	15	E10	Novorzhev	RUS	67	G11	Obrenovac	SRB	81	C11
Noia	E	22	C2	Novoselytsya	UA	78	A6	Ocaña	E	26	E5
Noicattaro	I	31	A9	Novovolyns'k	UA	73	C6	O Carballiño	E	22	D3
Noirmoutier-en-l'Île	F	14	G5	Novoyavorivs'ke	UA	73	D5	O Castelo	E	22	E2
Nokia	FIN	53	E12	Novska	HR	76	G2	Occhiobello	I	35	D8
Nomeland	N	48	D4	Nový Bor	CZ	41	C11	Ochsenfurt	D	40	F5
Nonancourt	F	15	D10	Nový Bydžov	CZ	74	D5	Ocna Mureș	RO	78	E2
None	I	19	A9	Nový Jičín	CZ	75	E8	O Convento	E	22	D2
Noordwijk-Binnen	NL	10	D5	Novyy Rozdil	UA	73	E6	O Corgo	E	22	C4
Nora	S	46	C6	Nowa Dęba	PL	73	C3	Ócsa	H	76	C6
Norberg	S	47	B7	Nowa Ruda	PL	74	C6	Odda	N	48	C3
Nordborg	DK	44	G3	Nowa Sarzyna	PL	73	D4	Odder	DK	44	E4
Norden	D	42	C2	Nowa Sól	PL	70	G5	Odense	DK	44	F4
Norderney	D	42	C2	Nowe	PL	71	C8	Oderzo	I	35	B9
Norderstedt	D	42	C5	Nowe Miasto Lubawskie	PL	71	D9	Odivelas	P	24	F2
Nordfjordeid	N	50	D2	Nowogard	PL	43	C12	Odobești	RO	79	F7
Nordhausen	D	40	A6	Nowy Dwór Gdański	PL	71	B9	Odobești	RO	83	B9
Nordholz	D	42	C4	Nowy Dwór Mazowiecki	PL	71	F11	Odorheiu Secuiesc	RO	78	E5
Nordhorn	D	11	C9	Nowy Sącz	PL	73	E1	Odry	CZ	75	E8
Nördlingen	D	38	A3	Nowy Targ	PL	75	E11	Odžaci	SRB	76	F6
Noreikiškės	LT	68	F6	Nowy Tomyśl	PL	70	F5	Oebisfelde	D	43	F7
Norheimsund	N	48	B3	Noyon	F	12	B3	Oelsnitz	D	41	C8

Paignton	GB	8	G4	Partinico	I	30	E3	Periș	RO	83	B10
Paimio	FIN	53	G11	Partizánske	SK	75	G9	Perișoru	RO	83	B12
Paimpol	F	14	D4	Pașcani	RO	79	C7	Peristeri	GR	89	B7
Paisley	GB	2	H5	Pasewalk	D	43	C10	Perleberg	D	43	D8
Pajęczno	PL	75	B10	Pasłęk	PL	68	G1	Përmet	AL	86	E3
Pakrac	HR	76	G2	Passau	D	39	B8	Pernik	BG	82	F5
Pakruojis	LT	68	C6	Pastavy	BY	69	E10	Péronnas	F	36	E2
Paks	H	76	D5	Pasvalys	LT	69	C7	Péronne	F	12	B3
Palafrugell	E	18	G2	Pásztó	H	77	B7	Perpignan	F	18	F1
Palagiano	I	31	B9	Pătârlagele	RO	78	G6	Perros-Guirec	F	14	D4
Palagonia	I	30	F5	Paterna	E	27	F10	Pershore	GB	8	C6
Palaikastro	GR	89	G11	Paternion	A	39	E8	Perstorp	S	45	D8
Palaiochora	GR	89	G7	Paternò	I	30	F6	Perth	GB	2	G6
Palaiokastritsa	GR	86	F2	Patos	AL	86	D2	Pertuis	F	18	D6
Palamas	GR	86	F6	Patra	GR	88	B4	Perugia	I	35	H9
Palamós	E	18	H2	Pattensen	D	42	F5	Perushtitsa	BG	83	G7
Palanga	LT	68	C3	Patti	I	30	E6	Pervomaisc	MD	79	D12
Palas de Rei	E	22	C3	Pau	F	20	B6	Pesaro	I	35	F10
Palau	I	32	C3	Pauillac	F	16	E3	Pescara	I	33	B8
Palavas-les-Flots	F	17	H11	Păunești	RO	79	E8	Pescia	I	35	F6
Palazzolo Acreide	I	30	G6	Pavia	I	34	C4	Peshkopi	AL	86	B3
Paldiski	EST	66	B5	Pavilly	F	15	B10	Peshtera	BG	83	G7
Palencia	E	23	E9	Pavlikeni	BG	83	E9	Pesnica	SLO	39	F11
Palermo	I	30	E3	Pavlovsk	RUS	65	H11	Pesochnyy	RUS	65	G11
Palestrina	I	32	D6	Pavullo nel Frignano	I	35	E7	Peso da Régua	P	22	F4
Palić	SRB	77	E7	Payerne	CH	13	H9	Pessac	F	16	E3
Palma Campania	I	30	B5	Pazardzhik	BG	83	G7	Peterborough	GB	9	C9
Palma del Río	E	28	C3	Pazin	HR	35	C12	Peterhead	GB	3	D8
Palma de Mallorca	E	29	F9	Peal de Becerro	E	29	C7	Peterlee	GB	5	D9
Palma di Montechiaro	I	30	G4	Peccioli	I	35	G7	Petersfield	GB	9	F8
Palmi	I	31	G7	Pécel	H	76	C6	Petilia Policastro	I	31	E9
Palombara Sabina	I	32	C6	Pechea	RO	79	F9	Petrești	RO	83	B9
Păltinoasa	RO	78	B6	Pechory	RUS	67	E9	Petrich	BG	87	B8
Pamiers	F	21	B9	Pecica	RO	77	E9	Petrila	RO	78	G1
Pamplona	E	20	C4	Pécs	H	76	E4	Petrinja	HR	76	G1
Panagyurishte	BG	83	F7	Pedro Muñoz	E	26	F6	Petrodvorets	RUS	65	H10
Panazol	F	17	C7	Pedroso	P	22	G2	Petroșani	RO	78	G1
Pančevo	SRB	77	H8	Peebles	GB	4	B6	Petrovac	SRB	82	B2
Panciu	RO	79	F7	Peer	B	11	F7	Petrovaradin	SRB	77	G7
Pâncota	RO	77	E10	Pegnitz	D	41	E7	Peyrehorade	F	16	H3
Pănet	RO	78	D3	Pego	E	27	G10	Pézenas	F	18	D2
Panevėžys	LT	69	D7	Peiraias	GR	89	C7	Pezinok	SK	75	H7
Pantelimon	RO	83	B10	Peitz	D	43	G11	Pfaffenhoffen	F	13	D10
Paola	I	31	E8	Pejë	RKS	81	G11	Pfarrkirchen	D	39	B7
Pápa	H	76	C3	Pelago	I	35	F8	Pforzheim	D	13	D11
Papenburg	D	11	B10	Pelhřimov	CZ	74	E4	Piacenza	I	34	D5
Parabita	I	31	C11	Pelplin	PL	71	C8	Piana degli Albanesi	I	30	E3
Paraćin	SRB	82	C2	Pembroke	GB	8	D2	Pianella	I	33	C8
Paralia	GR	88	E6	Pembroke Dock	GB	8	D2	Pianoro	I	35	E8
Paralia Avdiron	GR	87	C11	Peñafiel	E	23	E10	Piaseczno	PL	71	G11
Paralia Saranti	GR	88	B4	Peñaranda de Bracamonte	E	23	G8	Piatra Neamț	RO	78	D6
Paray-le-Monial	F	17	B11	Peñarroya-Pueblonuevo	E	24	G8	Piatra Olt	RO	83	B7
Parchim	D	43	D8	Penarth	GB	8	E5	Piazza Armerina	I	30	F5
Parczew	PL	72	G5	Peniche	P	24	D1	Picassent	E	27	F10
Pardubice	CZ	74	D5	Penicuik	GB	2	H6	Pickering	GB	5	E9
Parempuyre	F	16	E3	Peñíscola	E	21	H7	Piedimonte Matese	I	33	E8
Parets del Vallès	E	21	F10	Penmarch	F	14	F2	Piedrabuena	E	26	G4
Parga	GR	86	G3	Penne	I	33	B8	Piedras Blancas	E	23	B7
Pargas	FIN	53	G11	Penrith	GB	5	D7	Pieksämäki	FIN	65	C8
Pargolovo	RUS	65	G11	Penzance	GB	8	G1	Pieńsk	PL	41	B12
Paris	F	12	D2	Penzberg	D	37	B11	Piera	E	21	F9
Pârjol	RO	79	D7	Pëqin	AL	86	C2	Pierrelatte	F	17	F12
Parkano	FIN	53	D11	Perama	GR	89	C7	Piešťany	SK	75	G8
Parma	I	34	D6	Perechyn	UA	73	G4	Pietarsaari	FIN	56	G5
Pärnu	EST	66	D5	Peretu	RO	83	C8	Pietraperzia	I	30	F4
Paroikia	GR	89	D9	Perg	A	39	B9	Pietrasanta	I	34	F6
Parsberg	D	41	F7	Pergine Valsugana	I	35	B7	Pihlava	FIN	53	E10
Pârscov	RO	78	G7	Pergola	I	35	G10	Piła	PL	70	D6
Partanna	I	30	E2	Periam	RO	77	E9	Pilis	H	76	C6
Parthenay	F	16	B4	Périgueux	F	16	E6	Pilisszentiván	H	76	B5

P

P

Place	Country	No.	Grid	Place	Country	No.	Grid	Place	Country	No.	Grid
Pilisvörösvár	H	76	B5	Poddębice	PL	71	G9	Pont-l'Abbé	F	14	F2
Pinarhisar	TR	84	H3	Poděbrady	CZ	41	D12	Pontoise	F	12	C2
Pińczów	PL	73	C1	Podgorica	MNE	81	G9	Pontremoli	I	34	E5
Pineda de Mar	E	21	E11	Podoleni	RO	79	D7	Pont-St-Esprit	F	17	F12
Pinerolo	I	19	B9	Podstrana	HR	80	E4	Pontypool	GB	8	D5
Pineto	I	33	B8	Podu Iloaiei	RO	79	C8	Pontypridd	GB	8	D4
Pinkafeld	A	39	D11	Podujevë	RKS	81	F12	Poole	GB	8	F6
Pinoso	E	27	H9	Poduri	RO	78	E7	Popești	RO	77	C11
Pinos-Puente	E	28	D6	Podu Turcului	RO	79	E8	Popești-Leordeni	RO	83	B10
Pinto	E	26	D4	Poggiardo	I	31	C12	Popoli	I	33	C7
Piolenc	F	18	C4	Poggibonsi	I	35	G7	Popovo	BG	83	D10
Piombino	I	32	A2	Pogoanele	RO	79	H7	Poppi	I	35	F8
Pionerskiy	RUS	68	E2	Pogradec	AL	86	C3	Poprad	SK	73	F1
Piotrków Trybunalski	PL	71	H9	Poiana Lacului	RO	78	H4	Popricani	RO	79	C8
Pipirig	RO	78	C6	Poiana Mare	RO	82	C5	Porcuna	E	28	C5
Piran	SLO	35	C11	Poiana Mărului	RO	78	F5	Pordenone	I	35	B10
Pirkkala	FIN	53	E12	Poiana Teiuliu	RO	78	C6	Poreč	HR	35	C11
Pirna	D	41	B10	Poieni	RO	77	D12	Pori	FIN	53	E10
Pirot	SRB	82	E4	Poienile de Sub Munte	RO	78	B3	Porkhov	RUS	67	F12
Pisa	I	34	F6	Poitiers	F	16	B5	Pornic	F	14	G6
Piscu	RO	79	F9	Pokka	FIN	59	G8	Porozina	HR	80	B1
Piscu Vechi	RO	82	C5	Pola de Lena	E	23	B7	Porrentruy	CH	13	G9
Písek	CZ	41	E11	Pola de Siero	E	23	B7	Porsgrunn	N	49	D7
Pishchanka	UA	79	A10	Połaniec	PL	73	C2	Portadown	GB	4	E2
Pisticci	I	31	C9	Połczyn Zdrój	PL	70	C5	Portalegre	P	24	E5
Pistoia	I	35	F7	Polessk	RUS	68	F3	Port Askaig	GB	2	H3
Pisz	PL	68	H4	Polgár	H	77	B9	Port Ellen	GB	2	H3
Piteå	S	56	C3	Polgárdi	H	76	C4	Portes-lès-Valence	F	18	B5
Pitești	RO	78	H4	Poliçan	AL	86	D2	Portets	F	16	E4
Pithiviers	F	12	E2	Police	PL	43	C11	Porthcawl	GB	8	E4
Pitomača	HR	76	F3	Polichni	GR	87	D7	Portici	I	30	B5
Pizarra	E	28	E4	Polička	CZ	74	E6	Portimão	P	25	K3
Pizzo	I	31	F8	Policoro	I	31	C9	Portishead	GB	8	E5
Plaintel	F	14	E4	Polignano a Mare	I	31	B10	Port Láirge	IRL	7	M6
Plasencia	E	24	C7	Polistena	I	31	G8	Portlaoise	IRL	7	K5
Platanos	GR	89	F7	Polkowice	PL	70	H5	Portlethen	GB	3	E8
Plau	D	43	D8	Polla	I	31	B7	Portmarnock	IRL	4	G3
Plauen	D	41	C8	Pollença	E	29	E10	Portnahaven	GB	2	H2
Plenița	RO	82	C5	Pollenza	I	35	G11	Porto	P	22	F2
Plérin	F	14	D5	Polski Trŭmbesh	BG	83	D9	Porto Cervo	I	32	C3
Pleszew	PL	71	G7	Poltár	SK	75	G11	Porto do Son	E	22	C1
Pleven	BG	83	D7	Põltsamaa	EST	67	D7	Porto Empedocle	I	30	F3
Pljevlja	MNE	81	E9	Polva	EST	67	E8	Portoferraio	I	32	B2
Ploče	HR	80	F6	Polygyros	GR	87	D8	Portogruaro	I	35	B10
Płock	PL	71	F10	Polykastro	GR	87	C7	Pörtom	FIN	53	B10
Ploemeur	F	14	F4	Pomarance	I	35	G7	Porto Recanati	I	35	G11
Ploërmel	F	14	F5	Pombal	P	24	C3	Porto San Giorgio	I	35	H12
Ploiești	RO	78	H6	Pomezia	I	32	D5	Porto Sant'Elpidio	I	35	G12
Plön	D	42	B6	Pomorie	BG	84	F3	Portoscuso	I	32	G1
Płońsk	PL	71	E10	Pompei	I	30	B5	Porto Tolle	I	35	D9
Plopeni	RO	78	G6	Ponferrada	E	22	D6	Porto Torres	I	32	D1
Plopii-Slăvitești	RO	83	C7	Poniatowa	PL	73	B3	Porto-Vecchio	F	19	G11
Plopșoru	RO	78	H1	Ponsacco	I	34	G6	Portree	GB	2	D3
Plosca	RO	83	C8	Pont-à-Mousson	F	13	D8	Portrush	GB	4	C2
Ploudalmézeau	F	14	D2	Pontardawe	GB	8	D4	Portsmouth	GB	9	F8
Ploufragan	F	14	E5	Pontarlier	F	13	H8	Portstewart	GB	4	C2
Plouguerneau	F	14	D2	Pontassieve	I	35	F8	Port-St-Louis-du-Rhône	F	18	E5
Plouzané	F	14	E2	Pont-Audemer	F	15	C9	Port Talbot	GB	8	E4
Plovdiv	BG	83	G8	Pontcharra	F	36	G4	Portugalete	E	20	B1
Plungė	LT	68	C4	Pontchâteau	F	14	G6	Port-Vendres	F	18	F2
Pluvigner	F	14	F4	Pont-du-Château	F	17	C10	Porvoo	FIN	64	G6
Plyeshchanitsy	BY	69	F11	Ponteareas	E	22	C2	Posada	E	23	B7
Plymouth	GB	8	G3	Pontecagnano Faiano	I	30	B6	Posadas	E	28	C4
Plzeň	CZ	41	E9	Pontecorvo	I	33	D7	Pößneck	D	41	C7
Pniewy	PL	70	F5	Pontedera	I	34	G6	Poșta Câlnău	RO	79	G7
Pobiedziska	PL	70	F6	Ponteland	GB	5	C8	Postojna	SLO	35	B12
Pocking	D	39	B7	Pontevedra	E	22	D2	Potcoava	RO	83	B7
Pocklington	GB	5	F9	Pontinia	I	32	D6	Potenza	I	31	B7
Podari	RO	82	C6	Pontivy	F	14	E4	Potenza Picena	I	35	G11
Podbořany	CZ	41	D10					Potlogi	RO	83	B9

138

Potsdam	D	43	F9
Pottendorf	A	39	C12
Poulton-le-Fylde	GB	5	F7
Pouzauges	F	15	H7
Považská Bystrica	SK	75	F9
Póvoa de Varzim	P	22	F2
Poyrazcık	TR	85	F3
Požarevac	SRB	81	C12
Požega	HR	76	G3
Požega	SRB	81	D10
Poznań	PL	70	F6
Pozo Alcón	E	29	C7
Pozoblanco	E	26	H2
Pozuelo de Alarcón	E	23	H10
Pozzallo	I	30	G5
Pozzuoli	I	30	B5
Prabuty	PL	71	C9
Prachatice	CZ	41	F10
Prades	F	21	C10
Prado del Rey	E	25	L8
Prague	CZ	41	D11
Praha	CZ	41	D11
Praia a Mare	I	31	D7
Praia da Tocha	P	24	B2
Praid	RO	78	D4
Praszka	PL	75	B9
Prato	I	35	F7
Pravia	E	22	B6
Predappio	I	35	F9
Predeal	RO	78	F5
Preetz	D	42	B6
Preiļi	LV	69	C10
Prejmer	RO	78	F5
Preko	HR	80	D2
Premià de Mar	E	21	F10
Premnitz	D	43	E8
Prenzlau	D	43	D10
Přerov	CZ	75	E8
Preševo	SRB	82	G2
Presicce	I	31	D11
Prešov	SK	73	F2
Pressbaum	A	39	C11
Prestatyn	GB	4	G6
Přeštice	CZ	41	E9
Preston	GB	5	F7
Prestwick	GB	4	C4
Preutești	RO	78	C6
Preveza	GR	86	G4
Priboj	SRB	81	E9
Příbram	CZ	41	E10
Priego de Córdoba	E	28	D5
Prienai	LT	68	F6
Prievidza	SK	75	G9
Prijedor	BIH	76	H2
Prijepolje	SRB	81	E10
Prilep	MK	86	B5
Primorsk	RUS	65	G9
Priolo Gargallo	I	30	G6
Priozersk	RUS	65	E11
Prishtinë	RKS	82	F2
Priština	RKS	82	F2
Pritzwalk	D	43	D8
Privas	F	17	E12
Priverno	I	32	D6
Prizren	RKS	81	G11
Prizzi	I	30	E3
Prnjavor	BIH	76	H3
Probištip	MK	82	G3
Prokuplje	SRB	82	E2
Prostějov	CZ	75	E7
Proszowice	PL	73	D1
Provadiya	BG	83	E12
Provins	F	12	D4
Prudhoe	GB	5	D8
Prudnik	PL	75	C8
Prüm	D	11	H8
Prundeni	RO	83	B7
Prundu	RO	83	C10
Prundu Bârgăului	RO	78	C4
Pruszcz Gdański	PL	71	B8
Pruszków	PL	71	F11
Przasnysz	PL	71	E11
Przemków	PL	70	H5
Przemyśl	PL	73	E4
Przeworsk	PL	73	D4
Przysucha	PL	71	H11
Psachna	GR	89	A7
Psarades	GR	86	C4
Pskov	RUS	67	E10
Ptolemaïda	GR	86	D5
Ptuj	SLO	39	F11
Puchenii Mari	RO	83	A10
Puchheim	D	38	C5
Púchov	SK	75	F9
Pucioasa	RO	78	G5
Puck	PL	71	A8
Puçol	E	27	E10
Puente-Genil	E	28	D4
Puerto de Santa Maria	E	25	L7
Puertollano	E	26	G4
Puerto Lumbreras	E	29	D9
Puerto Real	E	25	L7
Pui	RO	77	F12
Puigcerdà	E	21	D10
Puig-reig	E	21	E9
Pula	HR	35	D12
Pula	I	32	H2
Puławy	PL	72	H4
Pulsano	I	31	C10
Pułtusk	PL	71	E11
Punta Umbría	E	25	K5
Purgstall an der Erlauf	A	39	C10
Pürvomay	BG	83	G8
Pushkin	RUS	65	H11
Pushkinskiye Gory	RUS	67	G11
Püspökladány	H	77	C9
Pustomyty	UA	73	E6
Puszczykowo	PL	70	F6
Pusztaszabolcs	H	76	C5
Putignano	I	31	B10
Putnok	H	73	H1
Puttgarden	D	43	A7
Pyle	GB	8	E4
Pyrgos	GR	88	C3
Pyrzyce	PL	43	D11
Pyskowice	PL	75	C9
Pytalovo	RUS	67	G10
Pythagoreio	GR	88	D2

Q

Quakenbrück	D	11	C10
Qualiano	I	30	B5
Quarrata	I	35	F7
Quarteira	P	25	K3
Quartu Sant'Elena	I	32	G3
Quedlinburg	D	43	G7
Querfurt	D	41	A7
Quiberon	F	14	G4
Quiliano	I	19	C11
Quimper	F	14	F3
Quimperlé	F	14	F3
Quintana de la Serena	E	24	F8
Quintanar de la Orden	E	26	F5
Quiroga	E	22	D4

R

Raahe	FIN	56	E6
Raalte	NL	11	C8
Rabastens	F	17	G7
Rabka	PL	75	E11
Răcăciuni	RO	79	E7
Racale	I	31	D11
Racalmuto	I	30	F4
Răcari	RO	83	B9
Racconigi	I	19	B9
Răchitoasa	RO	79	E8
Racibórz	PL	75	D9
Ráckeve	H	76	C5
Radashkovichy	BY	69	G11
Rădăuţi	RO	78	B6
Radebeul	D	41	B10
Radenthein	A	39	E8
Radlje ob Dravi	SLO	39	F10
Radnevo	BG	83	G10
Radom	PL	72	H3
Radomir	BG	82	F5
Radomsko	PL	75	B10
Radovanu	RO	83	C11
Radoviš	MK	82	H4
Radovljica	SLO	39	F9
Radstock	GB	8	E6
Răducăneni	RO	79	D9
Radviliškis	LT	68	D6
Radymno	PL	73	D4
Radziejów	PL	71	E8
Radzyń Podlaski	PL	72	G5
Raffadali	I	30	F3
Ragunda	S	52	B4
Ragusa	I	30	G5
Rahden	D	11	C11
Rahovec	RKS	81	G11
Rain	D	38	B4
Raisio	FIN	53	G10
Rakamaz	H	73	H2
Rakhiv	UA	78	A3
Rakitovo	BG	82	G6
Rákóczifalva	H	77	C8
Rakovník	CZ	41	D10
Rakovski	BG	83	G8
Rakvere	EST	67	B8
Ramacca	I	30	F5
Rambervillers	F	13	E8
Rambouillet	F	12	D2
Râmnicu Sărat	RO	79	G7
Râmnicu Vâlcea	RO	78	G3
Ramonville-St-Agne	F	17	H7
Ramsey	GBM	4	E5
Ramsgate	GB	9	E11
Ramsjö	S	52	D3
Rânåsfoss	N	46	B2
Randazzo	I	30	E6
Randers	DK	44	D4
Randsjö	S	51	D11
Randsverk	N	50	E6
Rankweil	A	37	C9
Raon-l'Étape	F	13	E9

R

R

Roskilde	DK 44	E6
Roskovec	AL 86	D2
Rosolini	I 30	G6
Rosporden	F 14	F3
Rossano	I 31	D9
Roßlau	D 43	G8
Ross-on-Wye	GB 8	D6
Røssvassbukta	N 55	C6
Rostock	D 43	B8
Rot	S 51	F11
Rota	E 25	L6
Rotenburg (Wümme)	D 11	B12
Roth	D 40	F6
Rothenburg ob der Tauber	D 40	E5
Rotherham	GB 5	G9
Rothesay	GB 2	H4
Rothwell	GB 5	F8
Rottenmann	A 39	D9
Rotterdam	NL 10	D5
Rottweil	D 13	E11
Roubaix	F 10	G3
Rouen	F 15	C10
Roulers	B 10	F3
Rovaniemi	FIN 61	E8
Rovato	I 34	C5
Rovereto	I 35	B7
Rovigo	I 35	D8
Rovinari	RO 78	H1
Rovinj	HR 35	D11
Royan	F 16	D3
Roye	F 12	B3
Røyrvik	N 54	E6
Royston	GB 9	D9
Rožaje	MNE 81	F10
Rozavlea	RO 78	B3
Rozdil'na	UA 79	D12
Rožňava	SK 73	G1
Roznov	RO 78	D7
Rozzano	I 34	C4
Rubano	I 35	C8
Rucăr	RO 78	G4
Ruciane-Nida	PL 68	H3
Rudne	UA 73	E6
Rudnik nad Sadem	PL 73	C3
Rudolstadt	D 41	C7
Rudozem	BG 87	B10
Rudzyensk	BY 69	H11
Ruelle-sur-Touvre	F 16	D5
Ruffano	I 31	D11
Rufina	I 35	F8
Rugby	GB 9	D7
Rugeley	GB 5	H8
Ruginoasa	RO 79	C7
Ruma	SRB 77	G7
Rumburk	CZ 41	B11
Rumia	PL 71	B8
Rumilly	F 36	F3
Runcorn	GB 5	G7
Ruona	FIN 53	B12
Rupea	RO 78	E4
Rusăneşti	RO 83	C7
Ruse	BG 83	C10
Ruše	SLO 39	F11
Rushden	GB 9	C8
Ruski Krstur	SRB 76	F6
Russi	I 35	E9
Rute	E 28	D5
Rüthen	D 11	E11
Ruthin	GB 4	G6
Ruurlo	NL 11	D8

Ruvo di Puglia	I 31	A8
Ružomberok	SK 75	F10
Rybnik	PL 75	D9
Rychnov nad Kněžnou	CZ 74	D6
Ryde	GB 9	F8
Rydułtowy	PL 75	D9
Rygnestad	N 48	D4
Ryki	PL 72	G4
Rýmařov	CZ 75	D7
Rypin	PL 71	E9
Rysjedal	N 50	F2
Rzepin	PL 43	F11
Rzeszów	PL 73	D3

S

Saalfeld	D 41	C7
Saalfelden am Steinernen Meer	A 39	D7
Saanen	CH 36	E5
Saarbrücken	D 13	C9
Saarenkylä	FIN 61	E8
Saarijärvi	FIN 64	B6
Saarlouis	D 13	C9
Šabac	SRB 81	B10
Sabadell	E 21	F10
Săbăoani	RO 79	C7
Sabaudia	I 32	E6
Sabiñánigo	E 20	D6
Sabinov	SK 73	F2
Sablé-sur-Sarthe	F 15	F8
Săcălăşeni	RO 78	B2
Săcălaz	RO 77	F9
Săcele	RO 78	F5
Sacile	I 35	B10
Săcueni	RO 77	C11
Sadova	RO 82	C6
Sæby	DK 44	B4
Säffle	S 46	C4
Saffron Walden	GB 9	D10
Săgeata	RO 79	C7
Sagna	RO 79	D7
Sagunto	E 27	E10
Šahy	SK 76	A5
St-Affrique	F 17	G9
St-Aignan	F 15	G10
St-Alban-Leysse	F 36	G3
St Albans	GB 9	D9
St-Amand-Montrond	F 12	H3
St-Amarin	F 13	F9
St-André-de-Cubzac	F 16	E4
St Andrews	GB 3	G7
St Apollinaire	F 12	G6
St-Astier	F 16	E5
St-Aubin-lès-Elbeuf	F 15	C10
St Austell	GB 8	G2
St-Avé	F 14	F5
St-Avertin	F 15	G10
St-Avold	F 13	C9
St-Benoît	F 16	B5
St-Berthevin	F 15	E7
St Brelade	GBJ 14	C5
St-Brieuc	F 14	D5
St-Chamas	F 18	D5
St-Chamond	F 17	D12
St-Christol-lès-Alès	F 17	G11
St-Claude	F 36	E3
St Cloud	F 12	D2
St-Cyprien	F 18	F2

St-Cyr-sur-Loire	F 15	G9
St-Denis	F 12	D2
St-Dié	F 13	E9
St-Dizier	F 12	D6
St-Doulchard	F 12	G2
Ste-Adresse	F 15	B9
Ste-Livrade-sur-Lot	F 16	F5
St-Éloy-les-Mines	F 17	C9
Ste-Maxime	F 19	E8
Saintes	F 16	C3
St-Étienne	F 17	D12
St-Étienne-de-Montluc	F 14	G6
St-Florentin	F 12	E4
St-Florent-sur-Cher	F 12	H2
St-Flour	F 17	E10
St-Galmier	F 17	D12
St-Gaudens	F 21	B8
St-Georges-de-Didonne	F 16	D3
St-Germain	F 12	E5
St-Germain-du-Puy	F 12	G2
St-Gilles	F 17	H12
St-Gilles-Croix-de-Vie	F 16	B1
St-Girons	F 21	C8
St Helens	GB 5	G7
St Helier	GBJ 14	C5
St-Herblain	F 14	G6
St-Hilaire-de-Riez	F 16	A1
St-Hilaire-du-Harcouët	F 15	D7
St Ives	GB 8	G1
St Ives	GB 9	C9
St-Jacques-de-la-Lande	F 14	E6
St-Jean-d'Angély	F 16	C4
St Jean du Cardonnay	F 15	C10
St-Jean-de-Luz	F 20	B4
St-Jean-de-Monts	F 14	H6
St-Jean-de-Védas	F 17	H11
St-Jean-d'Illac	F 16	E3
St-Jorioz	F 36	F4
St-Junien	F 16	C6
St-Just-en-Chaussée	F 12	B2
St-Laurent-de-la-Salanque	F 18	F1
St-Laurent-du-Var	F 19	D8
St-Lô	F 15	C7
St-Lys	F 17	H6
St-Macaire	F 16	F4
St-Maixent-l'École	F 16	B4
St-Malo	F 14	D6
St-Marcel-lès-Valence	F 18	A5
St-Marcellin	F 18	A5
St Margaret's Hope	GB 3	E10
St Martens Latem	B 10	F4
St-Maurice-l'Exil	F 17	D12
St Maximin	F 12	C2
St-Maximin-la-Ste-Baume	F 18	D6
St-Médard-en-Jalles	F 16	E3
St-Mihiel	F 13	D7
St-Nazaire	F 14	G5
St Neots	GB 9	C9
St-Nicolas-de-Port	F 13	D8
St-Pair-sur-Mer	F 14	D6
St-Paul-lès-Dax	F 16	G3
St-Péray	F 18	A5
St Peter Port	GBG 14	C5
St Petersburg	RUS 65	G11
St-Philbert-de-Grand-Lieu	F 14	G6
St-Pierre-d'Oléron	F 16	C2
St-Pierre-en-Faucigny	F 36	F4
St-Pierre-lès-Elbeuf	F 15	C10
St-Pierre-Montlimart	F 15	G7
St-Pol-de-Léon	F 14	D3

S

S

Sokobanja	SRB	82	D3	Spadafora	I	30	D6	Stebnyk	UA	73	F5
Sokółka	PL	72	D6	Spalding	GB	5	H10	Steenwijk	NL	11	C8
Sokołow Podlaski	PL	72	F4	Sparanise	I	30	A5	Ştefan cel Mare	RO	79	E7
Solarino	I	30	G6	Sparti	GR	88	D5	Ştefăneşti	RO	78	H4
Şoldăneşti	MD	79	B10	Spata	GR	89	C7	Ştefăneşti	RO	79	B8
Solec Kujawski	PL	71	E8	Spello	I	32	A5	Ştefan Vodă	MD	79	D12
Soleto	I	31	C11	Spennymoor	GB	5	D8	Ştei	RO	77	D11
Solihull	GB	9	C7	Spetses	GR	88	D6	Steinfurt	D	11	D9
Solin	HR	80	E4	Spezzano Albanese	I	31	D8	Steinheim	D	11	D12
Sollefteå	S	52	B5	Spiez	CH	36	D6	Steinkjer	N	54	F4
Sollentuna	S	47	C9	Spijkenisse	NL	10	D5	Stendal	D	43	E8
Söller	E	29	F9	Spilamberto	I	35	E7	Stenløse	DK	44	E6
Solofra	I	30	B6	Spilimbergo	I	35	B10	Stenungsund	S	46	F2
Solothurn	CH	13	G10	Spinazzola	I	31	B8	Šternberk	CZ	75	E7
Solsona	E	21	E9	Spinea	I	35	C9	Stes-Maries-de-la-Mer	F	18	D4
Solt	H	76	D6	Spinetoli	I	33	B7	Stevenage	GB	9	D9
Soltau	D	42	E5	Spišská Belá	SK	73	F1	Steyerberg	D	11	C12
Soltvadkert	H	76	D6	Spišská Nová Ves	SK	73	F1	Steyr	A	39	C9
Sölvesborg	S	45	E9	Spittal an der Drau	A	39	E8	Stiens	NL	11	B7
Soma	TR	85	F4	Spjelkavik	N	50	C3	Štip	MK	82	H3
Sombor	SRB	76	F6	Split	HR	80	E4	Stirling	GB	2	G5
Şomcuţa Mare	RO	78	B1	Spoleto	I	32	B6	Stjørdalshalsen	N	51	A8
Somero	FIN	53	G12	Spoltore	I	33	B8	Stockach	D	13	F12
Sommacampagna	I	35	C7	Spremberg	D	43	G11	Stockerau	A	39	B12
Sommatino	I	30	F4	Springe	D	42	F5	Stockholm	S	47	C9
Sömmerda	D	40	B6	Sprova	N	54	F4	Stockport	GB	5	G8
Sondalo	I	34	A6	Squinzano	I	31	C11	Stockton-on-Tees	GB	5	D9
Sønderborg	DK	44	G3	Srbobran	SRB	77	F7	Stöde	S	52	C4
Sondershausen	D	40	A6	Sredets	BG	83	F12	Stoke-on-Trent	GB	5	G8
Sondrio	I	34	B5	Srednogorie	BG	83	F7	Stolac	BIH	81	F7
Sonneberg	D	40	C6	Śrem	PL	70	G6	Stolberg (Rheinland)	D	11	G8
Sonseca	E	26	E4	Sremčica	SRB	81	C11	Stollberg	D	41	C9
Son Servera	E	29	F10	Sremska Kamenica	SRB	77	G7	Stolzenau	D	11	C12
Sonta	SRB	76	F6	Sremska Mitrovica	SRB	77	H7	Stone	GB	5	H8
Sonthofen	D	37	C10	Sremski Karlovci	SRB	77	G7	Stonehaven	GB	3	E8
Sopot	BG	83	F8	Środa Wielkopolska	PL	70	F6	Storby	FIN	47	A11
Sopot	PL	71	B8	Srpska Crnja	SRB	77	F8	Støren	N	51	B7
Sopron	H	76	B2	Stade	D	42	C5	Storkow	D	43	F10
Sora	I	33	D7	Staden	B	10	F3	Storlien	S	51	B9
Sorgues	F	18	C5	Stadskanaal	NL	11	B9	Stornoway	GB	2	C2
Soria	E	20	E2	Staffanstorp	S	45	E8	Storozhynets'	UA	78	A5
Soriano nel Cimino	I	32	B5	Staffelstein	D	40	D6	Storrington	GB	9	F9
Sorø	DK	44	F6	Stafford	GB	5	H8	Storuman	S	55	D10
Soroca	MD	79	A9	Staines	GB	9	E8	Storvreta	S	47	B9
Sorrento	I	30	B5	Stalowa Wola	PL	73	C3	Stourbridge	GB	8	C6
Sorsele	S	55	C10	Stâlpeni	RO	78	G4	Stourport-on-Severn	GB	8	C6
Sorso	I	32	D2	Stamboliyski	BG	83	G7	Støvring	DK	44	C3
Sortavala	RUS	65	D11	Stamford	GB	9	B9	Stowmarket	GB	9	C11
Sortino	I	30	G6	Stănileşti	RO	79	D9	Strabane	GB	4	D1
Sosnovyy Bor	RUS	65	H10	Stanišić	SRB	76	F6	Straja	RO	78	B5
Sosnowiec	PL	75	D10	Stanley	GB	5	D8	Strakonice	CZ	41	F10
Soto	E	22	B6	Stans	CH	13	H11	Straldzha	BG	83	F11
Sotrondio	E	23	B7	Staplehurst	GB	9	E10	Stralsund	D	43	B9
Soufli	GR	85	B1	Starachowice	PL	73	B2	Strängnäs	S	47	C8
Souk el Had el Rharbia	MA	28	H2	Stará Ľubovňa	SK	73	F1	Stranraer	GB	4	D4
Souk-Khémis-des-Anjra	MA	28	H3	Stara Moravica	SRB	76	F6	Strasbourg	F	13	D10
Souk Tleta Taghramet	MA	28	G3	Stara Pazova	SRB	77	H7	Strasburg	D	43	D10
Souppes-sur-Loing	F	12	E3	Stara Zagora	BG	83	F9	Străşeni	MD	79	C10
Soustons	F	16	G2	Stargard Szczeciński	PL	43	D12	Straßwalchen	A	39	C7
Southampton	GB	9	F7	Starogard Gdański	PL	71	C8	Stratford-upon-Avon	GB	9	C7
Southend-on-Sea	GB	9	E10	Starokozache	UA	79	E12	Strathaven	GB	2	H5
Southport	GB	5	F6	Staryy Sambir	UA	73	E4	Straubing	D	38	A6
South Queensferry	GB	2	G6	Staßfurt	D	43	G7	Straumen	N	59	B11
South Shields	GB	5	D8	Staszów	PL	73	C2	Strausberg	D	43	E10
Sovata	RO	78	D4	Stăuceni	MD	79	C10	Strážnice	CZ	75	F7
Soverato	I	31	F9	Staudach im Allgau	D	38	D2	Street	GB	8	E5
Sovetsk	RUS	68	E4	Stavang	N	50	E2	Strehaia	RO	82	B5
Sovetskiy	RUS	65	F9	Stavanger	N	48	E2	Strelcha	BG	83	F7
Sovicille	I	35	G7	Staveley	GB	5	G9	Stříbro	CZ	41	E9
Soyaux	F	16	D5	Stavsnäs	S	47	C10	Strommen	N	46	B1

Stromness	GB	3	E9
Strömstad	S	46	D2
Strömsund	S	55	G8
Strongoli	I	31	E9
Stropkov	SK	73	F3
Stroud	GB	8	D6
Struer	DK	44	D2
Struga	MK	86	C3
Strugi-Krasnyye	RUS	67	E11
Strumica	MK	87	B7
Stryn	N	50	D3
Stryy	UA	73	F6
Strzegom	PL	74	B6
Strzelce Krajeńskie	PL	70	E4
Strzelce Opolskie	PL	75	C9
Strzelin	PL	75	C7
Strzelno	PL	71	E8
Strzyżów	PL	73	E3
Studénka	CZ	75	E8
Stupava	SK	75	H7
Štúrovo	SK	76	B5
Stuttgart	D	13	D12
Suances	E	23	B10
Subiaco	I	32	C6
Subotica	SRB	77	E7
Suceava	RO	78	B6
Suchedniów	PL	73	B1
Suciu de Sus	RO	78	C2
Sudbury	GB	9	D10
Sudova Vyshnya	UA	73	E5
Sueca	E	27	F10
Sŭedinenie	BG	83	G7
Suhaia	RO	83	D8
Suharekë	RKS	81	G12
Suhl	D	40	C6
Sulechów	PL	70	G4
Sulęcin	PL	70	F4
Sulejów	PL	71	H10
Sulejówek	PL	71	F11
Sulingen	D	11	C12
Sully-sur-Loire	F	12	F2
Sulmona	I	33	C8
Sulzbach-Rosenberg	D	41	E7
Sumburgh	GB	3	C12
Sümeg	H	76	D3
Sumiswald	CH	13	G10
Šumperk	CZ	75	D7
Sundby	DK	44	C3
Sunde	N	48	C2
Sunderland	GB	5	D9
Sundsvall	S	52	C5
Sunnansjö	S	46	A6
Sunndalsøra	N	50	C5
Suolahti	FIN	64	B6
Supur	RO	77	C12
Surahammar	S	47	B7
Šurany	SK	76	A4
Surbo	I	31	C11
Surdulica	SRB	82	F3
Surgères	F	16	C3
Súria	E	21	E9
Surte	S	44	A6
Susa	I	19	A8
Sušice	CZ	41	F10
Susurluk	TR	85	E5
Susz	PL	71	C9
Sutton Coldfield	GB	9	C7
Sutton in Ashfield	GB	5	G9
Suvorovo	BG	83	D12
Suwałki	PL	68	G5

Suzzara	I	35	D7
Svalyava	UA	73	G4
Svedala	S	45	F8
Sveg	S	51	D12
Švenčionėliai	LT	69	E9
Švenčionys	LT	69	E9
Svendborg	DK	44	G4
Svenes	N	48	E5
Svenstavik	S	51	C12
Sveti Nikole	MK	82	G3
Světlá nad Sázavou	CZ	74	E5
Svetlogorsk	RUS	68	E2
Svetlyy	RUS	68	F2
Svetogorsk	RUS	65	E9
Svidník	SK	73	F2
Svilajnac	SRB	81	C12
Svilengrad	BG	83	H10
Svishtov	BG	83	D9
Svislach	BY	72	E6
Svitavy	CZ	74	E6
Svoge	BG	82	E5
Svolvær	N	57	D3
Svrljig	SRB	82	D3
Swaffham	GB	9	B10
Swanage	GB	8	F6
Swanley	GB	9	E9
Swansea	GB	8	D4
Swarzędz	PL	70	F6
Świdnica	PL	74	B6
Świdnik	PL	73	B4
Świdwin	PL	70	C5
Świebodzice	PL	74	B6
Świebodzin	PL	70	F4
Świecie	PL	71	D8
Swindon	GB	9	E7
Świnoujście	PL	43	C11
Swords	IRL	4	G2
Syców	PL	75	A8
Syston	GB	9	B8
Szabadszállás	H	76	D6
Szamotuły	PL	70	E6
Szarvas	H	77	D8
Százhalombatta	H	76	C5
Szczebrzeszyn	PL	73	C4
Szczecin	PL	43	D11
Szczecinek	PL	70	C6
Szczytna	PL	74	C6
Szczytno	PL	71	D11
Szécsény	H	75	H11
Szeged	H	77	E7
Szeghalom	H	77	C9
Szegvár	H	77	D8
Székesfehérvár	H	76	C5
Szekszárd	H	76	E5
Szentendre	H	76	B6
Szentes	H	77	D8
Szentőrinc	H	76	E4
Szerencs	H	73	H2
Szigetszentmiklós	H	76	C6
Szigetvár	H	76	E3
Szikszó	H	73	H2
Szolnok	H	77	C7
Szombathely	H	76	C2
Szprotawa	PL	70	H4
Sztum	PL	71	C9
Szubin	PL	71	E7
Szydłowiec	PL	73	B1

T

Taastrup	DK	44	E6
Tab	H	76	D4
Tábor	CZ	41	E11
Täby	S	47	C9
Tachov	CZ	41	E8
Tadcaster	GB	5	F9
Tafalla	E	20	D4
Taggia	I	19	D10
Taksony	H	76	C6
Talant	F	12	G6
Talavera de la Reina	E	26	E2
Talavera la Real	E	24	F6
Talayuela	E	24	C8
Talence	F	16	E3
Tälje	S	52	C3
Tallinn	EST	66	B6
Tălmaciu	RO	78	F3
Talmont-St-Hilaire	F	16	B2
Talsi	LV	66	G3
Tamási	H	76	D4
Tamaşi	RO	79	D7
Tampere	FIN	53	E12
Tamsweg	A	39	E8
Tamworth	GB	9	B7
Tanacu	RO	79	D9
Țăndărei	RO	83	B12
Tanger	MA	25	N7
Tangerhütte	D	43	F8
Tangermünde	D	43	E8
Tanna	D	41	C7
Țânțăreni	RO	82	B5
Taormina	I	30	E6
Tapa	EST	67	C7
Tápiószecső	H	77	C7
Tápiószele	H	77	C7
Tapolca	H	76	D3
Taraclia	MD	79	F10
Tarancón	E	26	E5
Taranto	I	31	C10
Tarare	F	17	C12
Tarazona	E	20	E3
Tarazona de la Mancha	E	27	F7
Tarbert	GB	2	C2
Tarbert	GB	2	G3
Tarbert	GB	2	H4
Tarbes	F	21	B6
Târgovişte	RO	78	H5
Târgu Bujor	RO	79	F9
Târgu Cărbuneşti	RO	78	H2
Târgu Frumos	RO	79	C7
Târgu Jiu	RO	78	G1
Târgu Lăpuş	RO	78	C2
Târgu Mureş	RO	78	D3
Târgu Neamţ	RO	78	C6
Târgu Ocna	RO	79	E7
Târgu Secuiesc	RO	78	E6
Târgu Trotuş	RO	79	E7
Tarifa	E	25	N8
Tărlungeni	RO	78	F5
Tărnăveni	RO	78	E3
Tarnobrzeg	PL	73	C3
Tarnos	F	16	H2
Târnova	RO	77	E10
Tarnów	PL	73	D2
Tarnowskie Góry	PL	75	C10
Tarquinia	I	32	C4

T

U

Uckfield	GB	9	F9
Uddevalla	S	46	E2
Udeşti	RO	78	B6
Udine	I	35	B11
Ueckermünde	D	43	C10
Uelzen	D	42	E6
Uetendorf	CH	13	H10
Uetersen	D	42	C5
Uetze	D	42	F6
Ugento	I	31	D11
Ugine	F	36	F4
Uherské Hradiště	CZ	75	F8
Uherský Brod	CZ	75	F8
Uig	GB	2	D2
Uithuizen	NL	11	A8
Újfehértó	H	77	B10
Újkígyós	H	77	D9
Újszász	H	77	C7
Ukmergė	LT	69	E7
Ulaş	TR	85	B4
Ulft	NL	11	D8
Ullånger	S	52	B6
Ullapool	GB	2	D4
Ulldecona	E	21	G7
Ulm	D	38	B3
Ulmeni	RO	77	C12
Ulmeni	RO	83	C11
Ulmu	RO	79	H8
Ulricehamn	S	45	A8
Ulsberg	N	51	C7
Ulsta	GB	3	B12
Ulucak	TR	85	G3
Ulverston	GB	4	E6
Umbertide	I	35	G9
Umbrăreşti	RO	79	F8
Umeå	S	56	F2
Umka	SRB	81	C11
Ungheni	MD	79	C9
Ungheni	RO	78	E3
Ungureni	RO	79	B7
Uničov	CZ	75	E7
Unirea	RO	78	E2
Unterägeri	CH	37	C7
Unterhaid b Bamburg	D	40	D6
Unterweitersdorf	A	39	B9
Uppingham	GB	9	C8
Upplands-Väsby	S	47	C9
Uppsala	S	47	B9
Urbania	I	35	G10
Urbino	I	35	F10
Urduña	E	20	C1
Urecheşti	RO	79	F7
Urganlı	TR	85	G4
Uricani	RO	77	G12
Urk	NL	11	C7
Urlaţi	RO	78	H6
Urziceni	RO	83	B11
Uskhodni	BY	69	G11
Uslar	D	42	G5
Ussel	F	17	D8
Ústí nad Labem	CZ	41	C10
Ústí nad Orlicí	CZ	74	D6
Ustka	PL	45	H12
Ustrzyki Dolne	PL	73	E4
Utbjoa	N	48	C2
Utena	LT	69	D9
Utiel	E	27	F9
Utrecht	NL	10	D6
Utrera	E	25	K7
Uttoxeter	GB	5	H8

Uusikaupunki	FIN	53	F10
Uxbridge	GB	9	E9
Uzès	F	17	G12
Uzhhorod	UA	73	G3
Užice	SRB	81	D10
Uzunköprü	TR	85	B2

V

Vaasa	FIN	53	B10
Vác	H	76	B6
Văcăreşti	RO	78	H5
Vado Ligure	I	19	C11
Vadsø	N	59	D11
Vadstena	S	46	E6
Vadul lui Vodă	MD	79	C11
Vadu Moldovei	RO	78	C6
Vadu Paşii	RO	79	G7
Vaduz	FL	37	C9
Våg	N	48	D2
Våge	N	48	G4
Vagney	F	13	E9
Vågsodden	N	54	C5
Vágur	FO	3	C9
Vairano Patenora	I	33	E8
Vaison-la-Romaine	F	18	C5
Valandovo	MK	87	B7
Valašské Klobouky	CZ	75	F8
Valašské Meziříčí	CZ	75	F8
Valbo	S	52	G5
Valby	DK	45	E7
Valdagno	I	35	C8
Valdemoro	E	26	D4
Valdepeñas	E	26	G5
Valderice	I	30	E2
Valdobbiadene	I	35	B9
Vale	GBG	14	C5
Valea lui Mihai	RO	77	B11
Valea Râmnicului	RO	79	G7
Valea Seacă	RO	79	C7
Valea Stanciului	RO	82	C6
Valence	F	16	G6
Valence	F	18	A5
Valencia	E	27	F10
Valencia de Alcántara	E	24	D5
Văleni	RO	79	D9
Vălenii de Munte	RO	78	G6
Valenza	I	19	A11
Valga	EST	67	F7
Valguarnera Caropepe	I	30	F5
Valjevo	SRB	81	C10
Valka	LV	67	F7
Valkeakoski	FIN	64	E5
Valkenswaard	NL	11	E7
Valladolid	E	23	E9
Vallauris	F	19	D8
Vallentuna	S	47	C9
Valletta	M	31	▢
Valli della Lucania	I	30	C6
Valls	E	21	F8
Valmiera	LV	66	F6
Valmontone	I	32	D6
Valognes	F	14	B6
Valozhyn	BY	69	G10
Valpovo	HR	76	F5
Valréas	F	18	C5
Valu lui Traian	RO	84	C4
Valverde del Camino	E	25	J6
Vama	RO	78	B5

Vammala	FIN	53	E11
Vámospércs	H	77	B10
Vânatori	RO	79	F8
Vânătorii Mici	RO	83	B9
Vänersborg	S	46	E3
Vânju Mare	RO	82	B4
Vannes	F	14	F5
Vannvikan	N	51	A7
Vansbro	S	49	B12
Vantaa	FIN	64	G6
Varallo	I	34	B2
Varapayeva	BY	69	E11
Vărăşti	RO	83	C10
Varaždin	HR	39	F12
Varazze	I	19	C11
Varberg	S	44	B6
Varde	DK	44	E2
Vårdö	FIN	53	G8
Varel	D	11	A11
Varėna	LT	69	G7
Varennes-Vauzelles	F	12	G3
Vareš	BIH	81	D7
Varese	I	34	B3
Vargön	S	46	E3
Variaş	RO	77	E9
Varkaus	FIN	65	C8
Varna	BG	84	E3
Värnamo	S	45	B9
Varnsdorf	CZ	41	B11
Várpalota	H	76	C4
Vasa	FIN	53	B10
Vásárosnamény	H	73	H4
Vasilaţi	RO	83	C10
Vaslui	RO	79	D9
Västansjö	S	55	C7
Västerås	S	47	B8
Västerhaninge	S	47	C9
Västervik	S	45	A12
Vasto	I	33	C9
Vasvár	H	76	C2
Vatican City	VAT	32	C5
Vatra Dornei	RO	78	C5
Vauldalen	N	51	C9
Vauvert	F	17	H12
Växjö	S	45	C10
Veauche	F	17	D12
Vecchiano	I	34	F6
Vechta	D	11	C11
Vecsés	H	76	C6
Veda	S	52	B6
Vedea	RO	83	D9
Veendam	NL	11	B9
Veenendaal	NL	11	D7
Vegadeo	E	22	B5
Vegarshei	N	48	E6
Veghel	NL	11	E7
Veglie	I	31	C11
Veidholmen	N	50	A5
Vejen	DK	44	F3
Vejer de la Frontera	E	25	M7
Vejle	DK	44	E3
Vela Luka	HR	80	F5
Velen	D	11	D9
Velenje	SLO	39	F10
Veles	MK	82	H3
Vélez-Málaga	E	28	C5
Vélez-Rubio	E	29	D9
Velika Gorica	HR	39	G11
Velika Kladuša	BIH	80	B3
Velika Plana	SRB	81	C12

Veliki Preslav	BG	83	E11	Vibo Valentia	I	31	F8	Villareal	E	27	E10
Velikiy Lyubin'	UA	73	E6	Vic	E	21	E10	Villarosa	I	30	F4
Veliko Tŭrnovo	BG	83	E9	Vícar	E	29	E8	Villarrobledo	E	26	F6
Velingrad	BG	82	G6	Vicchio	I	35	F8	Villarrubia de los Ojos	E	26	F5
Veľké Kapušany	SK	73	G3	Vicenza	I	35	C8	Villasana de Mena	E	20	B1
Velké Meziříčí	CZ	74	E6	Vichy	F	17	C10	Villa San Giovanni	I	31	G7
Veľký Krtíš	SK	75	H10	Vico del Gargano	I	33	D11	Villasimius	I	32	G3
Veľký Meder	SK	76	B3	Vico Equense	I	30	B5	Villasor	I	32	G2
Velletri	I	32	D6	Vicovu de Sus	RO	78	B5	Villaverde del Río	E	25	J7
Vellinge	S	45	F7	Victoria	RO	78	F4	Villaviciosa	E	23	B7
Velyka Mykhaylivka	UA	79	C12	Vidauban	F	19	D7	Villefontaine	F	36	F2
Velyki Mosty	UA	73	D6	Videle	RO	83	C9	Villefranche-de-Rouergue	F	17	F8
Velykyy Bereznyy	UA	73	G4	Vidin	BG	82	C4	Villefranche-sur-Saône	F	17	C12
Velykyy Bychkiv	UA	78	B2	Vidra	RO	79	F7	Villena	E	27	G9
Venafro	I	33	D8	Vidra	RO	83	C10	Villeneuve-lès-Avignon	F	18	C5
Venaria	I	19	A9	Vidzy	BY	69	D10	Villeneuve-sur-Lot	F	16	F6
Vence	F	19	D8	Viechtach	D	41	F9	Villeneuve-sur-Yonne	F	12	E4
Vendargues	F	17	H11	Vielsalm	B	11	H7	Villers-Cotterêts	F	12	C3
Vendas Novas	P	24	F3	Vienna	A	39	C12	Villeurbanne	F	36	F2
Vendôme	F	15	F10	Vienne	F	36	G2	Vilnius	LT	69	F8
Venelles	F	18	D6	Viersen	D	11	F8	Vilsbiburg	D	38	B6
Venezia	I	35	C9	Vierzon	F	12	G2	Vilshofen	D	39	B7
Vénissieux	F	36	F2	Vieste	I	33	D11	Vilyeyka	BY	69	F10
Vennesla	N	48	F5	Vietri sul Mare	I	30	B6	Vimianzo	E	22	B1
Vennesund	N	54	D4	Vievis	LT	69	F8	Vimmerby	S	45	A11
Venosa	I	31	B7	Vigevano	I	34	C3	Vimperk	CZ	41	F10
Venta de Baños	E	23	E9	Vignola	I	35	E7	Vinarós	E	21	H7
Ventimiglia	I	19	D9	Vigo	E	22	D2	Vinci	I	35	F7
Ventnor	GB	9	G7	Viişoara	RO	78	D2	Vineuil	F	15	F10
Ventspils	LV	66	F2	Vik	N	48	B2	Vinga	RO	77	E9
Vera	E	29	D9	Vikeså	N	48	E3	Vingåker	S	47	D7
Verbania	I	34	B3	Vikna	N	54	E3	Vinica	MK	82	G4
Vercelli	I	34	C3	Viksmon	S	52	B5	Vinje	N	48	A3
Verdalsøra	N	54	G4	Vila do Conde	P	22	F2	Vinjeøra	N	50	B6
Verden (Aller)	D	11	B12	Vilafranca del Penedès	E	21	F9	Vinkovci	HR	76	G5
Verdun	F	13	C7	Vila Franca de Xira	P	24	F2	Vinstra	N	51	E7
Vereşti	RO	78	B6	Vilagarcía de Arousa	E	22	C2	Vinţu de Jos	RO	78	E1
Vergato	I	35	E7	Vilalba	E	22	B4	Vipiteno	I	37	D11
Vergèze	F	17	G12	Vila Nova de Famalicão	P	22	F2	Vire	F	15	D7
Verín	E	22	E4	Vila Nova de Gaia	P	22	F2	Viriat	F	36	E2
Verkhovyna	UA	78	A4	Vila Nova de Ourém	P	24	D3	Virkkala	FIN	64	G5
Verneşti	RO	79	G7	Vilanova i la Geltrú	E	21	F9	Virovitica	HR	76	F3
Verneuil-sur-Avre	F	15	D10	Vilar de Andorinho	P	22	F2	Virrat	FIN	53	C12
Vernier	CH	36	E4	Vila Real	P	22	F4	Vis	HR	33	A11
Vernio	I	35	F7	Vila Real de Santo António	P	25	K5	Visaginas	LT	69	D10
Vernole	I	31	C12	Vilaseca de Solcina	E	21	F8	Visby	S	47	F9
Vernon	F	12	C1	Vila Viçosa	P	24	F5	Višegrad	BIH	81	D9
Veroia	GR	86	D6	Vilches	E	28	B6	Viseu	P	22	G3
Veroli	I	33	D7	Vilhelmina	S	55	E9	Vişeu de Sus	RO	78	B3
Verona	I	35	C7	Viljandi	EST	67	D7	Vişina	RO	83	B9
Versailles	F	12	D2	Vilkaviškis	LT	68	F5	Visoko	BIH	81	D7
Versoix	CH	36	E4	Villabate	I	30	E3	Visselhövede	D	42	E5
Vertou	F	14	G6	Villablino	E	22	C6	Viterbo	I	32	B5
Verzuolo	I	19	B9	Villacañas	E	26	E5	Vitez	BIH	81	D6
Veselí nad Lužnicí	CZ	41	F11	Villa Carcina	I	34	C6	Vitomiricë	RKS	81	G11
Veselí nad Moravou	CZ	75	F7	Villacarrillo	E	29	C7	Vitoria-Gasteiz	E	20	C2
Vesoul	F	13	F8	Villa Castelli	I	31	B10	Vitré	F	15	E7
Veszprém	H	76	C4	Villach	A	39	F8	Vitrolles	F	18	D5
Vésztő	H	77	D9	Villacidro	I	32	G2	Vitry-le-François	F	12	D5
Vetlanda	S	45	B10	Villadossola	I	34	B2	Vittel	F	13	E7
Vetovo	BG	83	D10	Villafranca del Bierzo	E	22	C5	Vittoria	I	30	G5
Vetralla	I	32	C4	Villafranca de los Barros	E	24	F6	Vittorio Veneto	I	35	B9
Vevey	CH	36	E5	Villafranca Tirrena	I	30	D6	Viveiro	E	22	A4
Veyre-Monton	F	17	D10	Villajoyosa-La Vila Joíosa	E	27	H10	Vize	TR	84	H3
Vezin le Coquet	F	14	E6	Villa Literno	I	30	A4	Viziru	RO	79	G9
Viana do Bolo	E	22	D5	Villamartín	E	25	L8	Vizzini	I	30	G5
Viana do Castelo	P	22	E2	Villanueva de Córdoba	E	28	B4	Vlaardingen	NL	10	D5
Viareggio	I	34	F6	Villanueva de la Serena	E	24	E7	Vladičin Han	SRB	82	F3
Viarmes	F	12	C2	Villanueva de los Infantes	E	26	G6	Vladimirescu	RO	77	E10
Viborg	DK	44	D3	Villaputzu	I	32	G3	Vlăhiţa	RO	78	E5

V

Z

152

Ø

Øksfjord	N	58	C5
Ølstykke	DK	44	E6
Ørsta	N	50	D3

Å

Åbo	FIN	53	G11
Åby	S	47	D7
Åfjord	N	54	G3
Ågskaret	N	57	G2
Åhus	S	45	E9
Åkarp	S	45	E8
Åkersberga	S	47	C10
Åkerstrømmen	N	51	E8
Åkrehamn	N	48	D2
Ålesund	N	50	C3

Åmot	N	48	D5
Åmål	S	46	D3
Åndalsnes	N	50	C4
Åre	S	51	A10
Århus	DK	44	D4
Ås	N	51	B9
Åsele	S	55	F10
Åseral	N	48	E4
Åstorp	S	45	D7
Åtvidaberg	S	47	E7

Ä

Älmhult	S	45	D9
Älta	S	47	C9
Älvros	S	51	D12
Älvsbyn	S	56	C3
Ängelholm	S	45	D7
Äänekoski	FIN	64	B6

Ö

Örebro	S	46	C6
Örnsköldsvik	S	53	A7
Östersund	S	51	B12
Överammer	S	52	A4